# The Identity of John the Evangelist

# The Identity of John the Evangelist

*Revision and Reinterpretation in Early Christian Sources*

Dean Furlong

LEXINGTON BOOKS/FORTRESS ACADEMIC
Lanham • Boulder • New York • London

Published by Lexington Books/Fortress Academic
Lexington Books is an imprint of The Rowman & Littlefield Publishing Group, Inc.
4501 Forbes Boulevard, Suite 200, Lanham, Maryland 20706
www.rowman.com

6 Tinworth Street, London SE11 5AL

Copyright © 2020 by The Rowman & Littlefield Publishing Group, Inc.

*All rights reserved.* No part of this book may be reproduced in any form or by any electronic or mechanical means, including information storage and retrieval systems, without written permission from the publisher, except by a reviewer who may quote passages in a review.

British Library Cataloguing in Publication Information Available

**Library of Congress Cataloging-in-Publication Data Available**
Library of Congress Control Number: 2020930538

ISBN 978-1-9787-0930-0 (cloth)
ISBN 978-1-9787-0931-7 (electronic)
ISBN 978-1-9787-0932-4 (pbk)

# Contents

| | |
|---|---|
| Abbreviations | vii |
| Introduction | 1 |
| Section 1: The Identity of the Evangelist | 3 |
|   1  Papias's Two Johns | 5 |
|   2  The Traditions of the Death of John | 19 |
|   3  John the Evangelist in the Earliest Sources | 37 |
| Section 2: Conflated Figures, Revised Narratives | 57 |
|   4  Hippolytus and the Claudian Exile Tradition | 59 |
|   5  Hippolytus, Gaius, and the Alogoi | 73 |
|   6  Eusebius and the Domitianic Exile Tradition | 89 |
| Section 3: Toward a Reconstruction of the Earliest Tradition | 107 |
|   7  The Tradition of John's Neronian Exile | 109 |
|   8  Papian Traditions on the Gospel of John | 123 |
|   9  John on the Τάξις of the Gospels | 139 |
|   10  Papias and the Publication of John's Gospel | 155 |
| Conclusion | 173 |
| Bibliography | 175 |
| Index | 187 |
| About the Author | 191 |

# Abbreviations

| | |
|---|---|
| ACCSNT | Ancient Christian Commentary on Scripture: New Testament |
| AB | Anchor Bible |
| ABD | *Anchor Bible Dictionary*, ed. D. N. Freedman (6 vols.; New York: Doubleday, 1992) |
| ACT | Ancient Christian Texts |
| ACW | Ancient Christian Writers |
| *AJT* | *American Journal of Theology* |
| ANF | *The Ante-Nicene Fathers: Translations of the Writings of the Fathers Down to A.D. 325*, ed. Alexander Roberts and James Donaldson (Buffalo: Christian Literature Publishing Company, 1885–1897; Grand Rapids: Eerdmans, 1951–56), 10 vols. |
| ArBib | The Aramaic Bible series |
| BAFCS | The Book of Acts in Its First Century Setting |
| *BBR* | *Bulletin for Biblical Research* |
| BDAG | Arndt, William, Frederick W. Danker, and Walter Bauer, eds. *A Greek-English Lexicon of the New Testament and Other Early Christian Literature*. 3rd ed. Chicago: University of Chicago Press, 2000. |
| BETL | Bibliotheca Ephemeridum Theologicarum Lovaniensium |
| *BJRL* | *Bulletin of the John Rylands University Library of Manchester* |

| | |
|---|---|
| BNTC | Black's New Testament Commentary |
| *BRCM* | *Biblical Review and Congregational Magazine* |
| *BTNT* | Biblical Theology of the New Testament |
| CBM | Chester Beatty Monographs |
| CCSA | Corpus Christianorum Series Apocryphorum |
| CCSL | Corpus Christianorum, Series Latina |
| CGTSC | Cambridge Greek Testament for Schools and Colleges |
| CRB | Cahiers de la Revue biblique |
| CSCO | Corpus Scriptorum Christianorum Orientalium |
| CSEL | Corpus Scriptorum Ecclesiasticorum Latinorum |
| *DTT* | *Dansk Teologisk Tidsskrift* |
| EAA | Collection des Études Augustiniennes. Série Antiquité |
| ECS | Early Christian Studies |
| EtB | Études bibliques |
| *Exp* | *Expositor* |
| *ExpT* | *Expository Times* |
| FC | Fathers of the Church |
| FRLANT | Forschungen zur Religion und Literatur des Alten und Neuen Testaments |
| GCS | Die Griechischen Christlichen Schriftsteller der ersten drei Jahrhunderte |
| *GS* | *Gesammelte Schriften* |
| *Herm* | *Hermathena* |
| HSem | Horae Semiticae |
| *HTR* | *Harvard Theological Review* |

| | |
|---|---|
| ICC | International Critical Commentary |
| ICQ | *Irish Church Quarterly* |
| JBL | *Journal of Biblical Literature* |
| JECS | *Journal of Early Christian Studies* |
| JEH | *Journal of Ecclesiastical History* |
| JETh | *Jahrbuch für evangelikale Theologie* |
| JETS | *Journal of the Evangelical Theological Society* |
| JSL | *Journal of Sacred Literature* |
| JSNT | *Journal for the Study of the New Testament* |
| JTS | *Journal of Theological Studies* |
| LCL | Loeb Classical Library |
| LSJ | Liddell-Scott-Jones, *Greek-English Lexicon* |
| MGH | *Monumenta Germania Historica* |
| NHMS | Nag Hammadi and Manichaean Studies |
| NICNT | The New International Commentary on the New Testament |
| NIGTC | New International Greek Testament Commentary |
| NovT | *Novum Testamentum* |
| NovTSup | Novum Testamentum Supplements |
| NPNF | *A Select Library of Nicene and Post-Nicene Fathers of the Christian Church*, ed. Philip Schaff (New York: Christian Literature Company, 1887–1900; Grand Rapids: Eerdmans, 1952–55), 28 vols. in 2 series |
| NTA | Neutestamentliche Abhandlungen |
| NTOA | Novum Testamentum et Orbis Antiquus |
| NTS | *New Testament Studies* |

| | |
|---|---|
| OAF | Oxford Apostolic Fathers |
| *ODCC* | *Oxford Dictionary of the Christian Church*, ed. F.L. Cross & E.A. Livingstone, 3rd ed. Oxford University Press, 2005 |
| OECT | Oxford Early Christian Texts |
| OLD | Oxford Latin Dictionary, ed. P. G. W. Glare (Oxford 1982; repr. 1983) |
| OSDHL | Oxford Studies in Diachronic and Historical Linguistics |
| OThM | Oxford Theological Monographs |
| *OTP* | James H. Charlesworth (ed.), *The Old Testament Pseudepigrapha* |
| OTRM | Oxford Theology and Religion Monographs |
| *PG* | *Patrologiae Cursus Completus, Series Graeca*, ed. J. P. Migne (Paris, 1857–66, 1894) |
| *PL* | *Patrologiae Cursus Completus, Series Latina*, ed. J. P. Migne (Paris, 1844–80) |
| PNTC | Pillar New Testament Commentary |
| PTS | Patristische Texte und Studien |
| *REAug* | *Revue des études augustiniennes* |
| *RevBén* | *Revue Bénédictine* |
| *RSPT* | *Revue des sciences philosophiques et théologiques* |
| *RTP* | *Revue de Théologie et de Philosophie* |
| SC | Sources Chrétiennes |
| SCHT | Studies in Christian History and Thought |
| *Scr* | *Scripture* |
| SH | Subsidia hagiographica |
| *SJT* | *Scottish Journal of Theology* |
| SP | Sacra Pagina |

| | |
|---|---|
| SPBS | Society for the Promotion of Byzantine Studies |
| *StP* | *Studia Patristica* |
| StT | Studi e Testi |
| ThH | Théologie historique |
| TNTC | Tyndale New Testament Commentaries |
| *TS* | *Theological Studies* |
| TU | Texte und Untersuchungen zur Geschichte der altchristlichen Literatur |
| *TZ* | *Theologische Zeitschrift* |
| *VC* | *Vigiliae Christianae* |
| VCSup | Supplements to Vigiliae Christianae |
| *VL* | *Vetus Latina; die Reste der altlateinischen Bibel* |
| WBC | Word Biblical Commentary |
| WGRW | Writings from the Greco-Roman World |
| *WTJ* | *Westminster Theological Journal* |
| WUNT | Wissenschaftliche Untersuchungen zum Neuen Testament |
| ZNW | *Zeitschrift für die neutestamentliche Wissenschaft und die Kunde der älteren Kirche* (1920–2005), *des Urchristentums* (1900–19) |

# Introduction

This study seeks to examine the reception of John the Evangelist in early Christian sources. It does not address the historicity of the various claims and traditions which sprang up around this figure, though no doubt some traditions were more historically grounded than others.

Traditionally, early Christian sources have been understood as reflecting a generally uniform Johannine narrative, according to which John the Evangelist, also identified as the Apostle John, the son of Zebedee,[1] settled in Ephesus (probably from Jerusalem in the mid-60s[2]), where he remained until the end of Domitian's reign, at which time he was banished to Patmos.[3] He later returned to Ephesus in the reign of Nerva and died there a few years later, early in the reign of Trajan.[4]

Challenging elements of this narrative, this study will seek to reconstruct the earliest traditions pertaining to John the Evangelist, delineating the development of the Johannine story in the period from Papias, who probably wrote in the early second century, to Eusebius in the early fourth century. It will argue that John the Evangelist of the earliest sources was most likely the John referred to by Papias as "the Elder," and that the Evangelist only later came to be widely identified with the Zebedean John, probably from the third century onwards. This identification, it will be argued, initiated further revision, as traditions previously associated with the separate figures of the Evangelist and Apostle came to be variously configured into new narratives, the most significant of which were those of Hippolytus of Rome (c. 170–c. 235) and Eusebius of Caesarea (c. 263–339).

Hippolytus of Rome's synthesis of the traditions seems to have favored the Apostle's early martyrdom as the template for its version of the Johannine story. This would have necessitated the early dating of the Patmos exile (associated with the Evangelist) and probably gave rise to the narrative of John's Claudian exile and death, found in a number of sources that appear to have been dependent on Hippolytus. Eusebius's later and more complex retelling of the Johannine story likewise identified the Apostle and Evangelist, but it favored the tradition of the Evangelist's long life and peaceful death at Ephesus for its template, leading to the displacement of the martyrdom narrative.

Early evidence supportive of John's late, natural death is relatively sparse compared to that of the Apostle John's early martyrdom. To bolster the narrative of John's long life, Eusebius seems to have constructed a context for John's exile in the unlikely setting of Domitian's persecution of the Roman nobility at the end of the first century, which he effected by conflating various unrelated accounts from secular and ecclesiastical sources and by misinterpreting ambiguous statements by Irenaeus and Clement of Alexandria.

The final section of this work will seek to reconstruct the earliest Johannine narrative. After laying out evidence that the earliest writers contextualized John's exile in Nero's reign, it will go on to argue that Papias identified the author of John's Gospel with John the Elder and that he placed the writing of this Gospel in Ephesus, late in Domitian's reign, in what was once a well-established narrative before it was displaced by Eusebius's.

## A NOTE ON TERMINOLOGY

In this work, "John the Evangelist" will refer to the John whom early tradition associated with Ephesus and the Fourth Gospel, irrespective of whether he is to be identified with the Elder, the son of Zebedee, or any other figure. The word "apostle" will be capitalized when referring to the twelve apostles and Paul but will be in lowercase when used of the wider circle of Jesus's eyewitness disciples.

## NOTES

1. E.g., J. H. Bernard, *A Critical and Exegetical Commentary on the Gospel According to St. John*, vol. 1 (ICC; New York: Scribner, 1929), xlvi; D. A. Carson, *The Gospel According to John* (PNTC; Grand Rapids: Eerdmans, 1991), 28, 68; Leon Morris, *The Gospel According to John* (NICNT; Grand Rapids: Eerdmans, 1995), 555; Andreas J. Köstenberger, *A Theology of John's Gospel and Letters: The Word, the Christ, the Son of God* (BTNT; Grand Rapids: Zondervan, 2009), 53, 72, 74; Craig S. Keener, *The Gospel of John: A Commentary*, vol. 1 (Grand Rapids: Baker, 2012), 220.

2. E.g., William Barclay, *Introduction to John and the Acts of the Apostles* (Philadelphia: Westminster Press, 1976), 19; Donald A. Carson and Douglas J. Moo, *An Introduction to the New Testament* (2nd ed.; Grand Rapids: Zondervan, 2005), 254; Köstenberger, *Theology*, 83. Eusebius, *Hist. eccl.* 3.1.1–3 which is often cited in support, does not state that John moved to Ephesus after the Jewish War any more than it places Peter's sojourn in Rome and Paul's ministry in Illyricum, which are also mentioned in the context, at that time. Rather, it speaks generally of the movements of the apostles after the ascension.

3. E.g., Carson and Moo, *Introduction*, 707–8; Andreas J. Köstenberger, L. Scott Kellum, and Charles L. Quarles, *The Cradle, the Cross, and the Crown: An Introduction to the New Testament* (Nashville: B&H, 2009), 822.

4. E.g., Carson and Moo, *Introduction*, 266; Köstenberger, *Theology*, 94.

# Section 1

## *The Identity of the Evangelist*

This section of the study will challenge the view that the identification of the Evangelist with the Apostle John, the son of Zebedee, informed the earliest sources of the Johannine tradition. Its starting point will be a discussion of Papias's John the Elder, a figure who is often considered to be obscure or whose historical existence as a separate John is denied altogether. After laying out evidence that Papias did intend to speak of a second John who had, like the Apostle, known and followed Jesus, it will argue that the principal authors of the second and early third century, including Papias, Justin Martyr, Polycrates, Irenaeus, Tertullian, and Clement of Alexandria, are best interpreted as presupposing an identification of the Evangelist with the Elder rather than the Apostle.

# ONE
## Papias's Two Johns

Any assumption that the earliest sources identified John the Evangelist with the Apostle John, the son of Zebedee, is potentially challenged by a fragment from the largely lost work of Papias, bishop of Hierapolis in Asia Minor (on dating see below), entitled *Explanation* (or *Account*) *of the Dominical Logia*, which speaks of two Johns who belonged to the circle of Jesus's disciples, namely the Apostle and the Elder.

The mention of this second John has elicited much discussion within scholarship. Some argue that the same John's name was listed twice, so that there never was a separate Elder John. According to others, there was a second John, though efforts at identifying him differ. While some consider him a relatively obscure and irrelevant figure, others posit that it is this second John, the Elder, rather than the Apostle, who is to be identified with John the Evangelist, the John who is said to have resided in Ephesus and who was associated with the authorship of the Fourth Gospel.

After introducing Papias and his work, this chapter will examine the question of whether Papias is better understood as having spoken of a single figure named John, or of two separate ones, considering at the same time the historical origins of each interpretation. It will conclude that Papias almost certainly did differentiate two Johns, and this will open up the way for later chapters to examine the question of whether the Apostle or the Elder better correlates with the Evangelist of early sources.

### PAPIAS'S LOST WORK

Only a limited number of fragments and allusions to Papias's lost work have been identified (with varying degrees of confidence[1]), and editors have adopted different parameters for what constitutes a Papian fragment. While the most complete edition, accompanied with extensive discussion of each fragment, is that of Enrico Norelli,[2] in this study the Papian fragments will be numbered where possible according to the more accessible Lightfoot-Harmer-Holmes edition.[3]

According to Eusebius, Papias's work consisted of five books (*Hist. eccl.* 3.39.1). This is probably the same work as that referred to by Agapius, a tenth-century Melkite bishop of Hierapolis in Syria (not Asia Minor), who mentions a "prominent teacher" in Hierapolis who wrote five treatises on the Gospel, noting that the last of these was concerned with the Gospel of John (Fragment 23). Papias's work may have contained commentary on the sayings of Jesus recorded in the Gospels.[4] This is consistent, at least, with some of the extracts preserved from the work. Thus, Andrew of Caesarea (563–637) provides a summary of Papias's exposition of the fall of Satan, possibly in explanation of Luke 10:18 which Andrew cites in the context (Fragment 24=Andrew of Caesarea, *Commentary on Revelation*, on Rev 12:7–9). In providing an exposition of Matt 26:29 (cf. Mark 14:25), which speaks of Christ's drinking of the vine in his coming kingdom, Irenaeus (c. 180) cites a tradition from Papias's fourth book concerning the great abundance of vines and wheat during the eschatological days of the kingdom (Irenaeus, *Haer.* 5.33.3–4).[5] Papias is also said by George the Sinner (or Georgios Hamartolos) (c. 840) to have related in his second book that John the son of Zebedee was killed by Jews, which may have been mentioned within the context of exposition of Mark 10:39–40, Christ's prediction of the martyrdom of the Zebedee brothers, which George goes on to cite.[6]

*The Date of Papias's Writings*

The seventh-century *Chronicon Paschale* claimed that Papias was martyred in the year 164, and for this reason Papias was once widely held to have written in the second half of the second century. This position has now largely been abandoned, as Lightfoot demonstrated that the *Chronicon Paschale* likely confused Papias with Papylas, an otherwise unknown martyr who is mentioned by Eusebius in a passage from which the *Chronicon Paschale* derived its information (cf. *Hist. eccl.* 4.15.48).[7] Indeed, Photius (c. 810–c. 893) distinguished a certain Methodius from Papias by stating that he won the crown of martyrdom (Fragment 22), which suggests that Papias had not been martyred.[8]

More recent studies often place Papias's activities in the reign of Hadrian (117–138) on the basis of a fragment of an epitome of the otherwise lost fifth-century Greek *Ecclesiastical History* of Philip of Sidé (Philip Sidetes), contained in a seventh- or eighth-century manuscript.[9] After relating a tradition of the Apostle John's martyrdom, for which it cites Papias's second book, it adds: "Concerning those resurrected from the dead by Christ: he says that they were living until the time of Hadrian" (Fragment 5). If Papias reported concerning those who lived into Hadrian's reign (117–138), then Papias himself must have been alive at this time or later.

However, the reference to those who lived into Hadrian's reign may have been taken by Philip from Eusebius's *Ecclesiastical History*, in which the same statement is made. Philip was familiar with this work, for he repeats from it Eusebius's views found in it concerning Papias's two Johns and his millennialism, which he summarizes before citing Papias on John the Apostle's martyrdom. In Eusebius, however, the statement is attributed to the second-century apologist Quadratus rather than to Papias, suggesting that Philip (or his epitomist) may have mistakenly attributed to Papias what had originally been related concerning Quadratus.[10] This puts the value of the statement for dating Papias's works into doubt.[11] Another possibility has been noted by Sanday, who suggests that "the sentence in the Fragment about the dead raised to life is really a new statement not connected with the sentences preceding which are referred to Papias."[12] This view does not seem to have gained any currency in more recent studies, however.

A more reliable indication as to the time of Papias's activities and writing is perhaps given by Eusebius, who discusses Papias at the end of the third book of his *Ecclesiastical History*, which narrates events from the deaths of Peter and Paul (c. 67) to the end of the bishopric of Evarestos of Rome (c. 109),[13] suggesting that he placed Papias's activities during this period. Furthermore, after mentioning the appointment of Evarestos in the third year of Trajan (100/101) and the martyrdom of Simeon, bishop of Jerusalem, he relates that at that time Papias "became well known" (ἐγνωρίζετο)[14] (possibly on account of his writings), along with Ignatius (*apud* Eusebius, *Hist. eccl.* 3.34.1–3.36.2), who is known to have been martyred around the year 107. Because of these considerations, many now favor a date of 110 CE or earlier for Papias's work.[15]

Eusebius provides further evidence for the earlier date a little later: after noting that Philip the Apostle and his daughters lived in Hierapolis, he refers to Papias as "their contemporary" (*Hist. eccl.* 3.39.9), employing the masculine pronoun (κατὰ τοὺς αὐτοὺς ὁ Παπίας γενόμενος), showing that Papias's life must have overlapped, at least, with that of Philip.[16] Eusebius elsewhere quotes from Polycrates, a bishop of Ephesus in the late second century (see chapter 3), who identifies this Philip as one of the twelve apostles; Eusebius seems to simultaneously think that this Philip was also Philip the Evangelist, spoken of in Acts 21:8–9 (*Hist. eccl.* 3.31.3), though his sources do not make this connection.[17] In either case, this would have made Papias quite old already by the turn of the second century.

# THE APOSTLE AND THE ELDER

Papias's double mention of the name of John is found in the lost preface to his work, which Eusebius quotes as follows:

> And if by chance someone who had been a follower of the elders should come my way, I inquired about the words of the elders (τοὺς τῶν πρεσβυτέρων ἀνέκρινον λόγους)—what Andrew or Peter said (τί Ἀνδρέας ἢ τί Πέτρος εἶπεν), or Philip, or Thomas or James, or John or Matthew or any other of the Lord's disciples, and whatever Aristion and the elder John (ὁ πρεσβύτερος Ἰωάννης), the Lord's disciples, were saying. For I did not think that information from books would profit me as much as information from a living and abiding voice. (Fragment 3.4 = Eusebius, *Hist. eccl.* 3.39.4 [Holmes])

Papias here describes a time when he was inquiring after the words of the elders, and in so doing he distinguishes between what Andrew, Peter and the others had said (εἶπεν) and what Aristion and John the Elder were saying (λέγουσιν). This change in tense suggests that he divided the disciples into those who were dead by the time of these inquiries and those who were still alive.[18] If prominent apostles had already died by this time, then he could not have made his inquiries much earlier than the last quarter of the first century. On the other hand, if two eyewitness disciples of Jesus were still alive, he could not have made them much later than the end of the first century.[19] Probably these inquiries were made in the period 75–100 CE, which is agreeable to Papias's claim that he had personally known the Apostle Philip's daughters, who were said to have resided with their father in Hierapolis (Fragment 3.9 = *apud* Eusebius, *Hist. eccl.* 3.39.9).[20]

Because Papias lists the first John alongside members of the twelve apostles, it is generally accepted that Papias was speaking here of John the son of Zebedee, the Galilean fisherman of the Synoptic Gospels. The identity of the second John, however, has engendered much debate. Many of those holding to the traditional view argue that Papias referred to the same John, the Apostle, twice,[21] and their views will be discussed below. If correct, this would remove from consideration the possibility that there was a second prominent disciple of Jesus named John. Most scholars, however, are unconvinced that Papias can be understood this way.[22] Thus, Munck claims it would have been "unnatural" for Papias to have repeated the name of the same John in his list, with barely more than a line's interval between them.[23] According to Charles, Papias "carefully distinguishes" the two,[24] while Barclay considers it "barely conceivable and highly improbable" that Papias speaks of only one John and "includes him among the disciples of the Lord who spoke, and the disciples of the Lord who still speak."[25] Schoedel views it as "very doubtful" that Papias identified the two,[26] while Cullmann affirms that "there is certainly a distinction here between two Johns."[27] Hengel states that the two Johns are for Papias, "zwei verschiedene Personen,"[28] while Ratzinger writes that the Elder is "evidently not the same as the Apostle"[29]

This distinction of the Apostle John and Elder John is also maintained among many who are favorable to the traditional view. According to McGiffert, the editor of the Ante-Nicene Fathers collection, "no other conclusion can be reached" than that Papias spoke of two Johns, "unless we accuse Papias of the most stupid and illogical method of writing."[30] He attributes the attempts at finding one John in the passage to the historical difficulties associated with positing a second John in Asia.[31] Lightfoot notes that the second John is "is distinguished as the 'elder' or 'presbyter,' this designation being put in an emphatic position before the proper name." He adds, "We must therefore accept the distinction between John the Apostle and John the Presbyter," despite its "inconvenience."[32] Beckwith is similarly insistent: "We are compelled to accept" the separate historical existence of the second John.[33] And Westcott, the staunch defender of the Zebedean authorship of the Fourth Gospel, referred to this as "the natural interpretation" of Papias's words,[34] while Brown admits that attempts to identify Papias's two Johns as the same person "seem forced."[35]

Nevertheless, attempts at resolving the difficulty have stalled on the question of whether Papias might have expressed himself poorly. Thus, Farrar claims that while the distinction of John's "would be the *natural* inference, it is by no means the *certain* inference."[36] Bruce too allows that Papias was "expressing himself clumsily" in only speaking of one John, and he consequently treats the question as an open one.[37] Papias does not seem to have been a clumsy or imprecise writer, however, for Jerome spoke of the beauty (*venustas*) of his writings and expressed his inability to worthily translate them (Fragment 8 = Jerome, *ad Lucinus*, Letter 71.5).

## *Origins of the Theory of a Single John*

It is not often noted that the identification of Papias's two Johns is built upon another questionable interpretation of Papias's words. Guericke in 1831 seems to have been the first to propose that the same John was mentioned twice.[38] Central to his proposal was his further identification of the elders whose words Papias inquired after with the apostles whose words were reported. That is, by the words, τοὺς τῶν πρεσβυτέρων ἀνέκρινον λόγους· τί Ἀνδρέας ἢ τί Πέτρος εἶπεν, κ.τ.λ., Guericke understood Papias as claiming: "I inquired about the words of the elders, namely, what [the elders] Andrew or Peter said, etc."[39] (the question of whether this rendering represents Papias's likely meaning will be discussed below). From this, he maintained that Papias's two Johns could be identified since the designation of "elder" was common to both the first John (since he was one of the apostles, identified by Guericke with the elders) and the second.[40] He then suggested that the designation was specifically included with the second mention of John to emphasize his later witness in the period after the death of the other apostles, in his old age, and during the time in which he exercised a "patriarchalisch" activity in Asia Minor.[41]

Farrar put forward similar arguments some decades later, alleging that Papias's elders were "the disciples of the Lord"[42] and that John's title of "the Elder" belonged to him both on account of his great age and because he was the last of the apostles (i.e., "elders").[43] Since, in his view, both Johns are spoken of as an "Elder" and as "a disciple of the Lord," he reasons that Papias would have given the second John a separate title had he wished to differentiate them.[44]

Petrie also follows this identification of the apostles and elders, and he interprets the definite article in ὁ πρεσβύτερος Ἰωάννης as anaphoric, that is, as pointing back to a previous mention of this figure, so that "it is naturally rendered, 'the (aforementioned) ancient worthy John,'" claiming: "The grammar and the general sense demand this rendering."[45] He adds that Papias names him a second time because he placed his activities both in a prior period and during his own time.[46] Shanks also understands the Greek text of Papias as requiring that the definite article have this anaphoric meaning,[47] claiming it "defies explanation" that scholars trained in Greek could conclude otherwise.[48]

Baum, though supportive of the identification both of the two Johns and of the apostles and elders, probably rightly rejects the interpretation of the article as anaphoric, pointing out that this would require a previous mention of a single elder rather than just a previous mention of John.[49] He instead takes the article to mean "der bekannte Presbyter,"[50] which, on the basis of the identification of the elders and apostles, he argues would refer to "the well-known apostle" (i.e., the son of Zebedee). He admits, however, that the use of a title before the second mention of John would quite naturally suggest that a different person was intended, were it not for the prior identification of the apostles and elders.[51] Thus, it is only the identification of the apostles and elders that allows Baum to identify the two Johns.

*The Distinction of Papias's Apostles and Elders*

While Guericke and others would understand Papias as identifying the apostles and elders, others interpret Papias as claiming that the elders were themselves reporting what the apostles had said, and would translate his words: "I inquired into the words of the elders regarding what [according to the elders] Andrew or Peter said, etc."[52] This interpretation distinguishes the apostles and elders and consequently leaves no room for the interpretations of the definite article in ὁ πρεσβύτερος Ἰωάννης which are necessary for identifying the second John with the first.

According to the interpretation of Guericke and others, the λόγους and τί are in apposition ("I inquired into the words of the elders, namely, what [the elders] Andrew or Peter said, etc.").[53] In the second interpretation, the indirect question acts as the complement of ἀνακρίνω ("I was inquiring into the words of the elders regarding what Andrew, or what Peter, had said etc."). The latter accords with similar constructions found in other writers. Plutarch (c. 45–120 CE), for example, writes that when Marcus Licinius Crassus was in hiding and was visited by two slave women, "he was inquiring of them regarding what they wanted and who they were" (ἀνέκρινον οὖν αὐτάς τί βούλονται καί τίνες εἰσίν) (*Crass.* 5.3),[54] with the two clauses introduced by τί and τίνες complementing the verb ("he was asking ... what ... and who ..."). The grammatical structure of Papias's statement is the same; in both, the verb ἀνέκρινον takes a direct object (λόγους in Papias, αὐτάς in Plutach) and is followed by indirect questions introduced by interrogative pronouns (τί and ἄ in Papias; τί and τίνες in Plutarch). Similarly, the book of Acts records that those at Berea were "inquiring into the scriptures if these things were so" (ἀνακρίνοντες τὰς γραφὰς εἰ ἔχοι ταῦτα οὕτως) (Acts 17:11), with the verb, a form of ἀνακρίνω, taking a direct object (τὰς γραφὰς) followed by the interrogative εἰ which introduces an indirect question complementing the verb.

By analogy with the usage of these passages, we would expect Papias to be inquiring into the words of the elders regarding what the apostles had said (the second interpretation), not placing the interrogatives in apposition with the words of the elders, as required by Guericke's interpretation.

*Further Difficulties with the Identification of the Apostles and Elders*

A number of other difficulties also confront any identification of Papias's apostles and elders. First, those whom Papias questioned were likely traveling through Hierapolis from other parts of Asia Minor, since the city was located at an important crossroads, with one road connecting Syrian Antioch to Ephesus and the other connecting Attalia in Pamphylia to Smyrna.[55] This seems to point to these elders as a revered group who were then resident in Asia Minor, for while Papias might have reasonably expected travelers to have had some familiarity with the teaching of leaders in the great centers of Christianity in Asia Minor, he could hardly have expected them to have had firsthand familiarity with the words of a former generation of apostles. He must have inquired of these travelers because he knew that they had sat under the teaching of these elders in their local communities.

Secondly, Luthardt, in his book defending the traditional authorship of John's Gospel, points out that the words "the disciples of the Lord" (οἱ τοῦ κυρίου μαθηταί) which further describe Aristion and John would be redundant if the reference to this John as "the elder" had already identified him as a disciple of the Lord.[56] Instead, he suggests, Papias would have referred only to Aristion as "the disciple of the Lord," and to John as the elder.[57] This point does not seem to have been addressed in more recent studies. Keener does attempt to meet the problem of why Aristion and John are referred to in this way, but he does not seem to recognize the redundancy:

> By calling Aristion and John "disciples of the Lord," Papias may also include them among eyewitnesses; but he almost certainly includes the elder John as one of the Twelve, who are also called "disciples" in the same quotation, probably tying them all (including Aristion) to the first generation.[58]

Keener goes on to argue (no doubt correctly) that they are set apart from the others in the list because they outlived them, but he does not explain why the epithet would have been repeated in John's case if he had already been spoken of as a disciple.[59]

Lastly, the identification of the elders and apostles seems to have been unknown before Guericke. The church historian Eusebius, writing in the early decades of the fourth century, distinguished Papias's apostles from his elders by interpreting Papias's claim to have learned carefully from the elders (*Hist. eccl.* 3.39.3) as meaning that Papias had received the words of the apostles from those who had followed them (3.39.7). Irenaeus, who was bishop of Lyon in Gaul in the latter quarter of the second century, also distinguished a group whom he calls "the elders" from the apostles by stating that some of the elders had also seen other apostles besides John, and he also relates that John remained among the elders until the reign of Trajan (98–117) (*Haer.* 2.22.5). In his letter to Florinus, Irenaeus speaks of "the elders who were before us, who also accompanied the apostles" (*apud* Eusebius, *Hist. eccl.* 5.20.4). He thus takes it for granted that there was a group called "the elders" who were distinct from the apostles.[60] Irenaeus elsewhere demonstrates familiarity with Papias's work by citing from it (*Haer.* 5.33.4), rendering it likely that Irenaeus was following Papias's distinction (see chapter 8 for evidence that the source of Irenaeus's statements concerning the elders was Papias).

Some have maintained that Eusebius took advantage of Papias's lack of precision in naming John twice to create the figure of the second John, for the purpose of suggesting a John other than the Evangelist as a potential author of Revelation, whose canonicity Eusebius evidently doubted (cf. chapter 6).[61] However, Irenaeus also distinguished the elders from the apostles, contrary to any interpretations that would identify the two Johns, rendering it very probable that he distinguished the two Johns also, just as Eusebius later did.

## Chapman's View

Chapman is an exception in attempting both to follow Irenaeus and Eusebius in distinguishing the apostles and elders and in maintaining that Papias spoke of only one John.[62] Chapman does not seek to associate the title of "the Elder" with Papias's previous mention of the elders, as others do, but rather argues that "the Elder" was used as a "surname of honour" and an *epitheton ornans*, or title that can be included or omitted without any risk of confusion (he provides the example of "the Grand Old Man" given to the nineteenth-century British Prime Minister William Gladstone).[63] But the provision of the title before the second occurrence of the name rather than the first would more naturally seem to suggest that a new person is in view. Furthermore, Chapman's view must still confront the redundancy of the designation of Aristion and the Elder as "disciples of the Lord," pointed out by Luthardt, when on his reading of the passage the second John had already been introduced as one of the apostles of Jesus.

## The Elder

Papias's employment of the title "the Elder" before the second mention of John can naturally be explained as intending to distinguish him from the first John,[64] a possibility that Baum only disregards on the basis of his (questionable) identification of Papias's elders with the apostles.[65] It likely denoted that this John enjoyed a revered status in old age.[66]

According to Eusebius, Papias had claimed to have been a hearer (αὐτήκοος) of both John the Elder and Ariston; he adds: "in fact (γοῦν),[67] mentioning them by name frequently, he puts their traditions in his writing" (*Hist. eccl.* 3.39.7). An example of this is likely found later in Eusebius, where he cites Papias as referring to what "the Elder was saying" (*Hist. eccl.* 3.39.15), in what is usually understood as a reference to John the Elder.[68] The reference simply to "the Elder" would again show that this was indeed a title by which this John was known and could be distinguished.

Since Papias had mentioned the Elder more frequently than others and had even heard him himself, it is likely that the Elder taught in Asia Minor.[69] This would also account for how travellers to Hierapolis were able to report on his words. Eusebius also associated him with Asia Minor, for he suggested that he was buried at one of two memorials in Ephesus bearing the name of John (*Hist. eccl.* 3.39.5–6).

As in Papias, two of the Johannine letters also employ the title of "the Elder" independently, without any qualification (2 John 1; 3 John 1). Both of these figures are also associated with the name of "John." Probably the reference in each case is to the same individual,[70] though Papias's familiarity with 2 and 3 John, in which the title is also used, cannot be proven.[71]

## CONCLUSION

Papias, who was likely active at around the turn of the second century, is best interpreted as having spoken of two Johns from among the disciples of Jesus. Some have argued that Papias spoke of the same John twice, but this modern reading of Papias's words requires that he spoke in a clumsy or unnatural manner. Furthermore, as Luthardt pointed out, the designation of both Aristion and the second John as "disciples of the Lord" would have been redundant in the Elder's case, had he already been listed as an apostle previously.

It was also pointed out that this interpretation is dependent in turn upon another questionable reading of Papias which interprets him as identifying his elders and apostles, contrary to his earliest readers. Nevertheless, the close association of the two related interpretations and their construction in tandem by Guericke has barely been noted within scholarship. Indeed, far from acknowledging the modern origin of the identification of the two Johns, those maintaining that Papias spoke of only one John often suggest that the interpretation that distinguishes them is the novel one.

The conclusion that Papias distinguished his two Johns and that he considered both to have been disciples of the Lord opens up the way for considering in later chapters the question of whether the Evangelist of early Christian sources was identified with the Apostle or with the Elder.

## NOTES

1. Cf. the discussion in Ulrich H. J. Körtner, *Papias von Hierapolis: Ein Beitrag zur Geschichte des frühren Christentums* (FRLANT 133; Göttingen, 1983), 25–43.

2. Enrico Norelli, *Papia di Hierapolis, Esposizione degli Oracoli del Signore: I frammenti* (Milan: Paoline, 2005).

3. Michael William Holmes, *The Apostolic Fathers: Greek Texts and English Translations* (Grand Rapids: Baker, 1999).

4. Cf. Armin Daniel Baum, "Papias als Kommentator evangelischer Aussprüche Jesu: Erwägungen zur Art seines Werkes," *NovT* 38 (1996): 257–76.

5. Cf. William R. Schoedel, *The Apostolic Fathers*, vol. 5, *Polycarp, Martyrdom of Polycarp, Fragments of Papias* (Camden, N.J.: Nelson, 1967), 94; Dennis R. MacDonald, *Two Shipwrecked Gospels: The* Logoi *of Jesus and Papias's* Exposition of Logia *about the Lord* (Atlanta: SBL, 2012), 5.

6. See, e.g., MacDonald, *Two Shipwrecked Gospels*, 5.

7. Joseph B. Lightfoot, *Essays on Supernatural Religion* (2nd ed.; London: Macmillan, 1893), 147–49; cf. Robert W. Yarbrough, "The Date of Papias : A Reassessment," *JETS* 26 (1983): 182.

8. Photius elsewhere calls Papias a "bishop and μάρτυς" (Fragment 17), where μάρτυς may mean "witness."

9. Martin Hengel places it 125–35 (*The Johannine Question*, trans. John Bowden [London: SCM Press, 1989], 16); R. Alan Culpepper around 130 (*John, the Son of Zebe-

*dee: The Life of a Legend* [Edinburgh: T. & T. Clark, 2000], 109); Enrico Norelli in 110–25 (*Papia di Hierapolis*, 54).

10. Schoedel, *Polycarp*, 119–20; Robert H. Gundry, *The Old Is Better: New Testament Essays in Support of Traditional Interpretations* (WUNT 178; Tübingen: Mohr Siebeck, 2005), 51.

11. . Cf. Norelli, *Papia di Hierapolis*, 39.

12. Cf. William Sanday, *The Criticism of the Fourth Gospel* (Oxford: Clarendon Press, 1905), 150 n. 2, citing the view of V. Bartlet (presumably Vernon Bartlet).

13. John B. Orchard, "Some Guidelines for the Interpretation of Eusebius' Hist. Eccl. 3.34–39," in *The New Testament Age: Essays in Honor of Bo Reicke*, ed. William C. Weinrich, vol. 2 (Macon, Ga.; Mercer University Press, 1984), 394.

14. Translated by the author from the Greek text in Kirsopp Lake, ed. and trans., *Eusebius: The Ecclesiastical History*, 2 vols (LCL; London: Heinemann; 1926), and so hereafter, unless otherwise noted.

15. So, e.g., Vernon Bartlet, "Papias's 'Exposition': Its Date and Contents," in *Amicitiae Corolla*, ed. H. G. Wood (London: University of London Press, 1933), 16–17, 20–22; Schoedel, *Polycarp*, 91–92; Körtner, *Papias von Hierapolis*, 89–94, 167–72, 225–26; Richard Bauckham, *Jesus and the Eyewitnesses: The Gospels as Eyewitness Testimony* (2nd ed.; Grand Rapids: Eerdmans, 2017), 13–14.

16. Norelli, *Papia di Hierapolis*, 46.

17. Polycrates is usually thought to have confused the Apostle Philip with Philip the Evangelist. This may be so, though it should be noted that the Apostle is said by Polycrates to have had three daughters, two of whom were virgins, whereas Philip the Evangelist is said to have had four virgin daughters who prophesied. See Frederic W. Farrar, *The Early Days of Christianity* (London: Cassell, 1885), 46–7.

18. Barclay, *Introduction to John*, 44; C. K. Barrett, *The Gospel According to St. John* (2nd ed.; Philadelphia: Westminster, 1978), 107–8; Hengel, *Johannine Question*, 27; Carson, *John*, 70; Culpepper, *John*, 110; Bauckham, *Eyewitnesses*, 17; Raymond E. Brown, *The Gospel According to John (I–XII): Introduction, Translation, and Notes* (AB 29; New Haven, Conn.: Yale University Press, 2008), xci.

19. Cf. Körtner, *Papias von Hierapolis*, 225. MacDonald places the *terminus ante quem* for their deaths at 90 CE (*Two Shipwrecked Gospels*, 47).

20. Cf. Körtner, *Papias von Hierapolis*, 225.

21. Carson, *John*, 70; John R. W. Stott, *The Letters of John: An Introduction and Commentary* (TNTC; Downers Grove, Ill.: IVP, 1988), 38–43; Stephen Smalley, *John, Evangelist and Interpreter* (2nd ed.; London: Paternoster, 1997), 81; Andreas J. Köstenberger and Stephen O. Stout, " 'The Disciple Jesus Loved': Witness, Author, Apostle — A Response to Richard Bauckham's *Jesus and the Eyewitnesses*," *BBR* 18 (2008): 219; J. Ramsey Michaels, *The Gospel of John* (NICNT; Grand Rapids: Eerdmans, 2010); 10–12; Keener, *Gospel of John*, 245; Monte A. Shanks, *Papias and the New Testament* (Eugene: Wipf and Stock, 2013), 19–21.

22. See, e.g., I. Howard Marshall, *The Epistles of John* (NICNT; Grand Rapids: Eerdmans, 1978), 44.

23. Johannes Munck, "Presbyters and Disciples of the Lord in Papias," *HTR* 52 (1959): 238.

24. Robert Henry Charles, *A Critical and Exegetical Commentary on the Revelation of St. John*, vol. 1 (ICC; New York: Scribner, 1920), xliii.

25. Barclay, *Introduction to John*, 89.

26. Schoedel, "Papias," in ABD 5:141.

27. . Oscar Cullmann, *The Johannine Circle*, trans. John Bowden (London: SCM, 1976), 69.

28. Martin Hengel, *Die johanneische Frage: Ein Lösungsversuch* (WUNT 67; Tübingen: Mohr Siebeck, 1993), 79.

29. Joseph Ratzinger, *Jesus of Nazareth: The Infancy Narratives*, trans. Philip J. Whitmore (New York: Doubleday, 2007), 226.

30. Arthur Cushman McGiffert, *NPNF* 2.1.170.

31. Arthur Cushman McGiffert, *NPNF* 2.1.170.
32. . Lightfoot, *Supernatural Religion*, 144.
33. Isbon Thaddeus Beckwith, *The Apocalypse of John* (New York: Macmillan, 1919), 366.
34. Brooke Foss Westcott, *A General Survey of the History of the Canon of the New Testament During the First Four Centuries* (Cambridge: Macmillan, 1855), 76 n. 3. He stated this even though he identified Papias' elders and apostles.
35. Brown, *John*, xci.
36. Farrar, *Early Days*, 620.
37. F. F. Bruce, "St John at Ephesus," *BJRL*, 60 (1978): 350.
38. Heinrich Ernst Ferdinand Guericke, *Die Hypothese von dem Presbyter Johannes als Verfasser der Offenbarung* (Halle, 1831), 6–8.
39. Guericke, *Die Hypothese*, 6–8.
40. Guericke, *Die Hypothese*, 7.
41. Guericke, *Die Hypothese*, 9. This also seems to be the view of Smalley (*John*, 81).
42. Farrar, *Early Days*, 620.
43. Farrar, *Early Days*, 620–22.
44. Farrar, *Early Days*, 620–22.
45. C. Stewart Petrie, "The Authorship of 'The Gospel According to Matthew': A Reconsideration of the External Evidence," *NTS* 14 (1967): 21. His views were largely followed by Carson, *John*, 70.
46. Petrie, "Authorship," 22.
47. Shanks, *Papias*, 19–21.
48. Shanks, *Papias*, 21.
49. Armin Daniel Baum, "Papias und der Presbyter Johannes: Martin Hengel und die johanneische Frage," *JETh* 9 (1995): 30.
50. Baum, "Papias und der Presbyter Johannes," 30.
51. Baum, "Papias und der Presbyter Johannes," 29. His other objections against are applicable only to Eusebius's particular interpretation of the passage (discussed in chapter 6 of this study).
52. John Chapman, *John the Presbyter and the Fourth Gospel* (Oxford: Clarendon Press, 1911), 9–27; Beckwith, *Apocalypse*, 363; Körtner, *Papias von Hierapolis*, 114–22; Hengel, *Die johanneische Frage*, 79; Norelli, *Papia di Hierapolis*, 42; Bauckham, *Eyewitnesses*, 15–16. Schoedel considers this reading "more likely" (William R. Schoedel, "Papias," in ABD 5:141).
53. This is clearly argued for by Gundry, *The Old is Better*, 53, though he seems to misunderstand the argument for the second interpretation where the τί is the direct object in an interrogative question, not an "accusative of general reference."
54. Translated by the author from the Greek text in Bernadotte Perrin, ed., *Plutarch, Lives*, vol. 3 (LCL 65; Medford, Mass.: Harvard University Press, 1916), 326.
55. Cf. Bartlet, "Papias's 'Exposition,' " 17; Schoedel, *Polycarp*, 91.
56. Christoph Ernst Luthardt, *St. John the Author of the Fourth Gospel*, rev. and trans. Caspar Rene Gregory (Edinburgh: T. & T. Clark, 1875), 137.
57. Luthardt, *St. John*, 137–38.
58. Keener, *Gospel of John*, 245.
59. Keener, *Gospel of John*, 245.
60. Contra Shanks, who states that the term "elder" and "apostle" were synonymous for Irenaeus (*Papias*, 143 n. 124).
61. E.g., Leon Morris, *Studies in the Fourth Gospel* (Grand Rapids: Eerdmans, 1969), 279; Stott, *Letters of John*, 38–41; Donald Guthrie, *New Testament Introduction* (4th rev. ed.; Downers Grove, Ill.: IVP, 1996), 280; Michaels, *The Gospel of John*, 12; Keener, *Gospel of John*, 245; Shanks, *Papias*, 19; cf. Baum, "Papias und der Presbyter Johannes," 24.
62. Chapman, *John the Presbyter*, 38–40; cf. 13–19.
63. Chapman, *John the Presbyter*, 39.

64. E.g., Munck, "Presbyters and Disciples," 238; Schoedel, *Polycarp*, 141; Hengel, *Johannine Question*, 28; Bauckham, *Eyewitnesses*, 422–23; Urban C. von Wahlde, *The Gospel and Letters of John*, vol. 3 (Grand Rapids: Eerdmans, 2010), 434.

65. Baum, "Papias und der Presbyter Johannes," 29. His other objections are applicable only to Eusebius' particular interpretation of the passage (discussed in chapter 6 of this study).

66. Cf. Hengel, *Johannine Question*, 28; Bauckham, *Eyewitnesses*, 422–23.

67. For the translation of γοῦν in Eusebius as "in fact" rather than "at least," see Chapman, *John the Presbyter*, 28–30; cf. Hengel, *Johannine Question*, 22; Norelli, *Papia di Hierapolis*, 265; Paul Trebilco, *The Early Christians in Ephesus from Paul to Ignatius* (Grand Rapids: Eerdmans, 2007), 250–51.

68. E.g., C. Clifton Black, *Mark: Images of an Apostolic Interpreter* (Minneapolis: Fortress, 2001), 202; John J. Gunther, "The Elder John: Author of Revelation," *JSNT* 11 (1981): 4. Others consider the identification at least likely; e.g., Bauckham, *Eyewitnesses*, 35; 204.

69. Hengel, *Johannine Question*, 22; *Die johanneische Frage*, 92.

70. Charles, *Revelation*, vol. 1, xliii; Georg Strecker, *The Johannine Letters: A Commentary on 1, 2, and 3 John*, trans. Linda M. Maloney (Hermeneia; Minneapolis: Fortress, 1996), xxxviii; Bauckham, *Eyewitnesses*, 422; von Wahlde, *Gospel and Letter*, 434. Michael J. Kok objects: "A single word, *presbyteros*, is a flimsy basis" for such an identification (*The Beloved Apostle? The Transformation of the Apostle John into the Fourth Evangelist* [Eugene: Cascade, 2017], 79), but the argument is based on more than the title alone.

71. Papias is said by Eusebius to have made citations "from John's former letter" (i.e., 1 John; *apud* Eusebius, *Hist. eccl.* 3.39.17); while this implies at least one later letter attributed to John, the terminology might belong to Eusebius rather than his source.

# TWO

# The Traditions of the Death of John

Two separate narratives concerning the death of a figure named John are known to early Christian sources: a martyrdom tradition which was associated with the Apostle John and a tradition of a natural death in old age which was associated with John the Evangelist. The existence of two narratives and the apparent attribution of each to the Apostle and Evangelist respectively is problematic for the traditional view which identifies the two figures. Consequently, the tradition of the Apostle's martyrdom, many of the sources for which only came to light relatively recently, has generally been discounted and dismissed.

After examining the principal early sources of these traditions, this chapter will argue that early Christian writings affirmed both narratives, and it will conclude that the evidence for the tradition of the Apostle's martyrdom has only been called into question on account of the assumption that early Christian writings identified the Apostle with the Evangelist, necessitating that a choice be made between the two narratives.

## THE DEATH OF JOHN THE EVANGELIST

A small number of sources either speak of the peaceful death of John the Evangelist in old age or seem to presuppose it. One of the earliest traditions is found in the second- or third-century[1] *Acts of John* (§§ 111–115) and reappears again in the late fourth- or early-fifth century[2] Monarchian prologue to John, both of which relate how John laid himself in his grave near Ephesus and expired. In the account found in the possibly third-century Harris fragments, John the Evangelist is depicted as contrasting his own peaceful death with Polycarp's martyrdom: "Since the Lord granted to me [i.e., John] that I die| on my bed, it is necessary that you [i.e., Polycarp]| die by the law | | [co]urt, so that an equilibrium might| [---]|."³

While Irenaeus does not specifically state that John died naturally in old age, he does claim that John remained with the elders until the times of Trajan (*apud* Eusebius, *Hist. eccl.* 3.23.3 = Irenaeus, *Haer.* 2.22.5), and the late placement of John's death along with Irenaeus's silence concerning any martyrdom are usually taken as reasonable indications that he held the Ephesian John to have died peacefully.⁴

## THE MARTYRDOM OF JOHN THE APOSTLE

While sources relating John the Evangelist's death in old age are relatively sparse, a comparatively copious number of sources seem to speak of the martyrdom of the Apostle John. These include Gospels, ancient martyrologies, and important early witnesses like Papias. Nevertheless, the interpretation or even the reliability of these sources is often a matter of dispute, and they will consequently be discussed in detail.

### *The Martyrdom Tradition in the Gospels*

In the Gospel of Mark (with a shorter version in Matthew's Gospel), the two sons of Zebedee come to Jesus and request from him that he would "Grant for us that we may sit in your glory, one by your right and one by your left." The account continues with Jesus's response, which contains a prophecy that many interpreters, ancient and modern, have understood as a prediction of the martyrdom of the Zebedee brothers.

> But Jesus said to them, "You do not know what you are asking; are you able to drink the cup which I am drinking, or to be baptized with the baptism with which I am being baptized?" They said to him, "We are able." But Jesus said to them: "You will drink the cup which I am drinking and be baptized with the baptism with which I am being baptized, but to sit at my right or at my left is not mine to give but is for them for whom it has been prepared (Mark 10:39; cf. Matt 20:23).⁵

The metaphors of the cup and baptism both seem to point to martyrdom as the intended meaning. The metaphor of drinking the cup is used elsewhere in the Gospels, including Mark's, specifically of Jesus's experience of being put to death (Matt 26:39, 42; Mark 14:36; Luke 22:42; John 18:11; Luke 12:50). The association of the cup with death is also found in other literature. In the *Martyrdom of Isaiah*, in a section probably dating to the first century CE or earlier, Isaiah, who is about to be cut in half, is depicted as warning the prophets to flee in order that they not share his fate: "Go to the district of Tyre and Sidon, because for me alone the LORD has mixed the cup" (*Mart. Isa.* 5.13, trans. *OTP* 1:164). The perhaps fourth-century Targum Neofiti similarly speaks of "the sons of man who die and taste the cup of death" (*Tg Neof.* Deut 32:1).[6] The possibly third-century *Martyrdom of Polycarp* understands Jesus's cup as a reference to death and may allude to Jesus's prophecy to the Zebedee brothers when it records Polycarp as saying: "I bless you that you have made me worthy of this day and hour, to receive a part among the number of the martyrs in the cup of Christ (ἐν τῷ ποτηρίῳ τοῦ Χριστοῦ)" (*Mart. Pol.* 14.2).[7]

Lastly, two early expositors understood the cup spoken of in the prophecy as a reference to death. Origen in the Latin *Vetus Interpretatio* version of his *Commentary on Matthew*, translated perhaps as early as the sixth century, comments on Jesus's words as follows: "Christ did not answer 'You are indeed able to drink my cup,' but looking to their future perfection (*perfectio*), he says: 'you will indeed drink of my cup and be baptized with my baptism.'"[8] Here, the cup is said to refer to John's "perfection," which was a common way of referring to martyrdom (cf. Ignatius, *Eph.* 3.1; Clement, *Strom.* 4.4).

Chrysostom (c. 349–407), who became patriarch of Constantinople, summarized Jesus's words in Matt 20:23, which speaks of only the cup, as follows: "you will be counted worthy of martyrdom and suffer those things that I suffer: you shall end your life (τὴν ζωὴν καταλύσετε) in a violent death (βιαίῳ θανάτῳ) and share with me in those things" (*Hom. Matt.* 20:23).[9] In another place, however, he writes that "James was beheaded, and John died oft" (*De. pet. fil. Zeb.*),[10] and Badham suggests that he either "wavered on the point" or changed his views.[11]

Baptism in the early Christian community was understood as a metaphor for being buried in death (cf. Rom 6:4; Col 2:12–13). Indeed, the Markan passage was utilized by Cyril of Jerusalem (fourth century) in support of the belief that someone confessing the faith as a martyr could be considered baptized, even if this person had not yet received water baptism,[12] on the basis that "the Savior calls martyrdom a baptism" (*cat.* 3.10, quoting Mark 10:38).[13] Similarly, the North African work, *Concerning Rebaptism*, traditionally attributed to Cyprian (c. 200–258), cites the prophecy of Jesus when it records (c. 250): "He said to the sons of Zebedee: 'Are you able?' For he knew the men had to be baptized, not only in water, but in their own blood" (*Rebapt.* 13).[14]

The probably fifth-century Latin *Incomplete Commentary on Matthew*, which places his martyrdom in Jerusalem, states: "The cup and the baptism are not the same. The cup is the suffering, but baptism is death itself. . . . To be sure, every death has some suffering in it, but not every suffering also has death. For they have been who suffered and yet were not killed, such as the confessors. They all indeed rank of the cup of the Lord, but they were not baptized by his death" (*Hom. 35 on Matt 20*).[15] This seems to leave little doubt that the work understood Jesus's prophecy as a reference to literal martyrdom.

Another early expositor, Aphrahat, the patriarch of Nineveh, may have been alluding to Jesus's words when he spoke of the martyrdom of James and John in a homily delivered in around the year 344:

> Great and excellent is the martyrdom of Jesus. . . . After Him was the faithful martyr Stephen, whom the Jews stoned. Simon also and Paul were perfect martyrs. And James and John walked in the footsteps of their Master Christ. . . . Also others of the apostles thereafter in diverse places confessed and proved themselves true martyrs (Aphrahat, *Dem.* 21.23).[16]

The reference to walking in Jesus's footsteps is perhaps informed by Jesus's prediction that the two sons of Zebedee would experience the same death that he was going to undergo.

*Reconciling Jesus's Prophecy and the Natural Death of John*

As the identification of the Apostle and Evangelist became generally accepted, the tradition of the Evangelist's peaceful death came to dominate the Johannine narrative (largely as a result of Eusebius's reconstruction; see chapter 6). Attempts were subsequently made at interpreting Jesus's words in terms of suffering rather than martyrdom. Thus, pointing to the tradition of John the Evangelist being placed in a vat of burning oil (cf. chapter 7), Jerome (347–420) argues that John "did not lack the spirit of martyrdom."[17] The second homily, *In Praise of St Stephen* by Gregory of Nyssa (335–394), has two readings, one of which interprets martyrdom in terms of suffering. Both recensions state:

> The blessed John, contending in many and diverse contests through his life, and distinguishing himself in all righteous acts of piety, being condemned into boiling water—this goal—was numbered in the choir of martyrs. Even thus was the manner of their death [i.e., of Peter, James, and John], who through death have bequeathed their deathless memory to the churches (*Altera Laudatio S. Stephani*).[18]

This seems to suggest that John was martyred in the boiling water ("oil" in other writers), in a likely attempt at conflating the Apostle John's martyrdom with the tradition of the Evangelist's being plunged into boiling oil, first found in Tertullian (see chapter 3).

One recension, however, "attenuates the force of the above quotation" by adding that martyrdom was accounted according to desire rather than outcome, which suggests that John had escaped martyrdom.[19] Badham reasons that "there would be strong reason why a scribe should insert such a gloss," adding that it would be unlikely that a scribe would excise it, had it been original.[20] In any case, it demonstrates an attempt at interpreting Jesus's prophecy in terms of suffering rather than literal martyrdom.

Such explanations continue to find expression among those favoring the traditional narrative, as, for example, when Guthrie claims that Jesus's prophecy "amounts to no more than a prediction of suffering."[21] Morris goes so far as to dismiss any argument for John's martyrdom from Jesus's prediction as "worthless."[22] But not all are convinced that this explanation can satisfy the meaning of Jesus's prediction. For Charles, "The meaning is unmistakable. Jesus predicts for James and John the same destiny that awaits Himself."[23] This is acknowledged by McDowell, even though he identifies the two Johns and favors the dominant tradition of John's peaceful death, for he writes that "the natural reading of this passage" is as a prediction of martyrdom.[24] It is doubtful that it would ever have become a point of contention, had not the Apostle and Evangelist, to whom belonged mutually exclusive traditions of death, been identified.

*Papias and the Martyrdom of John*

Two fragments were published during the nineteenth century which attribute to Papias the claim that the Apostle John was martyred. The first is from a copy of the *Chronicle* of the ninth-century monk George the Sinner (Hamartolos), preserved in Codex Coislinianus 305. The twenty-six or so other copies of Hamartolos's *Chronicle* relate John's death as follows:

> And after Domitian, Nerva reigned one year, who, having recalled John from the island, released him to dwell in Ephesus. He alone then remained alive of the twelve disciples, and, having written his Gospel, he fell asleep in peace (ἐν εἰρήνῃ ἀνεπαύσατο).[25]

But instead of, "he fell asleep in peace," Coislinianus 305 reads, "he was deemed worthy of martyrdom" (μαρτυρίου κατηξίωται), and continues:

> For Papias, the bishop of Hierapolis, having been an eyewitness of him [i.e., John], says in the second book of his *Dominical Sayings* that he was killed by Jews, having clearly fulfilled, along with his brother, Christ's prediction concerning them and their own confession and assent concerning this. For after the Lord said to them: "Are you able to drink the cup that I am drinking?" and after they readily assented and agreed, he says: "You will drink my cup and be baptized with the baptism that I am being baptized with." And reasonably so, for God cannot lie. And so also the much-learned Origen confirms in his interpretation of the Gospel according to Matthew, how that John was martyred (μεμαρτύρηκεν), indicating that he had learned it from the successors of the apostles. And indeed, the very-learned Eusebius in his *Ecclesiastical History* also says: "Thomas obtained Parthia by lot, but John Asia, and having spent his life there, he died in Ephesus" (Fragment 6).[26]

In this longer version, Hamartolos, who in common with writers of his age takes the Apostle and Evangelist to be one and the same, is apparently attempting to reconcile Papias's martyrdom tradition with that of the Evangelist's long life by placing the martyrdom in John's old age.[27]

Morris, who holds the traditional view, notes that this account is only found in one manuscript of Hamartolos and he suggests that it might have been inserted from another source,[28] though this would not invalidate the citation in any case. Nevertheless, Baum thinks that Coislinianus 305 is likely the oldest manuscript of Hamartolos's work,[29] and Dmitry Afinogenov, who specializes in Byzantine literature, has suggested that this manuscript may represent the "first and genuine version" of Hamartolos's chronicle.[30] Barclay, although rejecting the tradition of John's martyrdom, nevertheless admits that "it is the best manuscript," and he suggests that copyists were puzzled by the reference to his martyrdom and edited the text.[31]

A little later a second fragment came to light, this time from an epitome found in a seventh- or eight-century manuscript, believed to have been summarized from Philip of Sidé's lost *History*, which he published in thirty-six volumes between 434 and 439.[32] This epitome was noted briefly in chapter 1, in relation to the statement concerning those alive until the reign of Hadrian. It records:

> Papias in his second book says that John the Theologian and James his brother were killed by Jews. The aforementioned Papias recorded, as having received it from the daughters of Philip, that Barsabbas, who was also called Justus, having been tested by the unbelievers, suffered no harm when drinking the venom of a snake in the name of Christ. He also records other wondrous things, and especially one about the resurrection of the mother of Manaim from among the dead. Concerning those raised from the death by Christ, (he says) that they lived until the time of Hadrian (Fragment 5).[33]

There appears to be some shared literary relationship between this passage and Hamartolos's: each reads ἐν τῷ δευτέρῳ λόγῳ, using λόγος rather than βιβλίον;[34] both refer to Papias's book as κυριακὰ λόγια rather than λογίων κυριακῶν ἐξηγήσεις;[35] and both have ὑπό Ἰουδαίων ἀνῃρέθησαν, or ἀνῃρέθη.[36] Possibly Hamartolos used Philip's *History*;[37] possibly they both derived their information from a common source.[38]

One of Philip's sources was Eusebius's *Ecclesiastical History*, for he alludes to Eusebius's statement that the millennial views of Irenaeus and others were derived from Papias (cf. Eusebius, *Hist. eccl.* 3.39.13), but he seems to have supplemented his account by drawing independently from another Papian source, for he specifically cites Papias's second book, which Eusebius does not do, and he records details not found in Eusebius, such as the name of the person said by Philip's daughters to have been raised from the dead.

While many hold that Papias did speak of John's martyrdom,[39] others question the reliability of Philip's account due to his inaccuracies elsewhere. Lightfoot thus speaks of him as a "careless writer," noting that he makes Pantaenus the pupil of Clement and claims that Athenagoras's *Apology* was addressed to Hadrian and Antoninus rather than Aurelius and Commodus.[40] Schoedel refers to him as a "bungler" who cannot be trusted because he confuses Papias and Quadratus (though perhaps the mistake belonged to the epitomist, or was not a mistake at all; cf. chapter 1) and because his work was held in poor estimation by Photius (c. 810–c. 893).[41] Shanks, however, notes that while Photius was uncomplimentary in his critique of Philip, he criticized him "for being verbose, pedantic, diffuse, disorganized, and boring" rather than for being inaccurate;[42] he also notes that Socrates of Constantinople ("Scholasticus") (c. 380–after 439) criticized him for elucidating on too many fields instead of focusing on church history.[43]

On the other hand, Oberweis has noted the accuracy of Philip's quotations from Chrysostom, Theodore of Alexandria, and Pierius.[44] Indeed, Kelhoffer argues that Philip's account may preserve Papias's words more closely than Eusebius; he notes that where Eusebius records that Barsabbas drank "a noxious drug" (*Hist. eccl.* 3.39.9), Philip claims that Barsabbas ingested snake poison, and he suggests that Eusebius, knowing that snake poisons are only lethal if delivered into the bloodstream by a bite and not ingestion, clarified the account to preserve the miraculous element.[45]

Another objection sometimes raised against the reliability of the fragments is that Eusebius would have mentioned the tradition of the Apostle John's martyrdom had Papias related it.[46] However, Eusebius was not averse to passing over evidence irreconcilable with his own historical reconstructions,[47] and it is unlikely that he was not aware of the tradition, which was well-represented in the sources. Indeed, he demonstrates his familiarity with Clement of Alexandria's *Stromata* (*Hist. eccl.* 3.29–30), and in this work Clement claimed that the ministry of the apostles (Paul and the Twelve) ended with Nero (*Strom.* 7.17; cf. chapter 3), yet Eusebius, who identified the Apostle and Evangelist and privileged the tradition of John's peaceful death in the reign of Trajan (see chapter 6), makes no mention of this. He perhaps regarded the martyrdom tradition as nothing more than one of Papias's mythical tales (cf. Eusebius, *Hist. eccl.* 3.39.12).[48]

## Heracleon

A fragment attributed to the Valentinian teacher Heracleon (c. 170) by Clement of Alexandria in his *Stromata* may suggest awareness of the tradition of the Apostle John's martyrdom. According to Heracleon, "Matthew, Philip, Thomas, Levi and many others" escaped public confession of Christ (*Strom.* 4.9),[49] and as Charles notes, the name of John is conspicuous by its absence in the list, suggesting that he did not escape martyrdom, as the others did.[50] Morris objects that Heracleon had been speaking of those who confessed before authorities, irrespective of whether they were consequently martyred,[51] but this is incorrect, as Heracleon spoke of those who "confessed the confession of the voice and departed (ἐξῆλθον)."[52]

*The* Acts of Andrew

In the *Acts of Andrew*, perhaps written c. 200, Peter and John (who is not further identified) are depicted as appearing to Andrew in a vision (§ 20). In the account, Peter had already died, and Andrew is told that he would "drink Peter's cup," meaning that he would also be crucified. The appearance of John alongside Peter in the vision may suggest that John was conceived of as having died also, reflecting a tradition according to which John was outlived by at least one other apostle.

*The Martyrologies*

The ancient ecclesiastical calendars or martyrologies record the days on which different apostles and martyrs were remembered. Thus, the Syriac martyrology of Edessa, which dates from 411 but was based upon an earlier Greek work compiled in Nicomedia, probably in the period 360–375,[53] provides a long list of martyrs under the title: "The names of our Lords the Confessors and Victors and their days on which they gained (their) crowns."[54] It reads for 27 December:

> The first confessor at Jerusalem, Stephen the Apostle, the chief of the confessors. John and Jacob [i.e., James], the Apostles, at Jerusalem. In the city of Rome, Paul the Apostle, and Simon Cephas, the chief of the Apostles of our Lord. Hermes the exorcist became a confessor in the city of Bononia.[55]

The reference to Jerusalem situates James and John's martyrdom in the city, as it does with Stephen, and as the reference to Rome does with Paul and Peter.[56] The association of John's death with Jerusalem is also found in the eighth-century calendar of Reichenau, which records: "the sixth kalends of January (i.e., 27 December), in the basilica of the Mount of Olives, the birthday of John the Evangelist and of James the son of Alphaeus, the brother of the Lord."[57] Similarly, a ninth-century Sacramentary of Senlis in northern France reads: "the sixth kalends of January (i.e., 27 December), in the basilica of the Mount of Olives, on the birthday (*natal*) of saint John, apostle and evangelist."[58] The tenth-century Georgian calendar of Iovane Zosime similarly remembers John and James on 29 December and refers to a synaxis (a liturgy often held the day after the feast day of a saint) on the Mount of Olives on the following day.[59] Presumably the Mount of Olives was associated with the site of either John's death or burial.

Other martyrologies also remember the Apostle John on or around the same date. An Armenian martyrology which dates from perhaps as early as the third century thus remembers Peter and Paul on 27 December and "James and John, the Sons of Thunder" on 28 December.[60] A fragment of the Spanish *Martyrology of Carmona* (fifth or sixth century) inscribed on a marble column at the church *Sancta Maria la Mayor* remembers "John the Apostle" on 27 December, the day after the remembrance of "Stephen the martyr."[61] Similarly, the *Gothic Missal*, which is said to have derived much of its practice from Eastern sources, speaks of the day of the death (Latin, *natal* or "birth") of the apostles John and James as 27 December.[62] This is probably related to the mention of the "birthday of the apostles James and John" in the collection of sermons by Caesarius of Arles (d. 542).[63]

It has been objected that apostles were sometimes mentioned in the martyrologies even if they were not martyred, so that the martyrologies do not constitute conclusive evidence that John was held as a martyr.[64] This may be true, but it does not address the fact that many of these entries do specifically speak of John's martyrdom. Thus, the heading of the Syriac martyrology refers to the commemorative dates (including John's) as the days on which the confessors and victors received their crowns, denoting martyrdom, and both the *Gothic Missal* and the Sacramentary of Senlis speak of the day of remembrance as John's birthday (*natal*), which was a common way of referring to the day on which a martyr went to heaven.

The later marginalization of the martyrdom tradition is also reflected in the martyrologies. The calendar of Carthage (c. 505) may exhibit an attempt at correcting the martyrdom tradition by replacing the Apostle John with John the Baptist, for it reads for 27 December: "of St. John the Baptist, and of James the Apostle, whom (singular, Latin *quem*) Herod killed."[65] The same martyrology remembers John the Baptist on 24 June,[66] suggesting that the entry for 27 December originally pertained to John the Apostle, as in the other martyrologies.[67] The Hieronymian Martyrology, which was compiled in the sixth century from earlier sources,[68] removes any reference to martyrdom, reading for 27 December: "The assumption (*assumptio*) of John the Evangelist; and the ordination of James, brother of the Lord, as bishop."[69] Thus, one has identified the martyred John with the Baptist and one has removed reference to the martyrdom altogether, with both having apparently corrected an ancient tradition of the Apostle's martyrdom.

Eastern sources remember the repose of John the Evangelist on 26 September. Thus, the tenth-century *Menologium Graecorum* relates under this date the story of how John the Evangelist lay down in his grave near

Ephesus and how his body could not be found when his disciples returned (1.7).[70] This perhaps represents what was once the remembrance of a separate John, the Evangelist, on a different day. The Ethiopic tradition has, however, conflated both by observing 27 September as the feast day of the sons of Zebedee.[71]

## THE *A PRIORI* REJECTION OF THE MARTYRDOM TRADITION

Scholarly reception of the martyrdom tradition is polarized. On the one hand, Charles considers John's martyrdom to be a "reasonably established facts of history"[72] and Boismard similarly thinks it is "impossible de douter."[73] Hengel more cautiously opines that the tradition seems *"vertrauenswürdiger zu sein, als gemeinhin angenommen wird."*[74] On the other hand, scholars who follow the traditional Johannine narrative have tended to minimize or even dismiss the evidence for the Apostle's martyrdom. Thus, according to Morris, "the evidence cannot be said to be very impressive."[75] Bernard goes so far as to label the martyrdom tradition as "wholly untrustworthy,"[76] while Guthrie claims that the tradition may "be regarded as purely legendary."[77]

Skepticism toward the martyrdom tradition seems to be informed more by presuppositions than by the weakness of the evidence itself. The existence of two traditions of the death of John, pertaining to the Apostle and Evangelist respectively, is not in itself problematic.[78] It is rather the insistence that early sources identified the two Johns that necessitates that a choice be made between the two narratives, usually in favor of the tradition of the Evangelist's peaceful death, though Boismard favors the martyrdom narrative and calls Irenaeus's evidence into question, suggesting that he confused the apostle with another John.[79] Thus, Chapman dismisses the martyrdom tradition on the basis that "Papias could not possibly have" related it as it would contradict the tradition of his peaceful death,[80] while Barrett feels compelled to choose between "the veracity of Irenaeus and Eusebius on the one hand, and the intelligence and accuracy of Philip and George on the other."[81] Davies and Allison reject the tradition on the basis that it would "overthrow the testimony of Irenaeus,"[82] and Zuntz objects that Irenaeus records that John lived until Trajan's time.[83]

## THE JAMES WITH WHOM JOHN WAS REMEMBERED

Another assumption that is sometimes raised against the John's martyrdom is that it requires Schwartz's view that the Zebedee brothers' martyrdom took place at the same time.[84] Thus, Guthrie and Crossley object that the Apostle John was still alive several years after James's martyrdom (citing Gal 2:9) and that the account of James's martyrdom (in Acts

12:2) does not mention that of John.⁸⁵ This assumption is perhaps unnecessary,⁸⁶ though the James in question might have been another James who did die at around the same time as the Apostle John.

As discussed above, the epitome of Philip's *History* cites Papias as claiming that "John the Theologian and James his brother were killed by Jews" (Fragment 5), but the reference to James as John's brother (i.e., as the Zebedean James) may be a mistaken gloss (by Philip or his epitomizer) as the mention of John as "the Theologian" appears to be,⁸⁷ for the Zebedean James was put to death by Herod (cf. Acts 12:2), not Jews.⁸⁸ Furthermore, Baum points out that the placement of John before James does not agree with the order of the deaths of the Zebedee brothers, as James was martyred first.⁸⁹ Moreover, the Zebedean James's name is always placed before that of John in the Synoptics and in Acts (e.g., Matt 4:21; 17:1; Mark 1:29; 9:2; 10:35; 14:33 Luke 6:14; 9:54; Acts 1:13), an order that Papias himself maintains when speaking of them (Fragment 3).

The names of John and James, in that order, are also placed together in the martyrologies, possibly on account of dependence on Papias or a common source. While this James is usually identified either with the Zebedean James or with James the Lord's brother, the eighth-century calendar (i.e., martyrology) of Reichenau discussed above speaks of "the birthday of John the Evangelist and of James the son of Alphaeus, the brother of the Lord." It seems that the survival of the mention of Alphaeus here is due to his being wrongly identified with a more significant James, that is, with James the Just, the "brother of the Lord" (see below).

A number of other sources relate that James the son of Alphaeus was killed by Jews, just as Papias states of his James. Thus, the Latin *Incomplete Commentary on Matthew* (fifth century?), which places his martyrdom in Jerusalem, states: "[the Jews] stoned Stephen; they rejoiced in the death of James; again they stoned James, the son of Alpheus. Because of all these things, Jerusalem was destroyed by the Romans" (*Hom. 41 on Matt 22*).⁹⁰ Likewise, the work, *On the Twelve Apostles*, wrongly attributed to Hippolytus, claims that James the son of Alphaeus was stoned to death by Jews while preaching in Jerusalem and that he was buried on the spot, by the temple. This is likely related to the claim of Gregory of Tours (*gloria mart.* 26) that James was buried on the Mount of Olives (which was near the temple).⁹¹

James the son of Alphaeus was often mistakenly identified in sources with James the Just, Jesus's brother,⁹² and Hegesippus already in the second century seems to have conflated their martyrdoms into a single account. He relates that James was thrown from a tower in the temple and then stoned by bystanders; while this was happening, he was given a fatal blow with a fuller's club (*Hist. eccl.* 2.23.16–18). He was then buried near the temple, where his memorial was said to remain (2.23.18). As Martin observes, the "[m]ultiple attempts at killing James (a fall, stoning, being beaten over the head) suggest that this is a legendary combination of motifs."[93] Jerome describes Hegesippus as "weaving together (*texens*) all the histories of ecclesiastical deeds from the passion of the Lord until his own time" (*Vir.* 22.1),[94] and perhaps his "weaving" involved an uncritical combining of sources into a single conflated narrative.

Clement of Alexandria's account of James the Just's martyrdom only records him as having been thrown from the temple and beaten with a club (*apud* Eusebius, *Hist. eccl.* 2.1.5): there is no mention of the stoning or of his being buried near the temple, associated with the son of Alphaeus in other sources. Indeed, stoning would not have occurred in the sacred temple grounds and had to be administered away from the court, "outside the camp" (*m. Sanh.* 6.1). The condemned would be placed in a high spot, twice the height of a man (*m. Sanh.* 6.4), and it was perhaps this circumstance which suggested the conflation with the account of James being thrown from the pinnacle of the temple.[95]

That Hegesippus conflated two separate accounts would explain the two conflicting dates for James's martyrdom given by Epiphanius, whose account was likely dependent upon him.[96] Epiphanius thus relates that it took place twenty-four years after the ascension and immediately before the siege of Jerusalem, or around 70 CE (*Pan.* 78.14.5). Since Hegesippus records that Simeon, Jesus's cousin, was ordained bishop in James the Just's place following the return of the Jerusalem Christians to the city after the Jewish War (*Hist. eccl.* 3.11.1), it can be inferred that the later date represents the tradition associated with James the Just and that it was the son of Alphaeus whose martyrdom was placed twenty-four years after the ascension.[97]

The work entitled the *Contendings of the Apostles*, preserved only in an Ethiopic translation but based upon works perhaps composed in Coptic as early as the sixth century,[98] differentiates both James the son of Alphaeus and James the Just and relates the martyrdoms of each. It recounts that the son of Alphaeus was brought before "Claudius the king" by the multitudes in Jerusalem on account of his preaching, and that he was ordered to be stoned by Claudius and was subsequently buried near the temple.[99]

The placement of the narrative in Claudius's reign is also found in the *Lamp of Darkness*,[100] a work originally written in Coptic by Ibn Kabar in the thirteenth century and preserved in an Arabic translation. Epiphanius's placement of James's martyrdom twenty-four years after the ascension could also correspond to the end of the reign of Claudius, who died in October 54.

The *Contendings* further relates, like Clement, that James the Just was thrown from a pinnacle of the temple and beaten with a fuller's club.[101] It adds that James the Just was buried in a synagogue,[102] possibly referring to the Zion church in Jerusalem.[103]

The preservation of unconflated versions of martyrdoms in Clement and the *Contendings* point to their use of sources that predated Hegesippus's conflated account, which was written in the second half of the second century.[104] Budge suggested on independent grounds that the *Contendings* reflects traditions that date back possibly as far as the second century, adding that such sources would have been written in a Semitic dialect (he suggests Hebrew or Syriac),[105] which would agree with Eusebius's claim that Hegesippus had used Syriac and Hebrew sources (*Hist. eccl.* 4.22.8).

The Apostle John's death, like that of James the son of Alphaeus, is also associated with Jerusalem and with the Mount of Olives in some martyrologies, as noted above. Furthermore, chapter 4 will discuss evidence that the Apostle John's martyrdom was held to have occurred at the end of Claudius's reign, as James's seems to have been. Probably the original form of the tradition spoke of the martyrdoms of both the Apostle John and James the son of Alphaeus, possibly at the same time, and of their burial on the Mount of Olives, on account of which they were remembered together. But the mention of the two Zebedee brothers together in Jesus's prophecy of martyrdom probably facilitated some confusion of the James in question, as did the later identification of the son of Alphaeus with James the Just, leading to the later variations found in Philip and the martyrologies.

## CONCLUSION

The tradition of the Apostle John's martyrdom is well attested in an array of early Christian sources, including two Gospels, Papias, Aphrahat, Chrysostom, and the martyrologies. Indeed, it is better attested than the Evangelist's peaceful death. Those denying the existence of the martyrdom tradition have tended either to interpret the sources in ways that do not require a literal martyrdom or to question the reliability of the sources. But underlying all of these objections, it seems, is the assumption that the Apostle John of the early sources was identified with John the Evangelist, whose natural death in old age is attested in early Christian literature. If this assumption is removed, the evidence can be explained without difficulty on the supposition that there are two narratives because there were two separate figures with whom these narratives were associated.

## NOTES

1. Cf. Bauckham, *Eyewitnesses*, 463.
2. So, e.g., Bernard Orchard and Harold Riley, *The Order of the Synoptics: Why Three Synoptic Gospels?* (Macon, Ga.: Mercer University Press, 1987), 208; Geoffrey M. Hahneman, *The Muratorian Fragment and the Development of the Canon* (OThM; Oxford: Clarendon, 1992), 107. H. A. G. Houghton places them in the late fourth century (*The*

*Latin New Testament: A Guide to Its Early History, Texts, and Manuscripts* [New York: Oxford University Press, 2016], 157).

3. Frederick W. Weidmann, *Polycarp and John: The Harris Fragments and Their Challenge to the Literary Traditions* (Notre Dame, Ind.: University of Notre Dame Press, 1999), 47; cf. 74.

4. Barrett, *St. John*, 104; Davies and Allison, *Matthew*, 91; cf. Baum, "Papias und der Presbyter Johannes," 35.

5. Translated by the author from the Greek text in Michael Holmes, ed., *The Greek New Testament: SBL Edition* (Atlanta: Society of Biblical Literature, 2011–2013).

6. Martin McNamara, *Targum Neofiti 1: Deuteronomy* (ArBib 5; Collegeville, Minn.: The Liturgical Press, 1997), 147.

7. Translated by the author from the Greek text in Holmes, *Apostolic Fathers*, 238.

8. Origen, *Commentary on Matthew* according to the *Vetus Interpretatio*, 16.5; translated by the author from the Latin text in *PG* 13:1381–82.

9. Translated from *PG* 58:620; cf. Charles, *Revelation*, vol.1, xlvii; M.-É. Boismard, *Le martyre de Jean l'apôtre* (CRB 35; Paris, Gabalda, 1996), 51.

10. The translation is given by Francis Pritchett Badham, "The Martyrdom of John the Apostle," *AJT* 8 (1904): 541.

11. Badham, "Martyrdom of John," 541.

12. Henry Barclay Swete, ed., *The Gospel according to St. Mark: The Greek Text with Introduction, Notes and Indices* (London: Macmillan, 1898), 237–38.

13. Translated by the author from the Greek text in Swete, *St. Mark*, 237.

14. See Charles, *Revelation*, vol. 1, xlviii; cf. Robert Eisler, *The Enigma of the Fourth Gospel* (London: Methuen, 1938), 64; Barclay, *Introduction to John*, 31.

15. James Kellerman, trans., Thomas C. Oden, ed., *Incomplete Commentary on Matthew (Opus Imperfectum)*, vol. 2 (Downers Grove, Ill.: IVP, 2010), 286.

16. Translation in Charles, *Revelation*, vol.1, xlviii; cf. Eisler, *Enigma*, 64; Jean Colson, *L'énigme du Disciple que Jésus aimait* (ThH 10; Paris: Beauchesne, 1969): 74–75; Boismard, *Le martyre*, 52.

17. Jerome, *Comm. Matt.* 20.23; Latin text in D. Hurst and M. Adriaen, eds., *Commentariorum in Matheum libri IV* (CCSL 77; Turnhout, 1969), 178.

18. I have followed the translation in Badham, "Martyrdom of John," 541.

19. Badham, "Martyrdom of John," 541 n. 6; the Greek text is in *PG* 46:732.

20. Badham, "Martyrdom of John," 541 n. 6. Cf. Boismard, *Le martyre*, 47–9.

21. Guthrie, *Introduction*, 273. See also W. D. Davies and D. C. Allison, *A Critical and Exegetical Commentary on the Gospel according to Saint Matthew*, vol. 3 (ICC; Edinburgh: T. & T. Clark, 1997), 89; cf. Günther Zuntz, "Papiana," *ZNW* 82 (1991): 242–45.

22. Morris, *Studies*, 282.

23. Charles, *Revelation*, vol. 1, xlv.

24. Sean McDowell, "A Historical Evaluation of the Evidence for the Death of the Apostles as Martyrs for their Faith," (PhD diss., Southern Baptist Theological Seminary, 2014), 251.

25. Translated from *PG* 14:1532.

26. Author's translation.

27. Cf. Schoedel, *Polycarp*, 120–21; Charles E. Hill, *From the Lost Teaching of Polycarp* (Tübingen: Mohr Siebeck, 2006), 175–76); Norelli, *Papia di Hierapolis*, 440.

28. Morris, *Studies*, 281.

29. Baum, "Papias und der Presbyter Johannes," 36.

30. Dmitry Afinogenov, "The Story of the Patriarch Constantine II of Constantinople in Theophanes and George the Monk: Transformations of a Narrative," in *History as Literature in Byzantium: Papers from the Fortieth Spring Symposium of Byzantine Studies, University of Birmingham, April 2007*, ed. Ruth Macrides (SPBS 15; Farnham, UK: Ashland, 2010), 208.

31. Barclay, *Introduction to John*, 35.

32. Hengel, *Johannine Question*, 158 n. 121.

33. Author's translation.

34. Beckwith, *Apocalypse*, 382; Schoedel, *Polycarp*, 120.
35. Beckwith, *Apocalypse*, 382; Schoedel, *Polycarp*, 120; Norelli, *Papia di Hierapolis*, 437.
36. Beckwith, *Apocalypse*, 382.
37. Beckwith, *Apocalypse*, 382; Boismard, *Le martyre*, 56.
38. Schoedel notes both possibilities (*Polycarp*, 120).
39. Gunther, "The Elder John," 178–79; Ernst Haenchen, *John: A Commentary on the Gospel of John, Chapters 1–6*, trans. Robert W. Funk (Hermeneia; Philadelphia: Fortress Press, 1984), 10; Hengel, *Johannine Question*, 21; 158 n. 121b; James H. Charlesworth, *The Beloved Disciple: Whose Witness Validates the Gospel of John?* (Valley Forge, Penn.: Trinity Press, 1995), 240; Boismard, *Le martyre*, 57; Strecker, *The Johannine Letters*, 14 n. 30.
40. Joseph B. Lightfoot, *Biblical Essays* (London: Macmillan, 1893), 95.
41. Schoedel, *Polycarp*, 119–20.
42. Shanks, *Papias*, 217, citing Photius, *Bibliothèque*, 1.20–21.
43. Shanks, *Papias*, 217, citing *NPNF* 2 2.168.
44. Michael Oberweis, "Das Papias-Zeugnis vom Tode des Johannes Zebedäi," *NovT* 38 (1996): 283; cf. Boismard, *Le martyre*, 57.
45. James A. Kelhoffer, *Miracle and Mission: The Authentication of Missionaries and Their Message in the Longer Ending of Mark* (Tübingen: Mohr Siebeck, 2000), 437–43.
46. J. H. Bernard, "The Traditions as to the Death of John," *ICQ* 1 (1908): 57; Baum, "Papias und der Presbyter Johannes," 35; Culpepper, *John*, 155.
47. See, e.g., Robert M. Grant, "Eusebius and His Church History," in *Understanding the Sacred Text: Essays in Honor of Morton S. Enslin on the Hebrew Bible and Christian Beginnings*, ed. John Reumann (Valley Forge, Pa.: Judson, 1972), 233–47; Hengel, *Johannine Question*, 21; Richard Bauckham, *The Testimony of the Beloved Disciple: Narrative, History, and Theology in the Gospel of John* (Grand Rapids: Baker, 2007), 57–8; Eugenia Scarvelis Constantinou, *Guiding to a Blessed End: Andrew of Caesarea and His Apocalypse Commentary in the Ancient Church* (Washington, DC: Catholic University of America Press, 2013), 29–30.
48. Cf. H. Latimer Jackson, *The Problem of the Fourth Gospel* (Cambridge: Cambridge University Press, 1918), 145 n. 3.
49. Translated from the Greek text in Otto Stählin, ed., *Clemens Alexandrinus*, vol. 2: *Stromata 1–6* (GCS; Leipzig: Hinrichs, 1906), and so hereafter.
50. Charles, *Revelation*, vol. 1, 47; cf. Francis Pritchett Badham, "The Martyrdom of St. John," *AJT* 3 (1899): 731.
51. Morris, *Studies*, 282.
52. Cf. Edwin A. Abbott, *The Fourfold Gospel: Introduction* (Cambridge: University Press, 1913), 168 n. 1.
53. Boismard, *Le martyre*, 21–22.
54. William Wright, "An Ancient Syrian Martyrology," *JSL* 8 (1866): 423.
55. Translation in Wright, "Syrian Martyrology," 423; cf. Boismard, *Le martyre*, 22.
56. Boismard, *Le martyre*, 27.
57. C. L. Feltoe, "St John and St James in Western 'Non-Roman' Kalendars," *JTS* 40 (1909): 591; Boismard, *Le martyre*, 25.
58. Translated by the author from the Latin text as given by Feltoe, "St John and St James," 591.
59. Gérard Garitte, ed., *Le calendrier palestino-géorgien du Sinaiticus 34 (Xe siècle)* (SH 30; Brussels: Société des Bollandistes, 1958), 420–21. Thanks to Dr Daniel Galadza for drawing my attention to this work in private correspondence.
60. See Davies and Allison, *Matthew*, 91 n. 39; cf. Eisler, *Enigma*, 60.
61. Boismard, *Le martyre*, 36; cf. Eisler, *Enigma*, 61.
62. Feltoe, "St John and St James," 590; Boismard, *Le martyre*, 25.
63. See Boismard, *Le martyre*, 30.
64. Bernard, *St. John*, vol. 1, xliii; Morris, *Studies*, 281.
65. Translated from the Latin text in Eisler, *Enigma*, 60; Boismard, *Le martyre*, 28.

66. Eisler, *Enigma*, 60.
67. So, Barrett, *St. John*, 104; contra Guthrie, *Introduction*, 274.
68. Boismard thinks that its principal source was the Greek martyrology used for the Syriac martyrology of Edessa (*Le martyre*, 22).
69. Translated by the author from the Latin text in Bernard, "Traditions," 62. The Celtic calendars are said to have followed the same reading (Feltoe, "St John and St James," 592).
70. Greek text in *PG* 117:73; an English translation can be found in Culpepper, *John*, 235 n. 4.
71. Eisler, *Enigma*, 61.
72. Charles, *Revelation*, vol.1, xlix.
73. Boismard, *Le martyre*, 13.
74. Hengel, *Die johanneische Frage*, 88; idem, *Johannine Question*, 21; cf. 158–59.
75. Morris, *Studies*, 280.
76. Bernard, "Traditions," 52.
77. Guthrie, *Introduction*, 274.
78. Thus, Francis J. Moloney accounts for the differing traditions by positing that the Apostle and Evangelist were originally distinguished (*The Gospel of John* [SP 4; Collegeville, Minn.: Liturgical Press, 1998], 8).
79. Boismard, *Le martyre*, 77.
80. Chapman, *John the Presbyter*, 78.
81. Barrett, *St. John*, 104.
82. Davies and Allison, *Matthew*, 90–91.
83. Zuntz, "Papiana," 246.
84. Eduard Schwartz, "Über den Tod der Söhne Zebedäi. Ein Beitrag zur Geschichte des Johannesevangeliums" (*GS* 5; Berlin: de Gruyter, 1963), 48–123.
85. Guthrie, *Introduction*, 274; James G. Crossley, *The Date of Mark's Gospel: Insight from the Law in Earliest Christianity* (London: T. & T. Clark, 2004), 57.
86. Hengel, *Johannine Question*, 159 n. 121; Norelli, *Papia di Hierapolis*, 375–76.
87. See, e.g., Norelli, *Papia di Hierapolis*, 378.
88. . Bernard ("Traditions," 58) and Zuntz ("Papiana," 248) raise this point as evidence against the authenticity of Philip's Papian fragment.
89. Baum ("Papias und der Presbyter Johannes," 35) raises this objection as evidence that Papias likely spoke of the martyrdom of John the Baptist rather than of the Apostle.
90. Translation in Kellerman, *Incomplete Commentary*, 328.
91. Cited in Els Rose, *Ritual Memory: The Apocryphal Acts and Liturgical Commemoration in the Early Medieval West (c. 500-1215)* (Leiden: Brill, 2009), 133.
92. Roelof van den Broek, *Pseudo-Cyril of Jerusalem On the Life and the Passion of Christ: A Coptic Apocryphon* (VCSup 118; Leiden, Brill, 2012), 18; 28.
93. Ralph P. Martin, *James* (WBC 48; Dallas: Word, 1998), lii; so also, Painter, *Just James*, 119.
94. Translated from the Latin text in Cécile Lanéry, *Ambroise de Milan hagiographe* (Institut d'Études Augustiniennes, 2008), 471 n. 22, citing K. Siamake, ed., Ἱερωνυμοῦ, *De viris Illustribus* (Thessalonica, 1992). Cf. *PL* 23:674.
95. See also the discussion in Richard Bauckham, "For what Offence was James put to Death?," in *James the Just and Christian Origins* (NovTSup 98; Leiden: Brill, 2014), 203–04.
96. See, e.g., Joseph B. Lightfoot, *The Apostolic Fathers: Ignatius, and Polycarp*, part 1, vol. 1 (London: Macmillan, 1889), 328–30; James H. Ropes, *A Critical and Exegetical Commentary on the Epistle of St. James* (ICC; New York: Scribner, 1916), 66.
97. Eusebius likely merged the account of James's martyrdom with that of an unrelated James who was sentenced in 62 CE, along with others, to stoning by the Sanhedrin on the charge that he had broken the law (*Hist. eccl.* 2.23.20–22; cf. Josephus, *Ant.* 20.9.1 § 200–1); see, e.g., Nathaniel Lardner, *The Works of Nathaniel Lardner*, vol. 3 (London: Thomas Hamilton, 1815), 377; Homersham Cox, *The First Century of Chris-*

*tianity* (London: Longmans, 1886), 88; Richard Carrier, "Origen, Eusebius, and the Accidental Interpolation in Josephus, Jewish Antiquities 20.200," *JECS* 20 (2012): 489–514. The two accounts cannot be reconciled; Hegesippus's and Clement's James was thrown from the temple in an act of momentary rage, not judicially sentenced to stoning, and James the Just is said to have died immediately before the siege, not in 62 CE as in Josephus. Indeed, James's martyrdom occurred after that of Peter in the Clementine literature and in the first year of Vespasian (69 CE) according to the *Chronicon Paschale*. The tradition of the appointment of James's successor after the war also points to a later date. Josephus and Hegesippus were often confused (see, e.g., Rainer Riesner, *Paul's Early Period: Chronology, Mission Strategy, Theology*, trans. Doug Stott [Grand Rapids: Eerdmans, 1998], 185–86) and this is probably responsible for the misattribution of the death of an otherwise unknown James in Josephus to James the Just, whose martyrdom was related by Hegesippus.

98. E. A. Wallis Budge, ed. and trans., *The Contendings of the Apostles: Being the Histories and the Lives and Martyrdoms and Deaths of the Twelve Apostles and Evangelists*, vol. 2: *The English Translation* (Oxford: Oxford University Press, 1901), viii.

99. Budge, *Contendings*, 265–66.

100. There is no complete scholarly edition of this work; a translation of the section on James the son of Alphaeus can be found in Felix Haase, ed., *Apostel und Evangelisten in den orientalischen Überlieferungen* (NTA 9; Münster: Aschendorff, 1922), 298.

101. Budge, *Contendings*, 88–89.

102. Budge, *Contendings*, 89.

103. This church was associated with James and referred to as a synagogue (see Jerome Murphy-O'Connor, "The Cenacle—Setting for Acts 2:44–45," in *The Book of Acts in its Palestinian Setting*, ed. Richard Bauckham [BAFCS 4; Grand Rapids: Eerdmans, 1995]), 309).

104. The *Second Apocalypse of James*, in a probably separate conflation, relates that James was thrown from the temple (a tradition belonging to James the Just), adding that a stone was placed on his abdomen (See *m. Sanh.* 6.4; Bauckham, "For what Offence?," 203–4). After this, James was made to stand again and dig a hole; they then stoned him and buried him in the hole, reflecting the tradition of James, son of Alphaeus, being stoned and buried near the temple (2 *Apoc. Jas.* 61.1–62.14).

105. Budge, *Contendings*, viii.

# THREE
# John the Evangelist in the Earliest Sources

While it is commonly claimed that early sources identified the Evangelist with the Apostle John,[1] others note that writers before the third century do not explicitly identify them; on the contrary, they observe, descriptions of the Evangelist in this period often better correlate with Papias's Elder than to the Apostle.[2] The question is further complicated by the mention of the Seer of Patmos, the purported author of Revelation, by some early Christian writers, which raises the question of whether this figure was identified with the Apostle, the Evangelist, or a third and separate Johannine figure.

This chapter will examine these claims and survey the sources with a view to ascertaining which of these approaches best fits the evidence. It will also consider the position which the Seer of Patmos occupies in these writers. It will conclude that the Evangelist of the early sources was often identified with the Seer, and that this identification was never explicitly denied; it will further argue that the Evangelist was likely distinguished from the Apostle, and that the profile of the Evangelist found in early writers is consistent with Papias's John the Elder rather than with his Apostle.

## THE SILENCE OF IGNATIUS

Ignatius, bishop of Antioch, wrote letters to seven churches while being led to his execution in Rome, c. 107, including one to the church at Ephesus, in which he addressed disunity involving polarized views toward the bishop, Onesimus (Eph. 5.1–3). Ignatius only mentions Paul in his letter (12.2), and this has suggested to some that the tradition of John's residence in Ephesus was unknown to Ignatius.³ However, Paul is only mentioned once, within a martyrdom context which might not have been applicable to the John of the Asian tradition (Ign. *Eph.* 12.2).⁴ Ignatius's silence may also be mitigated by the possibility that it was a secondary John who was associated with the city, such as Papias's Elder,⁵ though it is more difficult to account for on the supposition that he identified John the Apostle with an Ephesian John.

## POLYCARP THE DISCIPLE OF JOHN

Polycarp (d. c. 155/6 or 167), bishop of Smyrna, demonstrates familiarity with 1 John 4:2–3; 3:8, and possibly 2 John 7 (*Phil* 7.1) in his extant letter to the church at Philippi,⁶ though he does not mention John by name. According to Irenaeus, however, who claims to have attended Polycarp's lectures as a young man, probably in the 130s–140s,⁷ Polycarp related anecdotes concerning his association with John the Evangelist. He thus repeats Polycarp's anecdote of John going to the baths at Ephesus, where he caught sight of the false teacher Cerinthus (*Haer.* 3.3.4), and he relates how Polycarp claimed to have known John and others who had "seen the Lord," adding that Polycarp declared all things as one who claimed to have received them from the eyewitnesses of the word of life (ὡς παρὰ τῶν αὐτοπτῶν τῆς ζωῆς τοῦ λόγου παρειληφώς) (*apud* Eusebius, *Hist. eccl.* 5.20.6), where the allusion is to 1 John 1:1.⁸ This likely identifies Polycarp's John with the author of 1 John, but Irenaeus does not provide any indication that Polycarp identified his John with the Apostle.

Perhaps Ariston was also one of those eyewitnesses whom Polycarp was said to have known, for the late fourth-century *Apostolic Constitutions* (7.46) identifies Ariston—probably the same as Aristion—as the first bishop of Smyrna,⁹ the city in which Polycarp later became bishop.

The few sources available concerning Polycarp's life suggest that he could have known John and other eyewitnesses in the latter part of the first century. The third-century *Martyrdom of Polycarp* famously records Polycarp's claim, made immediately before his martyrdom, to have served Christ for eighty-six years. Some hold that this refers to Polycarp's age at the time of his martyrdom,¹⁰ but it may instead refer to the number of years from his baptism (the time of which is unknown).¹¹ The latter interpretation may receive some support from the Coptic Harris fragments, which make Polycarp to have been 104 at the time of his death (line 10),¹² and from the third- or fourth-century *Life of Polycarp* which claims he was adopted as a child and instructed (and presumably later baptized) in the Christian faith. The date of Polycarp's martyrdom is variously placed between 155 and 167,¹³ which means that Polycarp may have been born as early as the middle of the first century, allowing him to have known John in the latter part of the first century. However, this chronological placement corresponds with Papias's Elder rather than his Apostle.

## JUSTIN MARTYR'S JOHN

Justin Martyr (c. 100–c. 165) was a native of Palestine who is said by Eusebius to have engaged in a discussion at Ephesus with a Jew named Trypho (*Hist. eccl.* 4.18.6), an account of which he later published (c. 160) while living in Rome. In this work, he speaks by name only of John the Seer, whom he refers to "one of the apostles of Christ" named John:

> A certain man among us (παρ' ἡμῖν ἀνήρ τις), whose name was John, one of the apostles of Christ (εἷς τῶν ἀποστόλων τοῦ χριστοῦ), prophesied in a revelation given to him that those believing in our Christ would accomplish a thousand years in Jerusalem (*Dial.* 81).[14]

Justin's reference to this John as being "among us" (παρ' ἡμῖν) may suggest that he had resided in Ephesus. Because Justin speaks of this John as "a certain man" named John, and as "one of the apostles of Christ," many have concluded that he was referring to John the son of Zebedee,[15] but it is unclear whether Justin limited the word "apostle" to the Twelve or whether he could employ it in a more extended sense of any eyewitness disciple that had been sent out by Christ. While he does refer to the "twelve apostles" (*Dial.* 42), in other places it is unclear whether he speaks only of the twelve when he refers to "the apostles" (e.g., *Apol.* 42.4). He also uses the word "apostle" of Jesus, referring to him as "the Apostle of God the Father" (*Apol.* 12.9; cf. 63.5, 10, 14), and elsewhere he calls the prophets sent to Israel "apostles" (*Dial.* 75.3).

### The Extended Use of the Word "Apostle" in Writers of the Period

The particular expression "apostles of Christ" occurs twice in Paul's writings, neither of which refer to members of the Twelve (1 Thess 2:6 cf. 2 Cor 11:13), though it is unclear whether this usage influenced Justin's terminology. The Apostle Paul employs the word "apostle" to describe a wider number of eyewitness disciples of Jesus (1 Cor 15:4, 7), and the book of Acts speaks of Barnabas and Paul as "apostles," though neither were of the Twelve (Acts 14:14; cf. 1 Cor 9:5–6). The book of Revelation referred to by Justin speaks of the "twelve apostles of the lamb" (Rev 21:14) but also seems to assume the existence of apostles in a wider sense, speaking of the "apostles and prophets" who are to rejoice over the fall of Babylon (Rev 18:20).[16] Elsewhere, the risen Christ is said to commend those who had tested those who claimed to be apostles and were not (Rev 2:2). If apostles were limited to the Twelve, the need for such testing would be superfluous; this seems to better make sense on the supposition that there were others outside of the Twelve who were apostles, necessitating that those claiming to be such were tested.

The *Didache*, perhaps half a century or more before Justin's statement, also seems to use the word "apostle" in an extended sense, for it directs its readers to receive "every apostle" that comes to them in the course of their travels, while going on to warn them that apostles who remained and took advantage of their hospitality by overstaying their visits were "false prophets" (11.4–5). Furthermore, the seventy disciples sent out by Jesus were regarded as apostles by Tertullian (*Marc.* 4.24) and Irenaeus (*Haer.* 2.21.1; cf. discussion below) a few decades after Justin wrote, and a Syriac source quoted by Eusebius speaks of "Thaddeus, an apostle, one of the Seventy" (*Hist. eccl.* 1.13.11 [Lake]).

In light of the extended use of the word both before and after Justin's time, there is a question as to whether Justin's reference to "a certain John" as "one of the apostles of Christ" necessitates that he understood him as one of the Twelve, though it is reasonable to conclude that he did hold the author of Revelation to have been an eyewitness disciple of Jesus.

## IRENAEUS'S JOHN, THE DISCIPLE OF THE LORD

Irenaeus, who spent his early life in Asia Minor, served as bishop of Lugdunum in Gaul (now Lyon in France), where he wrote his monumental work, *Against Heresies* (c. 185). He is the first extant writer to speak of John the Evangelist's residence in Ephesus (*Haer.* 3.1.1) and death during Trajan's reign (3.3.4; cf. 2.22.5). He identifies this John with the Beloved Disciple of the Fourth Gospel (cf. John 13:23), speaking of him as "John, the disciple of the Lord, who also leaned upon his chest" (*Haer.* 3.1.1; *apud.* Eusebius, *Hist. eccl.* 5.8.4); elsewhere he attributes to him the Gospel (*Haer.* 2.2.5), 1 John (*Haer.* 3.16.5), 2 John (*Haer.* 1.16.3), and Revelation (*Haer.* 4.20.11). He likely derived much of his knowledge both from his familiarity with Papias's writings (*Haer.* 5.33.4) and from listening to Polycarp's lectures as a young man in Asia Minor (*apud* Eusebius, *Hist. eccl.* 5.20.6).

Irenaeus thus did identify the Evangelist with the Seer of Patmos; however, while many hold that Irenaeus identified John the Evangelist with the Apostle,[17] he never unequivocally speaks of this John as the son of Zebedee or by any other designation that would have clearly indicated that he made this identification,[18] referring to him instead as "John, the disciple of the Lord," as "the disciple of the Lord," or simply as "John."[19]

In the five places in which Irenaeus does refer to John the son of Zebedee, he speaks of him simply as "John," though always in connection with narratives found in the Gospels and Acts (*Haer.* 2.24.4; 3.12.3 (twice); 3.12.5; 3.12.15), and with no allusion to him as the famous Evangelist. However, he likewise introduces John the Baptist as "John," without any epithet (1.3.5; 3.12.7), and in both cases the reader is alerted to which John is being spoken of by the texts which are quoted or alluded to in the context. Irenaeus similarly speaks simply of "James" elsewhere in his work, leaving it to the context to inform the reader whether he is referring to James the son of Zebedee (2.24.4) or James the brother of Jesus (3.12.14).

*John as Apostle*

The strongest evidence for Irenaeus's Zebedean identification of the Evangelist is no doubt his two references to the Evangelist as "the apostle," found in a section of his work in which he refutes the interpretations of the Fourth Gospel found in Ptolemy (fl. c. 160), a Gnostic teacher and disciple of Valentinus (*Haer.* 1.9.2, 3). Elsewhere in his work the designation of "the apostle" is used seventy-two times, always of Paul,[20] and the unique use of it of John in this section may reflect Ptolemy's terminology,[21] though Irenaeus in any case accepts and employs it himself. In other contexts, too, it is clear that Irenaeus places John among the apostles, as when he speaks of those elders who "saw not only John but other apostles also" (2.22.5; cf. 3.21.3; 3.5.1; 3.11.9; 3.3.4).

Watson, who views Irenaeus as the culmination of a tendency of writers to amalgamate the figures of the Seer, Elder, and Apostle,[22] argues that the designation of John as an apostle marks him as the son of Zebedee, since, he asserts, Irenaeus "barely deviates" from a conception according to which there are twelve apostles plus Paul.[23] This needs qualifying; while he does refer to the Twelve as an exclusive group, speaking of them as the "twelve-pillared foundation of the Church" (4.21.3), and while he does speak of both the twelve and Paul as apostles, he does not speak of the twelve and Paul as constituting an exclusive group.

Furthermore, Irenaeus used the word "apostle" in a wider sense, of any eyewitness proclaimer of Jesus, as illustrated in his statement that John the Baptist was more than just a prophet, but "an apostle and prophet," since he not only announced Jesus's coming but saw him himself and proclaimed him and persuaded others to believe on him (*Haer.* 3.11.14). Zelyck, who like Watson claims that for Irenaeus, the apostles were Paul and the twelve,[24] suggests that this "is simply related to his function as a reliable witness to Jesus, not that he is categorically equivalent to the twelve apostles."[25] This is no doubt the case, but then why cannot the same reasoning be applied to other eyewitness followers outside of the Twelve, such as (as proposed here) John, the disciple of the Lord, who is spoken of as an apostle but never as "John the Apostle," which might have indicated equivalency with the twelve?[26]

Furthermore, Irenaeus presupposes that the seventy disciples sent out by Jesus (Luke 10:1) were apostles. When addressing the Valentinian claim that the twelve apostles were chosen as a type of the twelve Aeons, which they called the Duodecad (*Haer.* 2.21.2), Irenaeus points out that if the twelve apostles were types of the twelve Aeons, then Jesus would have chosen further groups of eight and ten apostles to correspond to the Valentinian Ogdoad (eight Aeons) and Decad (ten Aeons) respectively. Instead, he notes that after Jesus chose the twelve, he "sent out seventy others," and he reasons that if the twelve were to signify the twelve Aeons, then the seventy would signify seventy Aeons (*Haer.* 2.21.1). His reasoning requires, based on the Valentinian argument that Apostles signify Aeons, that Irenaeus viewed the seventy disciples as apostles. This point is confirmed by his further comments in which he goes on to speak of Paul, asking his opponents of what Aeon he was a type (*Haer.* 2.21.2). He was not simply arguing that "numbered groups represent pleromic beings,"[27] as Zelyck claims, for this would not require that the seventy disciples be types of seventy Aeons.[28]

Zelyck also objects that Irenaeus did not specifically refer to the seventy as apostles,[29] but Irenaeus's terminology is informed by the Lukan account, which does not refer to the seventy as apostles as such (Luke 10:1). However, it does state that Jesus sent seventy "others," where the reference is to the previous sending of the Twelve (Luke 9:1–2). Furthermore, the twelve are not referred to specifically as "apostles" in that passage either, though both passages do state that Jesus "sent out" the twelve and "sent out" the seventy, using the related verb ἀποστέλλω.

Another indication that Irenaeus conceptualized apostles as a wider group than the Twelve and Paul is found in his discussion of the episcopal succession in the churches. After relating how the apostles went to the ends of the earth to preach the good news (3.1.1), he goes on to claim that the Christians were able to show the succession of the bishops from apostles (3.3.1). After furnishing the example of the episcopal succession at Rome, which he reckons up to the apostles Peter and Paul (3.3.2), he goes on to discuss Polycarp, who, he claims, was "not only instructed by apostles and associated with many who had seen the Lord, but was also appointed bishop of the church in Smyrna by apostles in Asia" (3.3.4). In his letter to Victor (c. 190), the bishop of Rome, Irenaeus states that Polycarp had observed Easter according to the Asian practice, "with John the disciple of the Lord and the rest of the apostles with whom he had associated" (*apud* Eusebius, *Hist. eccl.* 5.24.16; cf. the claim of the Coptic Harris fragments that Polycarp was the last surviving disciple of the apostles[30]).

Irenaeus must, therefore, have held Polycarp to have known at least three apostles, including John. But it is improbable that he would have held Polycarp, who lived past the middle of the second century, to have been instructed by several of the twelve apostles and personally appointed by them in Asia Minor, and it is therefore unlikely that Irenaeus restricted his generic references to "apostles" in this way. Instead, he likely conceived of "apostles" as encompassing a wider group of eyewitness disciples of Jesus, some of whom had been resident in Asia (such as John the Elder and Aristion).

Even though Irenaeus seems to have used the title of apostle in an extended sense, he did view the Twelve as apostles in a special and exclusive sense, and this may explain the reticence he exhibits in referring to John as an apostle. As Burney notes, in Irenaeus's discussion of the four Gospels, he speaks of "Matthew the Apostle" (3.9.1), of Luke as a "follower and disciple of the apostles" (3.10.1), and of Mark as "Peter's interpreter and follower" (3.10.5), clearly differentiating each one. He goes on to speak of "Paul the Apostle" (e.g., 3.11.9) and "Peter the Apostle" (3.12.1), yet when he speaks of John, he describes him as "the disciple of the Lord" (3.11.1).[31] This may indicate that this John was not viewed as an apostle in a "categorically equivalent" manner to Paul and the Twelve.

Zelyck counters that the epithet "disciple of the Lord" may have carried more "apologetic weight" than that of "apostle" as it identified John as the apostle with the especially close relationship with Jesus.[32] It is not clear, however, that this epithet has any direct connection with the designation of him as "the disciple whom Jesus loved" in John's Gospel (John 13:23; 19:26; 20:2; 21:7, 20), which Irenaeus could have expressed by using the terminology of John's Gospel or by referring to him, as in modern scholarship, as "the beloved disciple." Perhaps Burney is right when he suggests instead that his description of John as "the disciple of the Lord" was derived from Papias, just as his description of Mark as "Peter's interpreter and follower" was (cf. Eusebius, *Hist. eccl.* 3.39.15), and that it originated with Papias's reference to Aristion and John the Elder as "the disciples of the Lord" (Fragment 1). While the seven disciples mentioned earlier in Papias's list were also referred to as "the disciples of the Lord," he reasons that the title would have distinctively designated John the Elder since he was not of the Twelve and therefore could not have been called an Apostle in the same sense as the others in the list.[33] If correct, Irenaeus would have been specifically referring to Papias's second John, the Elder, when he designated the Evangelist as "the disciple of the Lord."

## John the Elder

While Irenaeus does not explicitly identify his John with Papias's Elder, he does identify the Evangelist as the author of 2 John (*Haer.* 1.16.3), who introduces himself as "the Elder" (2 John 1). Bauckham suggests that the title of "the Elder" might have fallen out of use for this John by Irenaeus's time in favor of "the disciple of the Lord," in order to differentiate John from the second generation of Christian leaders in Asia known as "the elders."[34]

A comparison of Papias and Irenaeus is suggestive that Irenaeus identified Papias's Elder with the Evangelist. On the one hand, Papias placed the Apostle John's activities in a previous generation to his own while making himself contemporary with the Elder, an eyewitness who probably lived no later than the turn of the second century; on the other hand, Irenaeus claimed that it was the Evangelist who died during Trajan's reign (98–117) (*Haer.* 2.22.5),[35] corresponding to Papias's chronological placement of his Elder.

Furthermore, while Papias claimed to have been the Elder's "hearer" (αὐτήκοος) (*Hist. eccl.* 3.39.7), Irenaeus, the reader of Papias, stated that Papias was the "hearer" (ἀκουστής) of John the Evangelist (*Haer.* 5.33.4). If Irenaeus made Papias a hearer of the Evangelist, while Papias himself claimed only to have been a hearer of John the Elder, the simplest conclusion is that Irenaeus identified Papias's John (the Elder) with the Evangelist.[36] Nevertheless, to maintain the traditional interpretation, not a few scholars have asserted that Irenaeus must have mistakenly identified Papias as a disciple of John.[37]

## POLYCRATES'S JOHN: PRIEST, WITNESS AND TEACHER

Around the year 190, Polycrates, bishop of Ephesus, wrote to Victor, bishop of Rome, concerning a dispute which had arisen between the Christians of Rome and Asia Minor[38] over the correct date for the keeping of Easter:

> Therefore, we keep the day without interfering, neither adding or subtracting, for in Asia great luminaries (στοιχεῖα) have fallen asleep, who will rise in the day of the coming of the Lord, in which he comes with glory from heaven to seek out all the holy ones: Philip, of the twelve apostles, who fell asleep in Hierapolis; and two of his daughters, who grew old as virgins; and his other daughter who rests in Ephesus, having conducted her life in the Holy Spirit; still yet there is also John, who reclined on the Lord's bosom, who was a priest wearing the sacerdotal plate (τὸ πέταλον), and a witness (μάρτυς) and teacher. He sleeps in Ephesus. There is also Polycarp in Smyrna, both a bishop and a martyr (μάρτυς), and Thaseus, both a bishop and martyr (μάρτυς), from Eumenaea, who sleeps in Smyrna (*apud* Eusebius, *Hist. eccl.* 5.24.2–5).[39]

Polycrates speaks of only one famous John at Ephesus, and while he bolsters his reputation by describing him as the one who leaned on the Lord's bosom and as a priest wearing the priestly plate; he does not identify him with the Zebedean John. Indeed, while Polycrates refers to Philip as one "of the twelve apostles," he refers to John only as a witness (μάρτυς) and teacher.[40] If he did not draw attention to John's status as one of the foremost of the twelve apostles, despite its evident apologetic value, then perhaps he did not so identify him.[41]

It is likely for this reason also that Polycrates lists Philip of Hierapolis, one of the Twelve, before John.[42] Hengel further notes that the Zebedean John is always named before Philip in the Gospels, likewise suggesting that Polycrates's John was a different one.[43] Hill counters that Polycrates might have named Philip and John chronologically, with John placed second because he died last,[44] but the apologetic intent of the letter would probably lead to the expectation that the most authoritative figure would be mentioned first, and in any case Hill does not address the problem of why Polycrates did not draw attention to this John's status as one of the Twelve.

*The Priest Wearing the Πέταλον*

Polycrates is the first extant writer to describe John as a priest. There is no hint in the Gospels or Acts that John the son of Zebedee served in this capacity, though Wenham tries accommodating Polycrates's statement to the traditional view by suggesting that there is "more than a possibility" that this John served as a priest in the temple,[45] a conclusion he reaches by a tortuous train of reasoning (Salome, who is possibly the Zebedean John's mother, might have been related to descendants of Aaron,[46] and this could have made her a suitable wife for Zebedee, had he been a priest).[47] On the other hand, Blomberg acknowledges the difficulty for the traditional view and tries mitigating it by speculating that Polycrates might have mistakenly confused the Evangelist with another John.[48] He thus concedes that Polycrates's John seems non-Zebedean.

The πέταλον seems to refer to the "golden plate" (χρυσοῦν πέταλον) worn by the high priest on the Day of Atonement (Exod 28:36, LXX; The Letter of Aristeas 98; Philo, Migr. 103; Moses 2.114), but the exact meaning has puzzled scholarship. Proposed solutions have varied: the πέταλον figuratively described John's "intercessory ministry"[49] or his spiritual authority;[50] John functioned as a temporary high priest, for which allowances were made if the actual high priest were unable to perform his duties, according to the Mishnah;[51] the plate may have occasionally been worn by ordinary priests[52] or by those within the priestly aristocracy;[53] or it was an exegetical inference drawn from Acts 4:6, where a certain John (some manuscripts read "Jonathan" here instead) is mentioned along with other members of the family of the high priest.[54] Whatever the origin of the πέταλον motif,[55] the description of John as a priest seems unlikely for the Zebedean John.

*John as Witness*

Lastly, Polycrates speaks of John as a "witness and teacher" (μάρτυς καὶ διδάσκαλος). The word μάρτυς may signify either a martyr or a witness, though it is usually taken in the latter sense,[56] and Bauckham, arguing for this meaning, notes that it is "sandwiched between ἱερεὺς and διδάσκαλος" whereas the martyr Polycarp, along with two other bishops, was referred to as ἐπίσκοπος καὶ μάρτυς, with μάρτυς "appropriately placed second in the pair."[57]

It has been suggested that the reference is to John's suffering as a "witness" on the island of Patmos,[58] or to the testimony of the Beloved Disciple in John's Gospel (John 21:24).[59] B. W. Bacon, however, thinks that the combination of priest, witness, and teacher may recall the work of the Palestinian chronicler Hegesippus,[60] who published his *Memoirs* (Ὑπομνήματα), now lost, at Rome, probably sometime in the period from 150 CE to 180 CE,[61] or a few decades or so before Polycrates wrote. According to Hegesippus, the descendants of Jude presided over the churches as "witnesses" and relatives of the Lord until the reign of Trajan (*apud* Eusebius, *Hist. eccl.* 3.20.6), where "witnesses" possibly distinguishes them as eyewitnesses of Jesus's ministry. Hegesippus also spoke of "false teachers" who became active at that time (*apud* Eusebius, *Hist. eccl.* 3.32.8), and he attributed priestly functions to James (*apud* Eusebius, *Hist. eccl.* 2.23. 4–7),[62] as Polycrates does to John.

## JOHN IN THE LOST WORKS OF MELITO, THEOPHILUS, AND APOLLONIUS

Eusebius mentions a number of early writers who made use of Revelation but whose works are no longer extant. He notes that Melito, bishop of Sardis (c. 161–180), wrote a commentary on "the Revelation of John" (*apud* Eusebius, *Hist. eccl.* 4.26.2), and that Theophilus, bishop of Antioch (c. 169–c. 183), made use of "the Apocalypse of John" in his now lost *Against the Heresy of Hermogenes* (*Hist. eccl.* 4.24.1). The John in question is not further identified by these two writers, however, even though they have been claimed for the traditional view.[63] While Theophilus is known to have written a number of commentaries and apologetic works, only his *Apology to Autolycus* has survived, in which he quotes from the opening words of the Fourth Gospel, attributing them to "John," whom he includes among "all the bearers of the Spirit" (πάντες οἱ πνευματόφοροι) (*Autol.* 2.22)[64] but whom does not explicitly identify with John the son of Zebedee.[65]

Lastly, Eusebius states that Apollonius of Ephesus (fl. c. 180–c. 210) made use of the Revelation of John in a work directed against the Montanists, adding that he related a tradition of John restoring a dead man to life in Ephesus (*apud* Eusebius, *Hist. eccl.* 5.18.14). No further information is provided by Eusebius; possibly Apollonius identified the Seer with the Evangelist, who was often associated with Ephesus, or with Papias's Elder, who likely taught in Asia Minor (see chapter 1).

## JOHN IN THE MURATORIAN CANON

The Muratorian Canon, named after its discoverer, Ludovico Antonio Muratori (1672–1750), contains a list of New Testament canonical books, sometimes accompanied by a short description of the book. It contains a Latin text of poor quality and is partially preserved in a manuscript dating from the late seventh or the eighth century;[66] it was probably originally written in Greek,[67] sometime in the late second or early third century.[68]

The work describes how John came to write the Fourth Gospel as follows:

> Of the fourth of the Gospels, (the one) of John, one of the disciples (*ex discipulis*). Having been urged by his fellow disciples and bishops, he said: "Fast with me today for three days, and if anything is revealed to anyone, let us reveal it to each other. On the same night it was revealed to Andrew, one of the apostles (*ex apostolis*), that with everyone reviewing, John should write down all things in his own name (ll. 9–16).[69]

The text goes on to quote from 1 John 1:1, which it attributes to the same John while noting that he had been an eyewitness of Jesus's ministry (ll. 26–34).

Some identify the John of the Muratorian Canon with the Apostle John, the son of Zebedee,[70] though this has been challenged on the basis of the text's apparent contrast between John as "one of the disciples" (*ex discipulis*) and Andrew as "one of the apostles" (*ex apostolis*).[71] Bauckham suggests that the reference to John as a disciple represents Papias's terminology, who spoke of the eyewitness followers of Jesus as the "disciples of the Lord," and that the text distinguishes John from the Twelve by not referring to him as an apostle, as it does with Andrew.[72] However, even if the terminology reflects that of Papias (cf. chapter 8), evidence to be discussed in chapter 4 suggests that the Muratorian Canon itself presupposed the identification of the Apostle and Evangelist.

## TERTULLIAN'S JOHN, THE SUCCESSOR OF PAUL

Tertullian (c. 200) attributes the Gospel of John, 1 John, and Revelation to the same author, whom he refers to as the "apostle John" (*apostolus Ioannes*) (*Marc.* 3.8, 14; 4.2, 5; 5.16).[73] While this is often viewed as conclusive evidence that Tertullian identified this John with the Zebedean one,[74] this is not necessarily the case, for Tertullian did not limit the apostles to the Twelve, referring to Jude, the brother of Jesus, as the "apostle Jude" (*Iudas apostolos*[75]) (*Cult. fem.* 1.3; 2.13).

Elsewhere, Tertullian speaks of John as the Lord's most beloved disciple, who leaned on his chest, the one to whom the Lord pointed out Judas as the traitor, and the one who was given to Mary as a son in the Lord's place (*Praescr.* 22); as with Irenaeus, these descriptions are drawn exclusively from John's Gospel, and he does not attribute to this John anything that would have identified him as the John of the Synoptic tradition.

Tertullian also associates this John with Asian Minor, making him the founder of the episcopal successions of the Asian churches:

> We also have John's foster (*alumnas*) churches. For even if Marcion rejects his Apocalypse, nevertheless the order of the bishops when reckoned to its origin will stand on John as the founder (*Marc.* 4.5).[76]

Similarly, in another work, Tertullian claims that a written record of Polycarp's ordination as bishop of Smyrna by John still existed in the church's archives (*Praescr.* 32).

Tertullian, who takes the Evangelist and Seer to be one and the same, is the first extant writer to speak of John's exile, claiming that after emerging unharmed from a vat of burning oil at Rome, he "is banished to an island" (*in insulam relegatur*) (*Praescr.* 36).[77] Sanders thinks that Tertullian, with his legal training, was aware of the distinction between *relegatio* and *deportatio* when he wrote *relegatur*.[78] This would be significant, for, unlike *deportatio*, *relegatio* was generally reserved for the *honestiores* or ruling classes[79] and did not involve a forfeiture of property and rights (including Roman citizenship).[80] On this account, Sanders suggests that John was a member of the Jewish aristocracy[81] (cf. Polycrates's description of John as a priest). Interestingly, William Ramsay draws the "unavoidable conclusion" that Tertullian must have been mistaken, and that John must have been sent to the mines instead, since *relegatio* "was reserved for persons of good standing and some wealth," adding that it is "utterly impossible" for John (i.e., the son of Zebedee) to have been such a person.[82]

## EVIDENCE FOR TWO JOHNS IN CLEMENT

Clement of Alexandria (c. 150–c. 215), like Irenaeus and Tertullian, also identified the Evangelist and Seer, crediting to "John" quotations from John's Gospel (*Strom.* 5.12), 1 John (*Paed.* 3.11, 12; *Quis div.* 37; *Strom.* 4.16), and Revelation (*Strom* 6.13). He refers to 1 John as John's "larger letter" (*Strom.* 2.15), suggesting that he knew of at least one smaller letter attributed to the same author.[83] Since both 2 and 3 John claim authorship by "the Elder," Clement almost certainly identified the author of the Johannine works as a John of this title.

Clement does speak of this John as "John the apostle" (Ἰωάννης ὁ ἀπόστολος) when relating the story of John's recovery of a robber captain to repentance (*Quis div.* 42), but as with other writers, this probably constitutes insufficient grounds for concluding that he identified this John as one of the twelve apostles, for he employs this title of persons who were not members of the Twelve; thus, he speaks of Barnabas as both "the apostle Barnabas" (ὁ ἀπόστολος Βαρνάβας) (*Strom.* 2.6) and "Barnabas the apostle" (Βαρνάβας ὁ ἀπόστολος) (*Strom.* 2.7), and he refers to Clement of Rome as "the apostle Clement" (ὁ ἀπόστολος Κλήμης) (*Strom.* 4.17).[84]

Furthermore, Clement seems to have known both the tradition of the Apostle's early death and that of the Evangelist's death in old age, suggesting that he did not identify the two. Thus, he relates how the teaching ministry of the Twelve and Paul came to an end in the reign of Nero (r. 54–68 CE):

> For the teaching of the Lord at his coming (Ἡ μὲν γὰρ τοῦ Κυρίου κατὰ τὴν παρουσίαν διδασκαλία), beginning from Augustus Caesar, is finished (τελειοῦται) in the midst of the times of Tiberius.[85] However, the teaching of his apostles, encompassing the ministry of Paul, is finished in the time of Nero (*Strom.* 7.17).[86]

As Charles notes, Clement's words "presuppose the death of all the apostles before 70 A.D."[87] Elsewhere, however, Clement relates that John settled in Ephesus following his return from Patmos, which occurred "after the death of the tyrant," and that he appointed bishops in the neighboring areas (*Quis div.* 42). The name of the tyrant is not given, though such a description would have been applicable to Nero or Domitian,[88] and in either case this would contextualize the story after Nero's death (68 CE), or after the period in which he places the death of the Twelve.

This presents a difficulty for the traditional view, which has not eluded its defenders. Badham (who favors the martyrdom tradition) thus remarks that Clement "is inconsistent on the point" of whether John died early or late,[89] and Barclay states that he "seems to be on both sides" of the question.[90] McDowell similarly acknowledges the "seeming contradiction,"[91] although Allison and Davies dismiss the passage as "irrelevant" (without further explanation) and deny that it "registers the date of John's death."[92] Kenneth L. Gentry interprets Clement as only limiting "apostolic revelation" to the period before Nero,[93] but the passage speaks of the apostles' teaching, not revelation. Hill suggests that Clement "simply slipped, momentarily forgetting about John" when he spoke of the apostles, or that he was "speaking in general terms."[94] The specific mention of Paul along with the apostles weakens the latter suggestion; the former requires attributing a mistake to Clement in order to maintain the traditional view, following a pattern already noted with respect to Irenaeus, Polycrates, and Tertullian. The most straightforward reading of Clement is that he dated the Apostle's death before the year 68 while he placed the Evangelist's activities at a later time.

## JOHN'S EXILE IN THE EASTERN HIPPOLYTUS

Sometime in the early third century a writer named Hippolytus, who may have been an eastern writer distinct from Hippolytus of Rome,[95] composed his *Treatise on Christ and Antichrist*, in which John is briefly mentioned:

> For this one [i.e., John], being on the island of Patmos, saw a revelation of mysteries to be shuddered at. Tell me, blessed John, apostle and disciple of the Lord, what did you see and hear about Babylon? Be alert and tell it, for she also banished you (*Antichr.* 36).[96]

The reference to Babylon may allude to Rome and be reflective of the tradition, found in Tertullian (*Praescr.* 36), that John was sent into exile from that city.

While Hippolytus does refer to this John as an apostle, it is unclear whether he identified this John with the Zebedean John.

## THE IDENTIFICATION OF THE EVANGELIST AND THE APOSTLE

The Evangelist begins to be identified with the son of Zebedee from at least the early third century. The great biblical scholar Origen (c. 185–c. 254) identifies John the son of Zebedee as both the author of John's Gospel (*Comm. John* 2.4) and Revelation (*Comm. John* 1.14; cf. *Comm. Matt.* 16.6). Origen's pupil Dionysius of Alexandria, who was bishop of the city from 248 to 264, also identified the Evangelist with the son of Zebedee, though he had reservations about Revelation and suggested that another John might have written it (*Hist. eccl.* 7.25.7–25).

Possibly the identification was already made during the second century. The *Acts of John*, which dates in its original form to the second or third century,[97] identifies the Beloved Disciple as John the brother of James (§§ 88–91) in a section which is generally considered an original part of the work, although Czachesz has suggested that it is an early third-century interpolation.[98] A little later in the work, John is included among the twelve (§ 95) in a section that is generally considered to be a later interpolation.

Later writers, including Hilary of Poitiers (c. 300–367),[99] Chrysostom (c. 346–407),[100] and Jerome (347–420)[101] did identify the Evangelist with the Zebedean John of the Synoptics. Jerome's John, however, seems to be a conflated figure. On the one hand, he is the Galilean fisherman; on the other, he shares the aristocratic status of Polycrates's and Tertullian's John. Thus, Jerome claims in a letter written in 417 that John "was known to the high priest (cf. John 18:15) on account of the nobility (*nobilitas*) of his birth" (*Epist.* 127.5).[102] This has been dismissed as "an early and desperate conjecture to explain an obscure passage"[103] (i.e., John 18:5, the

Beloved Disciple's being known to the high priest), but the reference to John's noble birth and aristocratic status is clearly discordant with Jerome's understanding of John as the Galilean fisherman of the Synoptics and may have been drawn from a source which depicted the Beloved Disciple as a Jerusalemite of aristocratic extraction.

A conflation of the two Johns is possibly also exhibited by Chrysostom. In one place he relates that the Jewish war against the Romans (66–70 CE) occurred "after the death of the apostles" (*Hom. Act.* 11:19)[104] (cf. Clement's reference to the ministry of the Twelve ending in Nero's reign), but elsewhere he makes the Evangelist John to have lived after the destruction of Jerusalem (*Hom. Matt.* 24:16–18). Chrysostom, who identified the Evangelist with the son of Zebedee (*Hom. Matt.* 24:16–18), may have been unaware of these inconsistencies or confused by them (cf. Chrysostom's apparent inconsistency as to whether John was martyred or not, discussed in chapter 2).

## CONCLUSION

Among early writers, Irenaeus, Tertullian, and Clement of Alexandria identify the Evangelist with the Seer; while others do not explicitly affirm this identification, they also do not exclude it as a possibility. On the other hand, the principal early witnesses to the Johannine tradition are silent regarding any identification of John the Evangelist with the John of the Synoptic Gospels. Furthermore, the suggestion that they identified them often involves imputing errors to the writers. Thus, Polycrates is said to have confused two Johns, Irenaeus to have wrongly made Papias a disciple of John, Tertullian to have mistakenly described John's exile as *relegatio*, and Clement to have spoken out of both sides of his mouth or to have made a momentary slip by claiming that the ministry of the Twelve was fulfilled by the end of Nero's reign (cf. the claim that Papias wrote "clumsily," similarly employed to maintain the traditional view).

The hypothesis that the Evangelist was identified with another John, such as Papias's Elder, can better accommodate Ignatius's silence and is not challenged by Polycrates's description of John as a priest or by Tertullian's claim that he received a sentence reserved for *honestiores*. It can account for Irenaeus's depiction of Papias as a hearer of John and can resolve Clement's otherwise contradictory statements.

The strongest argument in favor of the view that early sources identified the Evangelist with the Zebedean John is undoubtedly found in the references to the Evangelist as an apostle. However, in light of the wider use of the word in ancient sources, this alone is probably an insufficient basis upon which to draw this conclusion. Indeed, the subdued use of the title with respect to the Evangelist by Irenaeus and its avoidance by Polycrates would be consistent with the proposal that John, while an eyewitness, was not considered an apostle in the same sense as the Twelve.

## NOTES

1. E.g., Bernard, *St. John*, vol. 1, xlvi; Carson, *John*, 28, 68; Morris, *John*, 555.
2. Charles Fox Burney, *The Aramaic Origin of the Fourth Gospel* (Oxford: Clarendon, 1922) 134–41; Colson, *L'énigme*, 29–63; John J. Gunther, "Early Identifications of the Author of the Johannine Writings," *JEH* 31 (1980): 418–19; Bauckham, *Eyewitnesses*, 438–63; Trebilco, *Early Christians*, 242–58.
3. Barrett, *St. John*, 102; Andrew T. Lincoln, *The Gospel According to Saint John* (BNTC; London: Continuum, 2005), 19.
4. Cf. Bernard, *St. John*, vol. 1, lxxii; Culpepper, *John*, 109; Trebilco, *Early Christians*, 677–78.
5. Théodor Keim, *Geschichte Jesu von Nazara in ihrer Verkettung mit dem Gesamtleben seines Volkes*, vol. 1 (Zurich: Orell, 1867), 161–164; Burnett Hillman Streeter, *The Four Gospels: A Study of Origins* (London: Macmillan, 1964), 435; Trebilco, *Early Christians*, 676.
6. Cf. Charles E. Hill, *The Johannine Corpus in the Early Church* (New York: Oxford University Press, 2004), 354–55.
7. See Lightfoot, *Supernatural Religion*, 98; Hill, *Lost Teaching*, 18–21.
8. Hill, *Johannine Corpus*, 109.
9. See Bauckham, *Eyewitnesses*, 18.
10. E.g., Hill, *Lost Teaching*, 74 n. 9, who places Polycarp's birth in c. 83.
11. Bart Ehrman, ed., The *Apostolic Fathers*, vol. 1 (2 vols.; LCL; Cambridge, Mass.: Harvard University Press, 2003), 362; Paul Hartog, *Polycarp's Epistle to the Philippians and the Martyrdom of Polycarp: Introduction, Text, and Commentary* (OAF; Oxford: Oxford University Press, 2013), 9–10.
12. Weidmann, *Polycarp and John*, 44.
13. Hartog, *Polycarp's Epistle*, 192.
14. Translated by the author from Greek text found in *Iustini martyris Dialogus cum Tryphone*, ed. Miroslav Marcovich (PTS 47; Berlin: de Gruyter, 1997), 211.
15. E.g., Robert H. Mounce, *The Book of Revelation* (NICNT; Grand Rapids: Eerdmans, 1997), 11; David E. Aune, *Revelation 1–5* (WBC 52A; Dallas: Word, 1998), li; Craig R. Koester, *Revelation: A New Translation with Introduction and Commentary* (AB 38A; New Haven, Conn.: Yale University Press, 2014), 66.
16. J. Massyngberde Ford, *Revelation: Introduction, Translation, and Commentary* (AB 38; New Haven, Conn.: Yale University Press, 2008), 299.
17. See, e.g., Bernard, *St. John*, vol. 1, xlviii; Barrett, *St. John*, 101, 124; Culpepper, *John*, 124; George R. Beasley-Murray, *John* (2nd ed.; WBC 36; Dallas: Word, 2002), lxvi; Lincoln, *Saint John*, 19; Carson and Moo, *Introduction*, 230; Keener, *Gospel of John*, 237; Watson, *Gospel Writing*, 464.
18. Cf. Bauckham, *Eyewitnesses*, 458.
19. Cf. Bauckham, *Eyewitnesses*, 469.
20. Burney, *Aramaic Origin*, 141.
21. See Hengel, *Johannine Question*, 4; Bauckham, *Eyewitnesses*, 461–62.
22. Watson, *Gospel Writing*, 464; cf. Culpepper, *John*, 131; Kok, *Beloved Apostle?*, 59.
23. Watson, *Gospel Writing*, 464 n. 48.
24. Lorne Zelyck, "Irenaeus and the Authorship of the Fourth Gospel," in *The Origins of the Fourth Gospel*, ed. Stanley Porter and Hughson T. Ong (Leiden: Brill, 2016), 248.
25. Zelyck, "Irenaeus," 251.
26. Cf. Burney, *Aramaic Origin*, 70, 139–41. Cf. Bauckham, *Testimony*, 70.
27. Zelyck, "Irenaeus," 249.

28. Cf. Bauckham, *Eyewitnesses*, 462.
29. Zelyck, "Irenaeus," 248–49.
30. Weidmann, *Polycarp and John*, 44.
31. Burney, *Aramaic Origin*, 139–40.
32. Zelyck, "Irenaeus," 258.
33. Burney, *Aramaic Origin*, 141.
34. Bauckham, *Eyewitnesses*, 460.
35. Eusebius, in his *Chronicle*, specifies the time as the third year of Trajan (c. 100). See, August Helm, *Die Chronik des Hieronymus* (Berlin: Akademie-Verlag, 1956), 193.
36. Burney, *Aramaic Origin*, 141–42; Rupert Annand, "Papias and the Four Gospels," *SJT* 9 (1956): 47; A. C. Perumalil, "Papias," *ExpT* 85 (1974): 362, 366.
37. Barrett, *St. John*, 105; Culpepper, *John*, 109; Lincoln, *Saint John*, 19; Hill, *Lost Teaching*, 11 n. 24; Watson, *Gospel Writing*, 465 n. 50.
38. This probably involved Asian Christians living in Rome (see Alistair Stewart-Sykes [now Alistair C. Stewart], *Melito of Sardis: On Pascha* [Crestwood, N.Y.: St Vladimir's Seminary Press, 2001], 85–86). A local context would explain Irenaeus's claim that presbyters had sent the Eucharist to the Asian parishes (*apud* Eusebius, *Hist. eccl.* 5.24.15). Perhaps Polycrates was a bishop of one such parish in Rome (and not of Ephesus), explaining why he would assert that he was not afraid of Victor's threats (5.24.7) and accounting for why he had been commanded to summon all the bishops (i.e., of the Asian churches in Rome) (5.24.8).
39. Translated by the author.
40. Hengel, *Johannine Question*, 7.
41. Heinrich Karl Hugo Delff, *Das vierte Evangelium: ein authentischer Bericht über Jesus von Nazret* (Husum: Delff, 1890), 8; cf. Dwight Moody Smith, *The Fourth Gospel in Four Dimensions: Judaism and Jesus, the Gospels and Scripture* (Columbia, S.C.: University of South Carolina Press, 2008), 13.
42. Burney, *Aramaic Origin*, 134; Colson, *L'énigme*, 36; cf. Hengel, *Johannine Question*, 7.
43. Hengel, *Johannine Question*, 7.
44. Hill, *Johannine Corpus*, 119; cf. Bauckham, *Testimony*, 41.
45. John Wenham, *Easter Enigma: Are the Resurrection Accounts in Conflict?* (2nd ed., Grand Rapids: Baker, 1992), 41.
46. Wenham reaches this conclusion by identifying Salome (cf. Mark 15:40) as the mother of John and the sister of Mary, the mother of Jesus (*Easter Enigma*, 34–35). He argues that since Mary was the cousin of Elisabeth, a daughter of Aaron (Luke 1:5, 36), Salome might have had some Aaronic connection also (*Easter Enigma*, 41).
47. Wenham, *Easter Enigma*, 41.
48. Craig L. Blomberg, *The Historical Reliability of John's Gospel: Issues & Commentary* (Downers Grove, Ill.: IVP, 2001), 25–26.
49. Bruce, "St John at Ephesus," 343.
50. François-Marie Braun, *Jean le Théologien et son évangile dans l'Église ancienne*, vol. 1 (EtB; Paris: Gabalda, 1959), 3 40.
51. Delff, *Das vierte Evangelium*, 9–10.
52. Bernard, *St. John*, vol. 2, 596.
53. Colson, *L'énigme*, 37.
54. Bauckham, *Eyewitnesses*, 451–52; *Testimony*, 49–50.
55. I discuss my own theory in Dean Furlong, *The John also Called Mark: Reception and Transformation in Christian Tradition* (WUNT II; Tübingen: Mohr Siebeck, forthcoming).
56. Colson, *L'énigme*, 42; Hengel, *Johannine Question*, 144 n. 29; Trebilco, *Early Christians*, 244
57. Bauckham, *Testimony*, 40.
58. . Braun, *Jean le Théologien*, vol. 1, 339.
59. Bauckham, *Testimony*, 40.

60. Benjamin Wisner Bacon, *The Fourth Gospel in Research and Debate: A Series of Essays on Problems Concerning the Origin and Value of the Anonymous Writings Attributed to the Apostle John* (New York: Moffat, 1910), 263–64.
61. John Painter, *Just James: The Brother of Jesus in History and Tradition* (Edinburgh: Fortress, 1999), 180.
62. Bacon, *The Fourth Gospel*, 263–64.
63. E.g., Mounce (Melito: *Revelation*, 11 n. 54; Theophilus: *Revelation*, 23).
64. Translated from *PG* 6:1088.
65. Keener nevertheless cites this as evidence for the Zebedean identification (*Gospel of John*, 237).
66. Joseph Verheyden, "The Canon Muratori: A Matter of Dispute," in *The Biblical Canons*, ed. J.-M. Auwers and H. J. de Jonge (BETL 163; Leuven: Peeters, 2003), 487.
67. See the discussion in Verheyden, "The Canon Muratori," 492–93.
68. For discussion and partial bibliography, see Graham N. Stanton, "The Fourfold Gospel," *NTS* 43 (1997): 321–23; Verheyden, "The Canon Muratori," 491; Bauckham, *Eyewitnesses*, 425–26.
69. Translated and numbered according to the corrected Latin text in Alexander Souter, *The Text and Canon of the New Testament* (New York: Scribner, 1913), 208–11, and so hereafter.
70. Haenchen, *John*, 14; Culpepper, *John*, 129;
71. Colson, *L'énigme*, 43; Bauckham, *Eyewitnesses*, 428–29; Trebilco, *Early Christians*, 249; Ilaria Ramelli, "John the Evangelist's Work: An Overlooked Redaktionsgeschichtliche Theory from the Patristic Age," in *The Origins of John's Gospel*, ed. Porter and Ong (Leiden: Brill, 2016), 48.
72. Bauckham, *Eyewitnesses*, 429.
73. For the Latin text, see Ernest Evans, ed. and trans., *Tertullian: Adversus Marcionem*, vol. 1 (Oxford: The Clarendon Press, 1972), 246.
74. So, e.g., Mounce, *Revelation*, 11; Hill, *Johannine Corpus*, 145–46; Keener, *Gospel of John*, 249; Ian Boxall, *Patmos in the Reception History of the Apocalypse* (OTRM; Oxford: Oxford University Press, 2013), 32.
75. For the Latin text, see Marie Turcan, ed., *La toilette des femmes: Introduction, texte critique, traduction, et commentaire* (SC 173; Paris: Cerf, 1971).
76. Translated from the Latin text in Aemilianus Kroymann, ed., *Tertullianus: Opera I* (CCSL 1; Turnhout: Brepols, 1954).
77. Translated from the Latin text in Kroymann, ed., *Tertullianus*.
78. Joseph N. Sanders, "St John on Patmos," *NTS* 9 (1963): 76; cf. Konrad Huber, *Einer gleich einem Menschensohn: die Christusvisionen in Offb 1,9-20 und Offb 14,14-20 und die Christologie der Johannesoffenbarung* (NTA 51; Münster: Aschendorff, 2007), 93.
79. Sanders, "St John on Patmos," 76–77; John Anthony Crook, *Law and Life of Rome: 90 B.C.-A.D. 212* (London, Thames & Hudson, 1967), 272–73; Leonard L. Thompson, "Ordinary Lives: John and his First Readers," in *Reading the Book of Revelation: A Resource for Students*, ed. David L. Barr (Atlanta: SBL, 2003), 33.
80. Aune, *Revelation 1–5*, 79.
81. Sanders, "St John on Patmos," 76–77.
82. William Ramsay, *The Letters to the Seven Churches of Asia* (2nd ed.; London: Hodder & Stoughton, 1906), 84–85. Cf. Huber, *Menschensohn*, 93.
83. Cf. Hahneman, *Muratorian Fragment*, 15.
84. Cf. Colson, *L'énigme*, 44–45; Bauckham, *Eyewitnesses*, 466–67.
85. The manuscripts read Αὐγούστου rather than the corrected reading Τιβερίου found in the Greek edition of Fenton J. A. Hort and Joseph B. Mayor (*Clement of Alexandria, Miscellanies Book VII* [London: MacMillan, 1902], 188).
86. . Translated from the Greek text in Hort and Mayor, *Clement of Alexandria*, 188.
87. Charles, *Revelation*, vol.1, xlvii.
88. Cf. John A. T. Robinson, *Redating the New Testament* (London: SCM, 1976), 223.
89. Badham, "Martyrdom of John," 540.
90. Barclay, *Introduction to John*, 31.

91. McDowell, "A Historical Evaluation," 240.
92. Davies and Allison, *Matthew*, 91 n. 39.
93. Kenneth L. Gentry, *Before Jerusalem Fell: Dating the Book of Revelation* (2nd ed.; Atlanta: American, Vision, 1999), 84–85.
94. Hill, *Johannine Corpus*, 124 n. 131.
95. See J. A. Cerrato, *Hippolytus Between East and West: The Commentaries and the Provenance of the Corpus* (OThM; Oxford: University Press, 2002) esp. 4–5; 121–23; 255.
96. Translated from *PG* 10:756.
97. See Bauckham, *Eyewitnesses*, 463. E. Junod and J.-D. Kaestli date it between 150–200 (*Acta Iohannis*, vol. 2 [CCSA; Turnhout: Brepols, 1983], 695).
98. István Czachesz, *Commission Narratives: A Comparative Study of the Canonical and Apocryphal Acts* (Leuven: Peeters, 2007), 120–22.
99. Hilary of Poitiers, *On the Trinity*, 2.13.
100. Chrysostom, *Hom. John*. 2. 1, 4.
101. Jerome, *Vir.* 9.
102. Translated from the Latin text in I. Hilberg, ed., *Sancti Eusebii Hieronymi Epistulae* (CSEL 56; Vienna: 1918), 149–50. The standard translation is found in *NPNF* 2.6:255.
103. Abbott, *Fourfold Gospel*, 368.
104. Translated by the author from *PG* 60:194.

# Section 2

## *Conflated Figures, Revised Narratives*

In the early third century, a Johannine narrative emerges which seems to have conflated the Apostle and the Evangelist, indicating that the two Johns had by then come to be identified. This revised narrative, which was likely constructed by Hippolytus of Rome maintained the Apostle's early martyrdom as the template of its Johannine story but seems to have combined it with the Patmos tradition associated with the Evangelist by bringing John's life to an end on Patmos, at the end of Claudius's reign (41–54) (cf. chapter 4). Possibly Hippolytus constructed this narrative within the context of his defense of the Johannine writings against Gaius of Rome (cf. chapter 5).

This dispute over the Johannine writings seems to have left in its wake some residual distrust toward the canonical text of Revelation, which likely influenced Eusebius's revised narrative in the early fourth century. While Eusebius identified the Apostle and Evangelist, he favored the tradition of the Evangelist's natural death in Trajan's reign over the Apostle's early martyrdom for his narrative. His subsequent view that the Apostle died in Trajan's reign necessitated that Papias's Elder, who was active a generation later than the Apostle according to Papias, had lived too late to have been an eyewitness disciple of Jesus. The Elder, stripped of his eyewitness status, was then conveniently suggested by Eusebius as a potential author of Revelation, the canonicity of which he evidently doubted. To buttress his case for John's natural death in Trajan's reign (presumably against the rival martyrdom traditions), he constructed a late Domitianic context for John's exile (cf. chapter 6), which formed the basis of what would become the traditional Johannine story.

# FOUR
## Hippolytus and the Claudian Exile Tradition

An important variation of the Johannine narrative, found in sources believed by many to have been dependent upon Hippolytus of Rome (early third century), places John's exile and death in Claudius's reign (41–54). Scholarship often reacts to this idiosyncratic dating with bewilderment. Here it will be posited that this narrative arose as a result of the identification of the Apostle and the Evangelist, in which the Apostle's early martyrdom functioned as the template of the conflated narrative, necessitating in turn the early placement of the Patmos tradition which was associated with John the Evangelist.[1]

### THE CLAUDIAN EXILE IN EPIPHANIUS

The first unequivocal reference to John's Claudian exile is given by Epiphanius (c. 315–403) in his *Panarion* of Epiphanius: "the Holy Spirit compelled John to issue the Gospel in his old age when he was past ninety, after his return from Patmos under Claudius Caesar, and several years of his residence in Asia" (*Pan.* 51.12.2).[2] Later on, speaking of the church of Thyatira's defection to Montanism, Epiphanius writes: "He [the Holy Spirit] foretold it prophetically by the mouth of St. John, who prophesied before his falling asleep, during the time of Claudius Caesar and earlier, when he was on the isle of Patmos (*Pan.* 51.33.9)."[3] Both references are given within the context of Epiphanius's discussion of the Alogoi, for which it is generally accepted that he was dependent upon Hippolytus of Rome,[4] making it likely that he was dependent upon Hippolytus for the Claudian tradition also.[5]

The placement of the exile in Claudius's reign seems, as Barclay notes, "impossibly early,"[6] while Boxall observes that Epiphanius "oddly dates John's return from Patmos to the reign of Claudius."[7] Some suggest that Epiphanius was actually referring to Nero, who was called Nero Claudius Caesar,[8] but other sources of the Claudian tradition, including the Muratorian Canon which predates Epiphanius, seem to place John's banishment chronologically in the period corresponding to Claudius's reign (see below).

While Epiphanius places John's death after his return from Patmos, he also places John's prophesying at Patmos in temporal proximity to his death, stating that he prophesied "before his falling asleep."[9] This perhaps betrays a source which ended John's life at Patmos, though Epiphanius seems to have also been influenced by Irenaeus's tradition of John's death in Ephesus.[10]

Epiphanius also states that John was instructed in his old age by the Holy Spirit to preach in Asia in order to oppose the influence of Ebion and Cerinthus who were teaching in the region (*Pan.* 51.2.3–4). This is presumably related to Irenaeus's claim that John wrote his Gospel in Ephesus to refute Cerinthus (*Haer.* 3.11.1). But while Irenaeus places Cerinthus's activities at the end of the first century (see chapter 7), Epiphanius places them in Claudius's reign, claiming that Cerinthus, whose preaching commenced in Asia (*Pan.* 28.1.4), stirred up the controversy over circumcision at Jerusalem at the time when Peter returned to Jerusalem following the conversion of Cornelius (*Pan.* 28.4.1; cf. Acts 11:2–3) and that he criticized Paul because Titus was not circumcised (*Pan.* 28.4.1–2; cf. Gal 2:3–5). The Jacobite bishop of Amid, Dionysius bar Salibi (d. 1171), attributes the same anecdotes concerning Cerinthus's role in Jerusalem to Hippolytus (*intro. Comm. Apoc*),[11] supporting the likely Hippolytan origin of the narrative.

## PAUL'S "PREDECESSOR" IN THE MURATORIAN CANON

The Muratorian Canon (c. 200) also seems to presuppose a Claudian exile. Referring to John's seven letters to the Asian churches of Revelation (cf. ll. 57–59), it states: "the blessed apostle Paul, following (*sequens*) the order of his predecessor (*predecessor*,[12] or rather *precessor*[13]) John, writes to only seven churches by name" (ll. 47–50). It therefore places the writing of Revelation before the earliest of Paul's letters,[14] which would place its composition no later than the early 50s[15] and most likely during the reign of Claudius (41–54).[16]

Streeter refers to this claim as an "extraordinary suggestion"[17] and Barclay calls it an "astonishing statement."[18] John T. Fitzgerald observes that Paul is "strangely" said to have written before his predecessor John.[19] But the claim would lose its exceptional character if it arose from the conflation of the Patmos tradition with that of the Apostle John's early martyrdom, as Oberweis has suggested.[20] Charles has hinted at the same solution, suggesting that the Canon's claim represents "the survival of the older tradition" of John's early death.[21]

Some have denied that the Muratorian Canon dates Revelation before Paul's letters. According to Kruger, it only claims that John "legitimizes Paul's written corpus to seven churches by writing to seven churches of his own,"[22] while according to Hitchcock, it only claims that John was an apostle before Paul.[23] However, if Paul was "following" (*sequens*) John's order when he wrote, then John must have been conceived of as having composed first.

While there is no consensus on the question of the authorship of the Muratorian Canon, Hippolytus has often been proposed.[24] Favoring this is the similarity of the Canon's statement concerning the seven churches to one attributed to Hippolytus by Dionysius bar Salibi (d. 1171): "Hippolytus says: in writing to seven churches, he [John] has written just as Paul has written his thirteen letters to seven churches."[25] Bar Salibi adds that Hippolytus did not judge Hebrews to be Paul's,[26] a claim which is also attributed to Hippolytus by Photius.[27] The Muratorian Canon, which is silent with respect to Hebrews, attributes only thirteen letters to Paul.[28]

## THE COPTIC HOMILY OF SEVERUS

A probably related narrative is recounted by Severus, bishop of Nastrawa (mid-ninth century), in a Coptic homily preserved in an Arabic translation.[29] In discussing Paul's being forbidden to preach in Asia by the Holy Spirit (Acts 16:6), Severus explains that the apostle had wanted to preach in the region as he had learned that John was in exile on Patmos; the Spirit forbade him, however, as Asia was John's heritage and John was still alive; it was only after the death of John the son of Zebedee, it adds, that Paul began his work in Ephesus.[30] Thus, in Severus, Paul enters into John's heritage, while John is Paul's "predecessor" in the Muratorian Canon. Furthermore, Severus placed John's preaching in Asia and his death before Paul's Ephesian ministry (Acts 19:1–20), corresponding to a period late in Claudius's reign, which is consistent with the Muratorian Canon's apparent placement of John's death before Paul wrote.

Epiphanius also seems to have used a source that, like Severus, placed John's death in chronological proximity to his exile and which seems to have placed John's Asian preaching during Claudius's reign. Perhaps both come from a common source. If so, Epiphanius's claim that John "is instructed (ἐπιτρέπεται) by the Holy Spirit to preach" in Asia in his old age (*Pan.* 51.2.3–4) likely complemented Paul's being forbidden to preach in Asia by the Holy Spirit (cf. Acts 16:6) while John was there, as found in Severus.

Severus's John seems to die while in exile. Possibly his narrative is related to that found in an Arabic introduction to the *Death of St. John*, translated from a lost Coptic text,[31] which places John's death on the island on the fourth day of the month Tuba[32] (roughly corresponding to 12 January[33]). In an Ethiopic translation of the introduction, John's death on Patmos is instead placed on the fourth day of the month Ter, or 30 December,[34] which is closer to the date of the traditional feast day of John the son of Zebedee in other church calendars (see chapter 2). Ibn Kabar (thirteenth century) in the Arabic translation of the otherwise lost Coptic work, *The Lamp of Darkness*, states that some held that John died in Ephesus while others said that he died on Patmos, on the fourth of Tuba.[35]

## VICTORINUS, THE MURATORIAN CANON, AND THE *AD METALLA* NARRATIVE

Victorinus (d. 303 or 304), of Pettau in Ponnonia (modern-day Slovenia), wrote a commentary on Revelation in which he may have modified a tradition of John's Claudian exile and death. Commenting on the words that John must again prophesy to many nations, he writes:

> When John saw this revelation, he was on the island of Patmos, having been condemned to the mines by Caesar Domitian. There, it seems, John wrote the Revelation, and when he had already become aged [*et cum iam seniorem*], he thought that he would be received [into bliss] after his suffering. However, when Domitian was killed, all of his decrees were made null and void. John was, therefore, released from the mines, and afterward he disseminated the revelation that he had received from the Lord (*Comm. Apoc.* 10:11).[36]

Victorinus's commentary is the first extant source to claim that John was sentenced *ad metalla*, or to the mines. Unlike the relatively mild sentence of *relegatio*, *ad metalla* was conceived of as "a deferred death sentence."[37] Mattingly thus speaks of one particular mine in Phaino "where even a condemned murderer is hardly able to live a few days."[38]

There is, however, no evidence for the existence of mines on Patmos,[39] and had John been sent *ad metalla*, he would have had no leisure to write and little chance of survival.[40] Probably in Victorinus's source, John met his death in the mines of Patmos in what was likely an attempt at combining the tradition of John's early martyrdom with that of his Patmos exile. While Victorinus's John does not die on Patmos, his thoughts are nevertheless on death, perhaps reflecting an attempt on Victorinus's part at combining elements of the tradition of John's death on Patmos with Irenaeus's claim that John died in Trajan's reign.

Victorinus also depicts John as "already aged" toward the end of his exile, and Ellis thinks that the "already" (*iam*) implies that John had grown old on Patmos and had therefore been there for many years,[41] indicating that Victorinus may have placed the commencement of John's banishment early in Domitian's reign. Epiphanius also draws attention to John's old age, claiming that John was compelled by the Spirit "to issue the Gospel in his old age when he was past ninety, after his return from Patmos under Claudius Caesar, and several years of his residence in Asia" (*Pan.* 51.12.2). He likewise makes John an old man when he began preaching in Asia to oppose the influence of Ebion and Cerinthus (*Pan.* 51.2.3–4), and as already noted, Epiphanius (or his source) seems to have placed Cerinthus's activities in Claudius's reign.

The depiction of John as an old man on Patmos was probably an integral part of the Claudian narrative, by conflation of the Apostle who was martyred with the Evangelist who died in old age. It may have been a depiction of John as an old man during his exile in Claudius's reign that prompted Victorinus to move the exile into Domitian's reign (the first writer to unequivocally do so), to bring it into better conformity with Irenaeus, who placed John's old age at the end of the first century (*Haer* 3.3.4).

*Victorinus and the Source of the* Ad Metalla *Tradition*

Hippolytus has been suggested as a source for Victorinus's commentary,[42] and possibly Victorinus derived the *ad metalla* tradition from him. This would explain the similarities found in his comments with the Muratorian Canon, another source for which Hippolytan authorship has been suggested. Thus, speaking of the seven stars of Rev 1:16 ("he had seven stars in his right hand"), he explains them as follows:

> The seven churches, which he [i.e., John] calls by name (*nominatim*) with his own words, to whom he wrote letters, not because they alone are churches or even the chief ones, but because what he says to one he says to all; for it will differ nothing (*nihil enim differet*; cf. the Muratorian Canon's *nihil tam differt*[43] in line 18) whether one speaks to a cohort, of few soldiers in number, or through it to the whole army. Indeed (*denique*), whether in Asia or whether in the whole world, Paul has taught that all the seven churches, even the seven named ones, are one catholic [church][44] (*Comm. Apoc.* 1.7).[45]

Victorinus's discussion of the seven churches evokes the Muratorian Canon's claim that Paul "writes to seven churches by name (*nominatim*)" (47–50), and that "although John writes to the seven churches, he speaks to all" (ll. 58–59).[46]

Victorinus also seems to presuppose that John wrote before Paul, for he claims that Paul taught that the seven churches of Asia which are named (i.e., in Revelation) represent the one catholic church; he adds that Paul "did not go beyond the number of seven churches that he (himself) also might preserve this very thing (*ut servaret ipse et ipsum*)," where the *et* ("he *also* might preserve") may presuppose John's former writing to seven churches, a number which Paul "also" (i.e., like John before him) preserved. Victorinus may therefore unconsciously betray his use of a source that placed John's writing before Paul's, as in the Muratorian Canon, even though he himself placed John's exile in Domitian's reign.

It has been suggested that Victorinus was familiar with the Muratorian Canon[47] or even that he authored it.[48] The latter is unlikely, however, since the Muratorian Canon presupposes John's Claudian exile while Victorinus places it in Domitian's reign. And while Victorinus may have been familiar with the Canon, he could not have drawn his modified version of the *ad metalla* tradition from it. Another possibility is that he was drawing directly from Hippolytus, as the Muratorian Canon appears to have been, and that he derived the *ad metalla* tradition from his work. This sentence was used widely against Christians in the time of Hippolytus, and Hippolytus himself related how a Christian named Callistus was banished to the mines of Sardinia during the bishopric of Victor, in the late second century (*Haer.* 9.7).

Possibly the *ad metalla* tradition was constructed (whether by Hippolytus or not) to reconcile John's early martyrdom with the Patmos tradition, in accordance with the theory proposed here of the conflation of Johannine narratives. It may have also been intended as a corrective to the tradition known to Tertullian that John received the sentence of *relegatio*, which was generally given to *honestiores* or wealthier citizens, not to common fishermen (cf. Ramsay's comment discussed in chapter 3).

## COMMENTARY ON THE REVELATION OF THE APOSTLE JOHN

The Latin *Commentary on the Revelation of the Apostle John*, written by an unknown Irish author between the sixth and eighth centuries, also knows the *ad metalla* tradition and may betray knowledge of a Claudian exile:

> When on account of the word of the Lord he [John] had been thrown into the burning oil by his persecutors, and the Lord had led him out of there unharmed, they sent him there [Patmos], with his feet bound, for the iron mines (*ligatis pedibus metallis ferreis illuc transmiserunt*).[49]

It goes on to claim that Revelation was "written in the twenty-third year after the suffering of the Lord" (*XXIII anno post passionem domini scriptum est*), which could correspond to the end of Claudius's reign (52/53 CE), though it simultaneously places it during Domitian's reign. While the editor considers the reading XXIII a mistake for LXIII,[50] the sixty-third year, it is also possible that both chronological notices were found in different sources and combined by the writer.[51] Indeed, the date is close to that of the twenty-fourth year after the ascension given for the martyrdom of James the son of Alphaeus, who seems to have been remembered with John the Apostle, as discussed in chapter 2.

The work cites among its principle sources an "ancient book" (*liber antiquus*) written "in early times" (*priscis temporibus*) whose author was unknown, as well as Origen's twelve homilies on Revelation, Tyconius, and Primasius; it also quotes Jerome.[52] Origen's homilies and the preface of Tyconius's commentary on Revelation are lost, but Primasius (d. c. 560), bishop of Justiniapolis (Hadrumentum) in North Africa, assigns a Domitianic date to the *ad metalla* tradition,[53] and he may have been the source for the commentary's claim that Revelation was written in Domitian's reign.

## APRINGIUS, THE CLAUDIAN EXILE, AND THE ACTS NARRATIVE

Apringius, bishop of Pax in Portugal (or possibly of the town of the same name in Spain), places John's exile in the reign of Claudius in his *Tractate on the Apocalypse*, written during the reign of the Visigoth king Thendis (531–548):

> The ecclesiastical writers have taught that at the time of Claudius Caesar, when that famine which the prophet Agabus had announced in the Acts of the Apostles would come in ten years [sic] time was at its height, that during that difficulty this same Caesar, impelled by his usual vanity, had instituted a persecution of the churches. It was during this time that he ordered John, the apostle of our Lord, Jesus Christ, to be transported into exile (*exilium*), and he was taken (*deportatus*) to the island of Patmos, and while there confirmed this writing [i.e., Revelation].[54]

Apringius locates a historical context for John's exile in a Claudian persecution of the churches, which is said to have occurred at the time of the famine spoken of in Acts 11:28. According to Acts 18:2, Claudius expelled the Jews from Rome, and John's exile may have been associated with it based upon the tradition of John being exiled from Rome, found in Tertullian, and the notice of the Roman historian Suetonius (c. 70–c. 130) that Claudius banished Jews from Rome on account of "disturbances at the instigation of Christ (*Chrestus*)" (*Claud.* 25),[55] which is sometimes understood as a reference to a dispute within the Jewish community at Rome over the new religion of Christianity.[56] Evidence for Hippolytus's interest in the Acts narrative was separately seen in his probable placement of Cerinthus's activities at the time of the Jerusalem council.

## THE MARTYRDOM OF JOHN IN ORIGEN

Origen discusses John's banishment to Patmos within the context of his comments on Jesus's prophecy of the martyrdom of the Zebedee brothers, suggesting that he, too, may have held that John died in exile on the island:

> And the sons of Zebedee drank the cup and were baptized with the baptism, when Herod killed James, the brother of John, with the sword, and when the king of the Romans (Ῥωμαίων βασιλεύς), as tradition teaches, condemned John, witnessing on account of the word of truth, to the island of Patmos (κατεδίκασε τὸν Ἰωάννην μαρτυροῦντα διὰ τὸν τῆς ἀληθείας λόγον εἰς Πάτμον τὴν νῆσον). John teaches the circumstances of his testimony (or "martyrdom") (τὰ περὶ τοῦ μαρτυρίου αὐτοῦ), not recounting who condemned him, saying in Revelation these things: "I, John, your brother, and fellow partaker of the tribulation and kingdom and patience of Jesus, was in the island called Patmos on account of the word of God," etc. And he seems (ἔοικε) to have seen the apocalyptic vision on the island (Origen, *Comm. Matt.* 16.6).[57]

The statement that John "seems" (ἔοικε) to have seen the vision on Patmos is probably related to Victorinus's claim that "there [Patmos], therefore, John seems (*videtur*) to have written the Apocalypse" (*Comm. Apoc.* 10:11), which Jerome corrects to "there, therefore, he saw Revelation" (*ibi ergo vidit apocalypsin*). Victorinus may have been dependent upon Origen for the statement, for he is said to have used Origen's explanations of the Scriptures (*Epist.* 71.2), which may have included Origen's lost twelve homilies on the Apocalypse.

Origen relates that John was μαρτυροῦντα "on account of (διά) the word of God," where the verb μαρτυρέω can refer to testifying either by proclamation, by suffering, or by death. Thus, Origen could be saying that John was testifying on account of the word of truth,[58] or that he was suffering (as a martyr or otherwise) on account of the word of truth.[59]

The noun μαρτύριον used by Origen shares the ambiguities of its related verb and can refer to testimony in general (e.g., Matt. 24:14) as well as to martyrdom in particular (e.g., Origen, *Comm. John* 2.28). Origen uses it in the latter sense elsewhere in the context, arguing, for example, that martyrdom (μαρτύριον) was a form of baptism in which one receives forgiveness of sins (*Comm. Matt.* 16.6). Origen's use of it in this passage seems to have been a deliberate lexical choice, for the apocalyptic passage from which he draws (Rev 1:9) employs the related noun μαρτυρία (which likewise shares this ambiguity) in the sense of spoken "testimony," suggesting that Origen had John's martyrdom in mind.

According to Origen, John taught the circumstances of his μαρτύριον when he declared that he was on Patmos on account of the word of God. Possibly in making Patmos the scene of John's μαρτύριον, Origen was interacting with the *ad metalla* tradition, which was generally a *de facto* capital sentence. This would have been considered martyrdom, for the Liberian Catalogue (c. 354) counted Pontianus the bishop of Rome and a Roman presbyter named Hippolytus (probably Hippolytus of Rome) as martyrs after they died in exile in Sardinia, c. 235;[60] their remains were later deposited in Rome on the same day: Pontianus's in the cemetery of Callistus and Hippolytus's on the *Via Tiburtina* (where the Ligorio Statue associated with Hippolytus was later discovered).[61]

Further evidence that Origen was speaking of John's martyrdom is provided by the extant Latin version of this passage, found in the *Vetus Interpretatio* of his *Commentary on Matthew* (perhaps from the sixth century), discussed in chapter 2, in which Origen interprets Jesus's prophecy to the Zebedee brothers that they would drink his cup as a prediction of their "future perfection,"[62] where "perfection" denotes literal martyrdom (cf. Ignatius, *Eph.* 3.1; Clement, *Strom.* 4.4). Possibly this passage was removed from the Greek text to conform it to the tradition of John's peaceful death (as seems to have happened with Hamartolos's account, and perhaps also that of Gregory of Nyssa; see chapter 2).

*Revisions to Origen's Wording*

Evidence that Origen was speaking of martyrdom is indirectly provided by two later writers, both of whom seem to make subtle yet differing changes to Origen's wording in order to remove any reference to John's martyrdom. The first writer, Ps.-Dorotheus (sixth century), relates:

> James, the son of Zebedee, preaching Christ to the twelve tribes of Israel, is killed with a sword by Herod the tetrarch (ἀναιρεῖται μαχαίρᾳ ὑπὸ Ἡρῴδου τοῦ τετραάρχου) in Caesarea of Palestine. John, his brother, who has also written the Gospel, having preached Christ in Ephesus, is exiled (ἐξορίζεται) by Trajan the king (ὑπὸ Τραϊανοῦ τοῦ βασιλέως) to the island of Patmos (εἰς Πάτμον τὴν νῆσον), on account of the word of Christ (διὰ τὸν λόγον τοῦ Χριστοῦ). Having been lifted into heaven, he is said to have joined Enoch and Elijah in still consisting in the flesh.[63]

Thus, Ps.-Dorotheus speaks of John's exile by a Roman king rather than his condemnation by one, and he replaces the reference to John's μαρτυροῦντα on account of the word of truth with his exile on account of the word of Christ. Possibly the reference to "the word of Christ" rather than "the word of God" found in Revelation (1:2, 9) or "the word of truth" in Origen alludes to Jesus's prophecy of the martyrdom of the Zebedee brothers, representing an attempt at explaining Jesus's words in terms of John's banishment.

Ps.-Dorotheus's John does reach the end of his life on Patmos, but he is translated to heaven (cf. the reference to "the assumption of John the Evangelist" found in the sixth-century Hieronymian Martyrology, discussed in chapter 2) in what is likely a conflation of various Johannine traditions and motifs; i.e., Patmos as a place of revelatory ascent (see chapter 9), John's metastasis near Ephesus in *the Acts of John*, and John's martyrdom on Patmos.

The dependence of Theophylact (d. c. 1107), bishop of Ochrid (part of the Bulgarian empire, now in Macedonia), on Origen is more evident:[64] in his *Explanation of Matthew* (*apud* Matt 20:23), he writes: "for on the one hand, Herod killed (ἀπέκτεινεν) James; on the other hand, Trajan condemned (κατεδίκασε) John, witnessing to the word of truth (μαρτυροῦντα τῷ λόγῳ τῆς ἀληθείας)."[65]

As with Origen and Ps.-Dorotheus, Theophylact mentions the fates of James and John, assigning both to the personal agency of a ruler, and he associates Patmos with John's condemnation. Like Origen, Theophylact employs the verb ἀπέκτεινεν in relation to the death of James, rather than the ἀνεῖλεν used in Acts 12:2 (cf. Ps.-Dorotheus, following the wording of Acts, states that James ἀναιρεῖται μαχαίρᾳ ὑπὸ Ἡρώδου).

Also like Origen, but unlike Ps.-Dorotheus, Theophylact uses the verb κατεδίκασε and the present participle μαρτυροῦντα, as well as the expression "the word of truth," which is characteristic of Origen.[66] However, he has amended the text so that John is witnessing to the word of truth (τῷ λόγῳ τῆς ἀληθείας), not suffering martyrdom on account of the word of truth (διὰ τὸν τῆς ἀληθείας λόγον), as in Origen.

Thus, both Ps.-Dorotheus and Theophylact seem to have understood Origen's μαρτυροῦντα διὰ τὸν τῆς ἀληθείας λόγον as a reference to his suffering martyrdom on account of the word. While one has amended the reference to John's μαρτυροῦντα to make it refer to spoken testimony, the other has removed it entirely.

*A Common Source*

Both Ps.-Dorotheus and Theophylact seem to have known an intermediate source which maintained Origen's wording concerning John's martyrdom on Patmos and which identified Origen's king with Trajan, even though Origen himself referred only to "the king of the Romans."

Hamartolos may have known and modified the tradition of John's martyrdom in Trajan's reign by bringing it into conformity with Eusebius's account, which had John return to Ephesus following his exile, for he relates that John returned to Ephesus from exile in Nerva's reign (September 96 to January 98) and was martyred there after writing his Gospel (Fragment 6), probably early in Trajan's reign (98–117). Hamartolos's *Chronicle* was perhaps the source for the claim of Gregory Abul Faraj, or Bar Hebraeus (1226–1286), who stated in his *Chronography* that John was martyred in a persecution stirred up by Trajan.[67]

As discussed in chapter 2, Hamartolos was probably dependent upon Philip of Sidé for this account, presumably including his citations from Papias and Origen. Philip in turn is known to have used Eusebius's *History*,[68] which quotes Irenaeus's statement that John died in Trajan's reign (Irenaeus, *Haer.* 2.22.5 = *apud* Eusebius, *Hist. eccl.* 3.23.4). Philip could therefore have potentially combined Origen's statement concerning the martyrdom of the Apostle John in exile with Irenaeus's statement that John died in Trajan's reign to conclude that Trajan was the king of the Romans by whom John was condemned. This notice would then have later been variously recycled and modified by Ps.-Dorotheus, Theophylact, and Hamartolos.

## DIONYSIUS OF ALEXANDRIA AND THE CLAUDIAN DATING

Dionysius of Alexandria, Origen's student, may have also been working within the chronological framework of John's Claudian banishment. In his discussion of the authorship of Revelation, he is unable to suggest a potential alternative to John the son of Zebedee, with whom he identified the Evangelist (*Hist. eccl.* 7.25.7), but he dismisses the possibility of authorship by the John who is also called Mark on the basis that Acts 13:13 records that this John returned to Jerusalem rather than following Paul and Barnabas into Asia (7.25.15). Dionysius thus has his eye specifically on the Acts narrative in his quest for a potential author. He is not interested in the fact that two letters attributed to Paul do later place the John called Mark in the region of Asia: Colossians associates Mark with Paul's co-workers and prepares the churches in the Lycus Valley for a possible visit by him (Col 4:10), and 2 Timothy depicts Paul as summoning to himself both Timothy and Mark from Asia Minor (cf. 2 Tim 4:11–13; cf. 1:18; 1 Tim 1:3). J. Edgar Bruns refers to this omission on Dionysius's part as "very curious," adding: "Dionysius seems not to have realised that John Mark was the Mark of Col 4:10 and 2 Tim 4:11."[69] But the omission would be expected if he chronologically placed the writing of Revelation during the time in which Acts records John/Mark's movements, that is, during Claudius's reign, rendering John/Mark's later movements during the Neronian period, as represented by the Pauline letters, irrelevant for his purposes.

## CONCLUSION

The tradition of John's exile during Claudius's reign is either spoken of or presupposed by a number of sources that independently exhibit evidence of dependence upon Hippolytus. While the existence of this narrative has puzzled many, it can plausibly be explained on the supposition that as the Apostle and Evangelist came to be identified, so the widespread tradition of John's martyrdom in Claudius's reign occasioned an early placement of the Patmos narrative. Possibly the originator of the narrative had assumed that the then-dominant tradition of John's exile in Nero's reign (see chapter 7) had arisen as a result of Claudius being mistaken for Nero, who was called Nero Claudius Caesar.

The *ad metalla* narrative associated with the Claudian exile likely sought to correct Tertullian's claim that John was sentenced to *relegatio*, which was reserved for prominent citizens, by replacing it with a sentence given to common people. Because this sentence usually ended in death, it also represents an attempt at combining the martyrdom and Patmos traditions by effecting John's martyrdom on the island, rather than in Jerusalem, as appears to have been the case in the earlier form of the martyrdom narrative.

Some later writers evince evidence of attempts at merging the Claudian tradition with Irenaeus's narrative of John's natural death at Ephesus in old age, during Trajan's reign. Epiphanius thus maintained the Claudian exile but depicted John as later returning to Ephesus, presumably where he died a natural death; Victorinus, however, moved John's exile into the reign of Domitian, possibly on account of a depiction of John as aged during his time in exile.

Four important writers seem to have known the tradition via Philip of Sidé, who in turn seems to have drawn from Origen, though only two of these—Bar Hebraeus and Hamartolos—have maintained the original martyrdom context, while two—Ps.-Dorotheus and Theophylact—have separately sought to correct the account by removing any reference to martyrdom.

## NOTES

1. After developing this theory, I later came across the similar theory of Oberweis, who argues that it was the identification of the Seer with the Apostle which resulted in the claim that Revelation was written in Claudius's reign ("Das Papias-Zeugnis," 287).

2. Frank Williams, *The Panarion of Epiphanius of Salamis*, vol. 2, *Books II and III. De Fide* (2nd rev. ed.; NHMS 79; Leiden: Brill, 2013), 36.

3. Williams, *Panarion*, vol. 2, 65–66.

4. Benjamin Wisner Bacon, "The Elder John, Papias, Irenaeus, Eusebius and the Syriac Translator," *JBL* 27 (1908): 2 n. 6; Bernard, *St. John*, vol. 1, lxxiv; Smith, "Gaius," 259; Guthrie, *Introduction*, 956; Culpepper, *John*, 122; Watson, *Gospel Writing*, 488.

5. Eisler objects that according to bar Salibi, Hippolytus and Irenaeus placed John's exile in Domitian's reign (*Enigma*, 92), but bar Salibi was citing a certain Hippolytus of Bosra (in Theodore H. Robinson, "The Authorship of the Muratorian Canon," *Exp* 7 [1906]: 486; cf. Eusebius, *Hist. eccl.* 6.20.2), not Hippolytus of Rome.

6. Barclay, *Introduction to John*, 20.

7. Boxall, *Patmos*, 40.

8. Fenton J. A. Hort, *The Apocalypse of St. John 1–3: The Greek Text with Introduction, Commentary, and Additional Notes* (London: Macmillan, 1908), xviii; Robinson, *Redating*, 224; Aune, *Revelation 1–5*, 78.

9. So, Jan Stolt, "Om dateringen af Apokalypsen," *DTT* 40 (1977): 203.

10. Cf. William. H. Simcox, *The Revelation of S. John the Divine* (CGTSC; Cambridge: Cambridge University Press, 1893), xlv.

11. Translated by the author from CSCO, Scriptores Syri, 2.101.2; cf. Smith, "Gaius," 590; Robinson, "Authorship," 487.

12. Souter, *The Text and Canon*, 209.

13. This reading is attested in the excerpts of the Muratorian Canon found in a Prologue to Paul's Epistles, found in three eleventh-century and one twelfth-century manuscript (see Hahneman, *Muratorian Fragment*, 9).
14. Streeter, *The Four Gospels*, 452; Barclay, *Introduction to John*, 32; Oberweis, "Das Papias-Zeugnis," 287; Ramelli, "John the Evangelist's Work," 48.
15. The Muratorian Canon identifies 1 Corinthians (conventionally dated c. 53–55) as Paul's first letter (ll. 50–51).
16. Cf. Wilhelm Hartke, *Vier urchristliche Parteien und ihre Vereinigung zur apostolischen Kirche*, vol. 1 (Berlin: Akademie-Verlag, 1961), 135; Stolt, "Om dateringen," 204; Oberweis, "Das Papias-Zeugnis," 287.
17. Streeter, *The Four Gospels*, 452.
18. Barclay, *Introduction to John*, 32.
19. John T. Fitzgerald, "Theodore of Mopsuestia on Paul's Letter to Philemon," in *Philemon in Perspective: Interpreting a Pauline Letter*, ed. D. Francois Tolmie (Berlin: de Gruyter, 2010), 345 n.67.
20. Oberweis, "Das Papias Zeugnis," 287.
21. . Charles, *Revelation*, vol. 1, xlviii.
22. Michael J. Kruger, "The Reception of the Book of Revelation in the Early Church," in *Book of Seven Seals: The Peculiarity of Revelation, its Manuscripts, Attestation and Transmission*, ed. Thomas J. Kraus and Michael Sommer (WUNT 363; Tübingen: Mohr Siebeck, 2016), 164.
23. Mark L. Hitchcock ("A Defense of the Domitianic Date of the Book of Revelation" [PhD diss, Dallas Theological Seminary, 2005], 52), following William Milligan (*The Revelation of St. John* [London: Macmillan, 1886], 309).
24. See Hahneman, *Muratorian Fragment*, 30–31; cf.; Orchard and Riley, *Order of the Synoptics*, 138. Allen Brent suggests that Hippolytus contributed to its writing or editing (*Hippolytus and the Roman Church in the Third Century: Communities in Tension Before the Emergence of a Monarch-Bishop* [Leiden: Brill, 1995], 341–43).
25. Translated by the author from CSCO, Scriptores Syri, 2.101.2.
26. CSCO, Scriptores Syri, 2.101.2–3.
27. *PG* 103:1103.
28. Robinson, "Authorship," 489.
29. Jean Joseph Léandre Bargès, trans., *Homélie sur St Marc, Apôtre et Évangéliste par Anba Sévère, Évêque de Nestéraweh* (Paris: Leroux, 1877).
30. Bargès, *Homélie sur St Marc*, 31.
31. Agnes Smith Lewis, *The Mythological Acts of the Apostles* (HSem 4; London: Clay, 1904) xv.
32. Lewis, *The Mythological Acts*, 54.
33. Boxall, *Patmos*, 122.
34. Budge, *Contendings*, 253. Cf. Boxall, *Patmos*, 123.
35. Haase, *Apostel und Evangelisten*, 295–300 (here, 297).
36. Trans., William C. Weinrich, ed., *Revelation* (ACCSNT 12; Downers Grove, Ill.: IVP, 2005) 153.
37. David J. Mattingly, *Imperialism, Power, and Identity: Experiencing the Roman Empire* (Princeton: Princeton University Press, 2011), 187. Cf. Nancy H. Ramage and Andrew Ramage, *Ancient Rome* (London: British Museum, 2008), 66; Crook, *Law and Life of Rome*, 273.
38. Mattingly, *Imperialism, Power, and Identity*, 187, quoting Athanasius, *Orations against the Arians*, 60.765–66.
39. Sanders, "St John on Patmos," 76; Thompson, "Ordinary Lives," 33.
40. Sanders, "St John on Patmos," 76.
41. E. Earle Ellis, *The Making of the New Testament Documents* (Leiden: Brill, 2002), 211. Cf. the translation in ANF 3.417 ("and when at length grown old").
42. Weinrich, *Revelation*, xxii; Constantinou, *Blessed End*, 2–3.
43. The reading in Souter's text. Others read, *nihil tamen differt*.

44. The Latin text of this sentence reads: *denique sive in Asia sive in toto orbe, septem ecclesias omnes et septem nominates unam esse catholicam Paul docuit.*
45. Translated by the author from the Latin text in Johannes Haussleiter, ed. *Victorini Episcopi Petavionensis Opera* (CSEL 49. Vienna: Tempsky, 1916), and so hereafter.
46. Cf. Verheyden, "The Canon Muratori," 495.
47. Adolf von Harnack, "Über den Verfasser und den literarischen Charakter des Muratorischen Fragments," *ZNW* 24 (1925 11–12; Martine Dulaey, *Victorin de Poetovio, Premier Exégète Latin*, vol. 1 (2 vols.; EAA 139/140; Paris: Institut d'Études Augustiniennes, 1993), 36.
48. Jonathan J. Armstrong, "Victorinus of Pettau as the Author of the Canon Muratori," *VC* 62 (2008): 1–34.
49. Translated by the author from the Latin text in Roger Gryson, ed. *Variorum Auctorum Commentaria Minora in Apocalypsin Johannis* (CCSL 107; Turnhout: Brepols, 2003), 193, and so hereafter.
50. Gryson, *Variorum Auctorum*, 183.
51. Cf. Francis X. Gumerlock, *Revelation and the First Century: Preterist Interpretations of the Apocalypse in Early Christianity* (Powder Springs: American Vision, 2012), 31.
52. Gryson, *Variorum Auctorum*, 194.
53. See the Latin text in A. W. Adams, ed., *Primasius Episcopus Hadrumetinus, Commentarius in Apocalypsin* (CCSL 92; Turnhout, 1985), 6–7.
54. Apringius of Beja, *Tractate on the Apocalypse* 1.9, trans. Weinrich, *Revelation*, 7. Cf. Eisler, *Enigma*, 90. Cf. Boxall, *Patmos*, 59; Gumerlock, *Revelation and the First Century*, 30. The Latin text is taken from Gryson, *Variorum Auctorum*, 39.
55. Latin text in J. C. Rolfe, ed. and trans., *Suetonius*, vol. 2 (LCL; London: Heinamann, 1914).
56. See, e.g., Joseph A. Fitzmyer, *The Acts of the Apostles: A New Translation with Introduction and Commentary* (AB 31; New Haven, Conn.: Yale University Press, 2008), 619.
57. Translated by the author from the Greek text in Erich Klostermann and Ernst Benz, eds., *Origenes Werke*, vol. 10 (GCS 40; Leipzig: Hinrichs, 1935).
58. So, Boxall, *Patmos*, 36.
59. Simcox, *Revelation*, xlv, allows both possibilities.
60. See the Latin text in Theodor Mommsen, ed. *Chronica Minora*, vol. 1 (*MGH*; Berlin: 1892), 71–2, 74–5; cf. W. Brian Shelton, *Martyrdom from Exegesis in Hippolytus: An Early Church Presbyter's Commentary on Daniel* (SCHT; Eugene: Wipf and Stock, 2008), 24.
61. Mommsen, *Chronica Minora*, vol. 1, 72.
62. Origen, *Commentary on Matthew* according to the *Vetus Interpretatio*, 16.5; translated by the author from the Latin text in *PG* 13:1381–2.
63. Translated by the author from the Greek text in Theodor Schermann, ed., *Prophetarum Vitae Fabulosae Indices Apostolorum Discipulorumque Domini* (Leipzig: Teubner 1907), 154. There is significant variation within the manuscript tradition (see John Granger Cook, *Roman Attitudes Toward the Christians: From Claudius to Hadrian* [WUNT 261; Tubingen: Mohr Siebeck, 2010], 248–49). Cf. Eisler, *Enigma*, 98.
64. Cf. Swete, *The Apocalypse* (2nd ed.; New York: Macmillan, 1907), xcvi.
65. Translated by the author from *PG* 123:364.
66. See, e.g., Origen, *Comm. Matt.* 10.8; 10.10; 12.4; 12:33.
67. E. A. Wallis Budge, ed. and trans., *The Chronography of Gregory Abû'l Faraj, the Son of Aaron, the Hebrew Physician Commonly Known as Bar Hebraeus*, (London: Oxford University Press, 1932), 52.
68. See, e.g., the fragments of Philip in G. C. Hansen, ed., *Theodoros Anagnostes Kirchengeschichte* (GCS 54; Berlin: 1971), 160.
69. J. Edgar Bruns, "John Mark: A Riddle within the Johannine Enigma," *Scr* 15 (1963): 91.

# FIVE
# Hippolytus, Gaius, and the Alogoi

A possible context for Hippolytus's proposed identification of the Evangelist with the Apostle John is provided by a dispute concerning the Gospel and Revelation of John which arose within orthodox circles[1] at Rome during the early third century. While Hippolytus is said to have defended these works and to have attributed them to the Apostle John, his opponent, a certain Gaius of Rome, is said to have rejected them and to have attributed them to a heretical teacher named Cerinthus. Possibly Hippolytus identified the Evangelist with the Apostle in order to lend credence to the Johannine writings.[2]

While most scholars accept the historicity of this dispute,[3] it has been called into question from time to time, most recently and notably by Allen Brent,[4] who has been followed by Charles Hill and T. Scott Manor,[5] both of whom defend the traditional Zebedean identification of the Evangelist. The question of its historicity is an important one, for it would provide further grounds for doubting that the Johannine writings were associated with the Apostle John from an earlier period, since any works universally associated with this figure would likely not have struggled to find canonical acceptance.

A discussion of this debate will also provide the necessary background both for understanding Eusebius's construction of the Johannine narrative (to be discussed in the following chapter) and for demonstrating (in the final two chapters) the likelihood that Papias identified the Evangelist and Elder.

### THE STATUS OF THE FOURTH GOSPEL IN ROME

Culpepper notes the "nearly complete absence" of references to the Gospel of John in the first half of the second century.[6] This is particularly noticeable in Justin, who lived at Rome during the mid-second century. While his works are marked by a distinctive Logos theology, he clearly alludes to the Fourth Gospel no more than half a dozen times while referring to the Synoptic Gospels hundreds of times.[7] As Bauer observes, Justin "seeks laboriously to press the synoptics into the service" of proving the preexistence of Christ,[8] so that "[t]he miraculous birth or the confession of Peter must bear the brunt of providing a proof which John could have given with no difficulty."[9] J. N. Sanders concludes that Justin did not regard John's Gospel as scripture or as apostolic,[10] while Culpepper accounts for Justin's tentative use of the Fourth Gospel by suggesting that either its "origin was suspect" or "it had not gained widespread recognition as an apostolic writing."[11] Keener, who favors the traditional view, acknowledges that "it is difficult to understand why it took second-century 'orthodox' Christians so long to accept the Gospel," and he refers to the late acceptance of John's Gospel as "probably the most persuasive objection of Johannine authorship"; he suggests that a limited circulation and its use by Gnostics may explain the situation.[12]

Some apparently rejected the Fourth Gospel altogether, for Irenaeus, in the late second century refers to a group whom he accuses of setting aside John's Gospel and the Prophetic Spirit (*Haer.* 3.11.9).[13] That he was speaking of a group in the church is shown by his complaint that they rejected the prophetic grace from the church and withdrew from fellowship with those "brothers" who were outside their circles.[14] Possibly he was referring to Gaius[15] or Epiphanius's Alogoi[16] (see below). Smith suggests that Irenaeus did not identify Gaius by name because he was orthodox, and it would have been inappropriate to name him in a Gnostic heresiology.[17]

The Muratorian Canon (c. 200) possibly indicates the existence of controversy over John's Gospel in the Roman church. While it devotes seven lines to the Gospel of Luke, it takes up twenty-five lines discussing the Gospel of John, which may indicate apologetic intent.[18]

## GAIUS OF ROME

Eusebius is silent concerning any dispute between Hippolytus and Gaius over the Johannine writings, though he does mention Gaius, stating that he was prominent in the Roman church during the bishopric of Zephyrinus (199–217) (*Hist. eccl.* 2.25.6; 6.20.3) and describing him as "very learned" (λογιωτάτου) (6.20.3) and as "a man of the church" (ἐκκλησιαστικὸς ἀνήρ) (2.25.6), which may suggest that he held an ecclesiastical office. He adds that Gaius wrote a work against the Montanist leader Proclus, entitled the *Dialogue of Gaius* (6.20.3). According to Photius, Gaius was a presbyter in the Roman church during the episcopates of Victor (189–199) and Zephyrinus (199–217); he also claims that he was ordained "bishop of the nations" (ἐθνῶν ἐπίσκοπον),[19] though he may have confused Gaius with another figure.[20]

In one of the two quotations from Gaius's *Dialogue* given by Eusebius, Gaius alleges that he can point out the tombs of Peter and Paul at Rome (*apud* Eusebius, *Hist. eccl.* 2.25.7). He likely asserted this to bolster Roman church's claims to orthodoxy against the innovations of the Asian Christians of the city, among whom Montanism seems to have been popular.

In the second quotation, Gaius attributes spurious revelations to Cerinthus, which included the idea of a thousand-year reign in Jerusalem after the resurrection:

> But Cerinthus too, through revelations which he claims were written by a great apostle, introduces marvelous tales, speaking falsely, claiming they were shown to him [the apostle] through angels, saying that after the resurrection the kingdom of Christ is to be on earth (μετὰ τὴν ἀνάστασιν ἐπίγειον εἶναι τὸ βασίλειον τοῦ Χριστοῦ) and that the flesh, living in Jerusalem, would again serve desires and pleasures. And being an enemy of the scriptures of God, he says, wishing to deceive, that there will be a numbering of a thousand years for a wedding festival (*apud* Eusebius, *Hist. eccl.* 3.28.2).

These spurious revelations are usually understood as a reference to the canonical book of Revelation,[21] though this has been challenged.[22] More light is perhaps thrown on the question by Eusebius's discussion of a similar charge found in a now lost treatise entitled *Concerning Promises* by Dionysius, bishop of Alexandria (248–265), which Dionysius is said to have penned in reply to the work of an Egyptian bishop and chiliast named Nepos entitled *Refutation of the Allegorists* (*Hist. eccl.* 3.28.3; 7.24.1–3). In his account, for which he was dependent upon "an earlier tradition" (3.28.3), Dionysius claimed that Cerinthus employed Revelation "to attach a trustworthy name to his own fiction" (3.28.4).

Dionysius's "earlier tradition" was probably Gaius's work, for like Gaius (3.28.2), Dionysius's source also relates Cerinthus's claim that "the kingdom of Christ" would be "on the earth" (ἐπίγειον) (3.28.4; 7.25.3). Furthermore, whereas Cerinthus added, according to Dionysius's source, that this would be accompanied by "food and drink and weddings" (σιτίοις καὶ πότοις καὶ γάμοις) (3.28.5; 7.25.3) and "holy feasts, sacrifices and the slaughter of offerings" (ἑορταῖς καὶ θυσίαις καὶ ἱερείων σφαγαῖς) (7.25.3), he added according to Gaius that there would be a wedding feast of a thousand years following the resurrection, with people once again serving, in Gaius's words, desires and pleasures (3.28.2).

In the same context, Dionysius spoke of those before him who had gone over the canonical book of Revelation chapter by chapter (καθ' ἕκαστον κεφάλαιον) and had thoroughly rejected it. He adds that they had declared it to be "unknowable and illogical" (ἄγνωστόν τε καὶ ἀσυλλόγιστον), claiming that it was not written by John or by an apostle, or even by someone belonging to the church, but was a work of Cerinthus (7.25.1–2). Thus, Dionysius's source was referring to the canonical book of Revelation, and those who were criticizing it were within the church. If Gaius was Dionysius's source,[23] then Gaius must have attributed Revelation to Cerinthus.[24]

## DIONYSIUS ON REVELATION

While Dionysius refrains from fully endorsing these criticisms of Revelation, he does so only to avoid giving offence to the many brothers who esteemed it (7.25.4).[25] While he does not attribute Revelation to Cerinthus, as his source does, he does reject authorship by the Evangelist (whom he identifies with the son of Zebedee), and he suggests that another John wrote it (7.25.7). He notes in support that there were two monuments (μνήματα) associated with the name of John in Ephesus, from which he infers that there had been two Johns in Asia (7.25.16). He was unable to cite any authority for this supposition, however, and earlier sources only associated one famous John with the city.

According to Jerome, many claimed that both memorials belonged to John the Evangelist (*Vir.* 9).[26] Eisler notes that one manuscript of the *Acts of John* seems to betray knowledge of the removal of John's remains from their original resting place to a church, and these two sites may correspond to the two memorials.[27] This church is probably the site of the basilica referred to by the Byzantine historian Procopius of Caesarea (c. 500–c. 554), which was built over a church that had been set up "in early times" and dedicated to the Apostle John, but which "was small and in a ruined condition because of its great age" (Procopius, *De Aedificis* 5.1.5–6 [Dewing and Downey, LCL]). Eisler observes that before their expulsion in 1920, the Greeks of Ephesus would honor what they believed to have been the original resting place of John at a cave near the ancient stadium of the city, rather than at the Church of St. John near the ruins of the ancient basilica.[28]

## EPIPHANIUS'S ALOGOI

In his *Panarion*, Epiphanius (c. 315–403), who was bishop of Salamis in Cyprus, discusses a group called the Alogoi who rejected the Johannine writings. It is in this section that Epiphanius places John's exile in Claudius's reign, and as noted in the previous chapter, this part of his work is generally thought to have been derived from Hippolytus

According to Epiphanius, these Alogoi rejected the books of John and attributed them to Cerinthus (*Pan.* 51.3.6); the similarity of this attribution to the claims of Gaius and Dionysius's source concerning Revelation raises the question of whether the Alogoi was an epithet given to Gaius and his party. Eusebius does not mention Gaius's rejection of the Gospel of John, but he may have glossed over this so as not to undermine his use of Gaius's criticisms of Revelation.[29]

Epiphanius adds that according to the Alogoi, neither the Gospel nor Revelation had any rightful place in the church (*Pan.* 51.3.6), and this presupposes that they themselves were members of the church, just as those referred to by Irenaeus and Dionysius evidently were.[30] Indeed, Epiphanius does not accuse them of any heresy beyond the rejection of John's books but concedes: "they seem to believe the same things as us," other than that they do not hold those things revealed "through the preaching of saint John" (*Pan.* 51.4.3).[31]

## The Appellation, "Alogoi"

The nickname Alogoi was coined as a pun on the Greek word λόγος, referring both to the (divine) Word spoken of in John 1:1 and to "reason" generally. Thus, the Alogoi were accused of being both "Anti-Logosites" and "Irrationalists."[32] Epiphanius might have coined the pun himself, since he states: "this is the nickname I put on them" (*Pan.* 51.3.1), though it is also possible that he is reproducing Hippolytus's text here.[33] Lightfoot points out that Epiphanius does quote his authorities verbatim at times, without always modifying or adapting their words to his own context.[34] Thus, in one place, Lightfoot notes that he "refers back to 'the catalogue' in which the name of Anicetus had been mentioned already.... But no catalogue has been given previously."[35]

Another such wordplay is known to have been found in Epiphanius's source:

> But they are called Merinthians too, I am told. Whether the same Cerinthus was also called Merinthus I have no idea; or whether there was someone else named Merinthus, a colleague of his, God knows! (*Pan.* 28.8.1).[36]

As Lightfoot points out, Μήρινθος means "noose," making this another probable example of Hippolytus's play on words, this time on the name of Cerinthus.[37] But as Harris observes: "Epiphanius has failed to see the Hippolytean joke," since he wonders whether Merinthus was a separate person.[38]

Hippolytus also employs a pun to caricature his opponent in his *Against Noetus*,[39] speaking of Noetus (Νοητός), meaning "mentally perceptible," or "intelligible," as the one "not perceiving (νοῶν) the truth" (*Noet.* 8), where the related verb is used.[40] Another pun is employed in the *Refutation of All Heresies*, which was possibly authored by Hippolytus.[41] Speaking of the Docetists, the writer "plays upon the words δοκεῖν 'to seem' and δοκός 'a beam,' contending that they are so named, not because they 'seemed to be of importance', but because of 'the beam in their eye'" (*Refut.* 8.11).[42]

Perhaps Hippolytus was responsible for the appellation of "Alogoi," though it is also possible that Epiphanius was imitating his style. The former, however, is perhaps indicated by the added qualification: "for *from now on* they will be called in this way" (ἀπὸ γὰρ τῆς δεῦρο οὕτως κληθήσονται) (*Pan.* 51.3.1; italics added), which suggests that they had been discussed previously, though not under this epithet: Epiphanius had not previously discussed them, but perhaps his source had. Similarly, Epiphanius speaks in one place of what "he says" (φησίν), in the singular, perhaps referring to Gaius of Rome, but no figure had previously been introduced in Epiphanius's account (*Pan.* 51.4.6).[43]

Interestingly, Hill infers a connection of this appellation with the criticism of those spoken of by Dionysius of Alexandria who went over the canonical book of Revelation "chapter by chapter" and concluded that it was "unknowable and impenetrable," using the alpha privatives ἄγνωστος and ἀσυλλόγιστος (*apud* Eusebius, *Hist. eccl.* 7.25.1). He suggests that the term Alogoi (Ἄλογοι), another alpha privative, was coined (he says by Epiphanius, but perhaps by Hippolytus) in response to these assertions.[44] This suggests that those referred to by Dionysius, who criticized Revelation and attributed it to Cerinthus, were the group known as the Alogoi.

*The Problem of the Alogoi*

The difficulty which the existence of the Alogoi presents for the traditional view has not been lost on its proponents, who have sometimes sought to minimize their significance or to deny their historical existence. Lightfoot thus diminishes their importance by characterizing them as "an obscure sect,"[45] while Brown considers the Alogoi just one of a number of "fringe groups."[46] Bruce speaks of "the eccentric views of Gaius and the Alogoi"[47] whose "negative attitude," he maintains, had "no influence on catholic thought, in Rome or elsewhere."[48] This seems inconsistent, however, with Gaius's status and with the prominent place Hippolytus gives to them in his work. Gaius's criticisms also do seem to have yielded a significant influence on later writers, including Origen, Dionysius, Eusebius, and Epiphanius, as will be discussed in this chapter and later ones.

Others label the Alogoi as heretics,[49] but this can be quickly dismissed, for as noted above, even Epiphanius, their arch critic, acknowledged that they held ecclesiastical communion (*Pan.* 51.3.6) and were otherwise orthodox in their beliefs (*Pan.* 51.4.3).

Perhaps the most potentially damaging claim raised against the group is that it was a constructed heresy with no historical existence and no association with Gaius.[50] The foremost proponent of this view, Allen Brent, asserts that Epiphanius "makes it clear that he is constructing a heresy."[51] He adds that Epiphanius "makes it clear" that the title of "Alogoi" is a generic one for anyone who rejects the Johannine books, so that Epiphanius even includes Porphyry and Celsus as members of the Alogoi.[52]

Brent's claims are built upon a misunderstanding of Epiphanius's position. It is true that Epiphanius mentions Porphyry and Celsus, two early critics of Christianity, while discussing the Alogoi, but he does so not because they were Alogoi, as Brent thinks, but because they alleged discrepancies between Matthew and Luke (cf. Origen, *Against Celsus*, 1.40; 48; 91.5-7), just as the Alogoi alleged discrepancies between John and the Synoptics.[53]

Furthermore, Epiphanius indicates that he considered the Alogoi to have had a real historical existence as a distinct group by stating that they otherwise believed as he did (*Pan.* 51.4.3) and by placing their rise chronologically after the Phrygians (i.e., Montanists), Quintillianists, and Quartodecimans (*Pan.* 51.1.1), that is, in or after the second half of the second century, or at about the time of Gaius and Hippolytus. For Epiphanius, the title of "Alogoi" was not simply a convenient label attachable to any group rejecting the Johannine books, "orthodox" or not, as Brent maintains.

## THE LIGORIO STATUE

Further evidence for a dispute over the Johannine writings at Rome was provided by a statue discovered in 1551 by Pirro Ligorio at Rome, near the catacomb of Hippolytus. The headless figure, seated on a throne, was originally reconstructed as Hippolytus but it is now thought to have originally been female. Inscribed on the plinth is a list of thirteen books, the first two of which are now illegible, containing titles often associated with Hippolytus.[54] Paschal calculations inscribed on the base of the throne give dates for Easter, commencing from the first year of Alexander Severus (i.e., the year 222) until the year 333 CE;[55] these calculations would have become inaccurate after 235,[56] providing important evidence for the dating of the inscriptions.

Among the works listed is one entitled [τ]ὰ ὑπὲρ τοῦ κατὰ Ἰωάννην εὐαγγελίου καὶ ἀποκαλύψεως;[57] Brent, noting that ὑπὲρ can mean "concerning," translates this as "matters concerning the Gospel according to John... etc.," rendering the title devoid of any apologetic intent.[58] But while ὑπὲρ followed by a genitive can function as the equivalent of περί ("concerning"), it more often has the nuance of "in defense of" or "on behalf of,"[59] which would render the title: "The things in defense of the Gospel and Revelation of John."[60]

Additional evidence for this connotation is provided by a Syriac listing of biblical and ecclesiastical books written by Ebed-Jesu in 1298, which lists among works attributed to Hippolytus one entitled *Chapters against Gaius* and another called *Defense of the Revelation and Gospel of John, Apostle and Evangelist.*[61] As Watson notes, the Syriac title suggests an original ἀπολογία ὑπέρ which has been abbreviated to ὑπέρ on the statue.[62] Thus, the evidence from the statute is suggestive of a debate concerning the Johannine writings in the early third century, associated with Hippolytus.

## BAR SALIBI

Further evidence for a dispute between Gaius and Hippolytus over the Johannine writings came to light in the form of fragments which were published in the late nineteenth century from a commentary on Revelation written by the Jacobite bishop Dionysius bar Salibi (d. 1171), containing answers to Gaius attributed to Hippolytus of Rome.[63] Brent dismisses the fragments as a "pseudepigraphic dialogue,"[64] but they are nevertheless generally regarded as genuine.[65]

In this work, bar Salibi's Hippolytus relates that "a man named Gaius appeared who used to claim that the Gospel was not of John, nor Revelation, but that they were of Cerinthus the heretic," echoing the charge raised by Epiphanius's Alogoi (*Pan.* 51.3.6).[66] Bar Salibi goes on to repeat Gaius's objections to Revelation, and there are correspondences between these and the objections raised against the book by the Alogoi, though, as Watson points out, where Gaius and the Alogoi overlap, bar Salibi provides a more detailed account, suggesting that he is independently drawing from a Hippolytan source.[67]

This overlap is found in Gaius's fourth objection against Revelation, namely that Rev 9:15, which speaks of the four angels being released to kill a third of mankind, portrays angels as making war, whereas scripture say nations make war (cf. Matt 24:7). Hippolytus answers by identifying the four angels as four nations which arise from the region of the Euphrates.[68] Epiphanius, however, does not record the objection but simply says: "If he [John] speaks of the four angels who are seated at the Euphrates, it is to show the different nations there, residing at the Euphrates, who are the Assyrians, Babylonians, Medes and Persians" (*Pan.* 51.34.3).[69] Bar Salibi thus provides that which must be inferred from Epiphanius.

Interestingly, Epiphanius employs the first-person singular personal pronoun in one of these objections: "What good does John's Revelation do me by telling me about seven angels and seven trumpets?" (*Pan.* 51. 32. 1–2).[70] Possibly the "me" was Gaius himself,[71] as in bar Salibi.

The objections of Gaius against Revelation recorded by bar Salibi are likely the same ones spoken of by Dionysius, who related that some before him had "set aside and demolished (ἠθέτησαν καὶ ἀνεσκεύασαν) the book entirely, correcting it chapter by chapter (καθ' ἕκαστον κεφάλαιον)" (*apud* Eusebius, *Hist. eccl.* 7.25.1). Indeed, this "chapter by chapter" approach may have inspired the title of Hippolytus's rejoinder, *Chapters against Gaius*, listed by Ebed-Jesu.

Bar Salibi also wrote a commentary on John which exists both in the original Syriac and in a Latin translation, neither of which have been published. In this work "a certain heretic" points out the same apparent discrepancies between the Johannine narrative and the Synoptics that the Alogoi did. This "heretic" is sometimes identified in the manuscript tradition with Gaius,[72] though in any event the preface to bar Salibi's commentary on Revelation does name Gaius as the opponent of Hippolytus who rejected the Gospel and Revelation of John.

Thus, where the Alogoi faulted the Fourth Gospel for passing over the period from Jesus's baptism by John to the wedding of Cana without mentioning the forty days' temptation of Jesus in the wilderness (*Pan.* 51.4.5–12), "a certain heretic (or "Gaius the heretic") criticized John because he did not agree with his fellow evangelists in that he says that after the baptism he went to Galilee and performed the miracle of the wine at Cana."[73]

It must be noticed, too, that in making this criticism, both the "certain heretic" and the Alogoi interpreted the day on which Jesus came to John and was declared by him to be the Lamb of God (John 1:9–34) as the day of Jesus's baptism. The following journey to Cana in Galilee in John's Gospel (John 1:43; 2:1–2) was consequently correlated with the commencement of Jesus's Galilean ministry following his baptism, as recorded in the Synoptics. The Synoptics, however, place a forty-day period of temptation between the baptism and the commencement of the Galilean ministry (Matt 3:13–4:12; Mark 1:9–14; Luke 3:21, 4:1–2, 14), leading to the charge that the Johannine account had omitted the forty days and was therefore in error.

Nevertheless, the solutions to the problem of the forty days proposed by bar Salibi's Hippolytus and by Epiphanius differ. Bar Salibi's Hippolytus takes the various references to numbered days and to the "next day" in the Johannine account and organizes them into two sets of three days, between which he inserts the forty days. He consequently claims that the Pharisees from Jerusalem came to the Baptist on the first day (cf. John 1:19–28) and that Jesus was baptized by John on the "second day," when John declared Jesus to be the Lamb of God (called the "next day" in John 1:29), after which he went into the wilderness for forty days. The second "first day" (called the "next day" in John 1:35) was the day following Jesus's return from the desert, when John pointed out Jesus to two of his disciples and again declared him to be the Lamb of God (John 1:35–36).[74] The second "second day" was the day on which Jesus departed to Galilee (cf. the "next day" of John 2:43), and the "third day" was the day of the wedding feast in Cana of Galilee (called the "third day" in John 2:1).[75]

Hippolytus finds support for this scheme in the words, "behold the lamb of God," which he addressed to his two disciples, (cf. John 1:36), inferring from them that John was pointing out Jesus to his disciples and to the people, as they had been searching for him for the forty days, during which time he could not be found as he had been hidden in the wilderness.[76]

Epiphanius on the other hand answers the Alogoi by differentiating the day on which Jesus was pointed out by the Baptist from the day of Jesus's baptism (*Pan.* 51.13.9–10). He suggests instead that Jesus immediately journeyed to Galilee following the baptism and forty days of temptation before returning to John at the Jordan, where he was pointed out by him (*Pan.* 51.13.4–8; 51.16.1–5). Nevertheless, Epiphanius continued (now unnecessarily) to correlate the subsequent wedding at Cana with the beginning of Jesus's Galilean ministry, as bar Salibi's "heretic" and the Alogoi had done.

Thus, according to Epiphanius, after Jesus went to the wedding at Cana of Galilee he settled in Capernaum, where he healed Peter's mother-in-law, a miracle association with the commencement of Jesus's Galilean ministry in the Synoptics (Luke 4:38–39). After that, Epiphanius adds, Jesus went into the synagogue at Nazareth and read from the scroll of Isaiah, which again is associated with the beginning of the Galilean ministry in the Synoptics (Luke 4:14–30) (*Pan.* 51.15.1–6).

Probably a better correlation with the Galilean ministry is instead provided by the return of Jesus to Galilee following the imprisonment of John, since this is mentioned both later in the Johannine narrative (John 2:11–13; 3:22–24) and in the Synoptics (cf. Matt 4:12 and Mark 1:14). Luke 4:14 could be read as making Jesus's Galilean ministry commence immediately after the forty days but it does not necessitate it.

## EPIPHANIUS AND ORIGEN'S DISCUSSION OF THE JOHANNINE CHRONOLOGY

Besides drawing from Hippolytus, Epiphanius also appears to be interacting with the discussion of the variance of the Gospels found in Origen's *Commentary on John*. It will be argued below that it is this interaction that explains why his solution to the problem of the variance between the Gospels differs from that attributed to Hippolytus.

T. Scott Manor draws attention to evidence suggesting that Epiphanius had Origen's *Commentary* before him when he wrote. After noting that Origen had discussed his preference for the reading of "Bethabara" in John 1:28 over "Bethany," found "in nearly all of the other copies" (σχεδὸν ἐν πᾶσι τοῖς ἀντιγράφοις) (*Comm. John* 6.24), he observes that Epiphanius (*Haer.* 51.13.1) likewise employs "Bethabara" while speaking of "Bethany" as the reading found "in the other copies" (ἐν δὲ ἄλλοις ἀντιγράφοις); Epiphanius also remarks, like Origen, that Cana means "the bride" (*Haer.* 51.30.10; cf. *Comm. John* 13.62).[77]

Origen had also discussed the issue of the apparent discrepancies between the Synoptics. Unlike Epiphanius, however, Origen does not deny that there were discrepancies between the accounts; rather he resolves the problem by claiming that the Johannine narrative must be understood "in an anagogical sense" (διὰ τῆς ἀναγωγῆς), or as allegory, and not "in the outward letters" (ἐν τοῖς σωματικοῖς χαρακτῆρσιν), or as a historical account (*Comm. John* 10.2).[78]

Thus, Origen correlates Jesus's visit to Capernaum following the wedding at Cana (John 2:12–25) with the Synoptic account of Jesus going to Capernaum from Nazareth after the forty days of temptation in the wilderness (Matt 4:11–13; Mark 1:12–15, 21; Luke 4:13–16, 30–31). This creates a contradiction between the accounts, since they differ on the question of where Jesus was prior to Capernaum (*Comm. John* 10.1), which Origen then employs in support of reading John anagogically.

Origen goes on to speak of those who hold a historical understanding of John's Gospel and who receive the four Gospels, but who are unable to resolve the chronological difficulty (*Comm. John* 10.2), and he challenges them to explain the difficulty concerning the forty days of temptation as well as that concerning when Jesus came to Capernaum (*Comm. John* 10.2),[79] asserting that no room "at all" (οὐδαμῶς) could be found in John's Gospel for the period of forty days, because (as he claims) the wedding at Cana was on the sixth day after the baptism of Jesus (*Comm. John* 10.2). Presumably he had discussed the succession of days between Jesus's encounter with the Baptist (which he identifies as the day of Jesus's baptism) and the wedding at Cana (John 1:29–2:1) in a preceding section of his commentary, since much of this work is no longer extant (the extant sixth book ends with comments on John 1:29 and the extant tenth book begins with a discussion of John 2:12: the seventh, eighth and ninth books are lost).

It is noteworthy that Origen had raised the very same passage in objection to the historicity of the Fourth Gospel as bar Salibi's "heretic" and Epiphanius's Alogoi. Perhaps he himself was familiar with the controversy between Gaius and Hippolytus.[80] Indeed, his objection relies upon the faulty correlation of the day on which Jesus was pointed out by John with Jesus's baptism by John, just as theirs evidently did, and like them he correlates the subsequent journey to Galilee with the commencement of the Synoptic Galilean ministry. It may also not be a coincidence that Origen is the earliest extant writer to specifically identify the Evangelist with the Apostle (Origen, *Comm. John* 2.4; Dionysius, *apud* Eusebius, *Hist. eccl.* 7.25.7–26), as Hippolytus evidently did; his familiarity with Hippolytus's work would also account for his apparent acceptance of the Patmos martyrdom narrative (chapter 4).

Origen's claim that he had shown that no room could be found for the forty days might have answered Hippolytus's attempt (according to bar Salibi) at inserting the forty days into the Johannine narrative. Hippolytus had divided the narrative into two sets of three days, but Origen's reference to the day of the wedding at Cana as being on the "sixth day" may indicate that he had argued for the continuity of the sequence of days in the Johannine account.

The evidence can thus be explained by positing that Epiphanius drew his account of the Alogoi from Hippolytus while also taking into account Origen's refutation and avoiding, unlike Hippolytus, any attempt at inserting the forty days into the Johannine narrative. This, in turn, argues for the authenticity of the bar Salibi fragments and against Hill's suggestion that bar Salibi's Hippolytan dialogue was constructed from Epiphanius,[81] since Hippolytus's argument represents the stage of the debate against which Origen seems to have been arguing, and it does not take account Origen's rebuttal or Epiphanius's response.

## CONCLUSION

The presence of reticence or suspicion toward the Fourth Gospel raises doubts concerning the thesis that the Johannine works were associated with the last surviving of the twelve apostles by the early Christians. Knowledge of the involvement of such a revered figure in its publication would no doubt have assured the work's widespread acceptance. Instead, at Rome at least, the Gospel seems to have been merely tolerated at best and rejected as a forgery of Cerinthus (along with Revelation) at worst.

Possibly the charge that Cerinthus authored the Gospel and Revelation was answered by an equally innovative attribution of the authorship to the Apostle John, the son of Zebedee, which was designed to invest the works with the Apostle's authority in the hope of setting aside, once and for all, lingering doubts and suspicions.

The existence of a group called the Alogoi who were evidently influential in the Roman church and who rejected the Gospel and Revelation of Rome is problematic for proponents of the traditional view, though it is more easily reconcilable with the supposition that the John associated with the Gospel and Revelation was a secondary figure whose fame was initially confined to Asia and whose works were at first only distributed among local audiences. Hill attempts to deal with the difficulty posed by the Alogoi by appealing to Brent's hypothesis that the group was a constructed heresy,[82] though he does not seem entirely convinced and refrains from fully endorsing it, holding it "somewhat lightly."[83] The specific details provided by Epiphanius concerning their activities and doctrines would seem to rule out such a theory, however.

The controversy involving the Alogoi was far from peripheral, engaging some of the most important ecclesiastical writers of that period and beyond, namely Hippolytus, Origen, Dionysius, Epiphanius, and probably Irenaeus (as well as Eusebius, as argued in Chapter 9). While Hippolytus responded to Gaius's criticisms of the Fourth Gospel by attempting to insert the forty days of temptation into the narrative, Origen seems to have answered Hippolytus by showing that the forty days could not be reconciled with the Johannine narrative. Epiphanius's response to the arguments of the Alogoi seem in turn to have taken into account Origen's objections, which he meets by distinguishing the day of Jesus's baptism by John from that of his encounter with the Baptist.

## NOTES

1. This terminology, despite its inherent problems, is used only to distinguish the dominant (or "catholic") Christianity of the time from other less-established forms. See Hill, *Johannine Corpus*, 3–10.
2. So, e.g., Gunther, "Early Identifications," 413.
3. Walter Bauer, *Orthodoxy and Heresy in Earliest Christianity*, ed. Robert A. Kraft and Gerhard Kroedel, trans. Paul J. Achtemeier (Philadelphia: Fortress, 1971), 209–10; A. F. J. Klijn and G. J. Reinink, *Patristic Evidence for Jewish-Christian Sects* (NovTSup 3; Leiden: Brill, 1973), 6; Haenchen, *John*, 23–24; F. F. Bruce, *The Canon of Scripture* (Downers Grove, Ill.: IVP, 1988), 168–69, 257; Culpepper, *John*, 121; Hengel, *Johannine Question*, 5–6, 183; Constantinou, *Blessed End*, 23; Watson, *Gospel Writing*, 477–89.
4. Brent, *Hippolytus*.
5. Hill, *Johannine Corpus*, 172–204; T. Scott Manor, *Epiphanius' Alogi and the Johannine Controversy: A Reassessment of Early Ecclesial Opposition to the Johannine Corpus* (VCSup 135; Leiden, Brill, 2016).
6. Culpepper, *John*, 108.
7. Streeter, *The Four Gospels*, 441.
8. Bauer, *Orthodoxy*, 206.
9. Bauer, *Orthodoxy*, 206.
10. Joseph N. Sanders, *The Fourth Gospel in the Early Church* (Cambridge: Cambridge University Press, 1943), 31.
11. Culpepper, *John*, 113; Hill's response to Culpepper frames the discussion only in terms of whether Justin knew the Fourth Gospel (*Johannine Corpus*, 313–14).
12. Keener, *Gospel of John*, 250.
13. See Joseph D. Smith, "Gaius and the Controversy over the Johannine Literature" [PhD diss., Yale University, 1979], 141–68.
14. Contra Hill, who maintains that "Irenaeus considered them to be not fellow orthodox believers but heretics" (*Johannine Corpus*, 174).
15. Smith, "Gaius," 167–68; Hengel, *Johannine Question*, 5; Culpepper, *John*, 121.
16. Haenchen, *John*, 23, Hahneman, *Muratorian Fragment*, 102; Carson and Moo, *Introduction*, 232.
17. Smith, "Gaius," 168. Irenaeus's language assumes that they associated with the church, for he accuses them of rejecting the "prophetic grace" (*charisma*) from the church and of separating from their brethren.
18. Streeter, *The Four Gospels*, 439–40; Arnold Ehrhardt, *The Framework of the New Testament Stories* (Manchester: Manchester University Press, 1964), 18; Culpepper, *John*, 129.
19. Photius of Constantinople, *Bibliotheca* 48, cited by Hill, *Johannine Corpus*, 178.
20. See Hill, *Johannine Corpus*, 196–98.

21. See, e.g., Klijn and Reinink, *Patristic Evidence*, 5; Aune, *Revelation 1–5*, iii; Weinrich, *Revelation*, xviii; Wilfrid J. Harrington, *Revelation*, ed. Daniel J. Harrington (SP 16; Collegeville, Minn.: Liturgical Press, 2008), 8; Watson, *Gospel Writing*, 479; Koester, *Revelation*, 67. According to Smith, Gaius is to be read as claiming that Cerinthus, like the Montanists, also appeals to Revelation in support of his doctrines, not that Gaius attributed Revelation to Cerinthus ("Gaius," 331).

22. Brent, *Hippolytus*, 133–36; Hill, *Johannine Corpus*, 174–75; cf. 185.

23. Raymond E. Brown thinks that either Dionysius depended on Gaius or both depended on a common source (*The Epistles of John: Translated, with Introduction, Notes, and Commentary* [AB 30; New Haven, Conn.: Yale University Press, 2008], 769).

24. To avoid this conclusion, Hill suggests that Dionysius was reliant upon an intermediate, possibly Egyptian source which had access to Gaius and which "made the leap from Cerinthus' 'revelations' to the Revelation of John" (*Johannine Corpus*, 175). This adds another layer of conjecture into his proposed construction of the controversy, alongside his claims that Epiphanius constructed the Alogoi (185–90), bar Salibi his Hippolytan dialogue (179), and Ebed-Jesu his list (184–85).

25. See, e.g., Constantinou, *Blessed End*, 27, especially n. 44.

26. Cf. Gundry, *The Old is Better*, 67.

27. Eisler, *Enigma*, 125–26.

28. Eisler, *Enigma*, 126–27.

29. Cf. Constantinou, *Blessed End*, 29–30.

30. Cf. Hengel's similar comment about Gaius (*Johannine Question*, 6; *Die johanneische Frage*, 27).

31. Translated by the author from the Greek text in Karl Holl, ed., *Epiphanius* (*Ancoratus und Panarion*), vol. 2, *Panarion haer. 34–64* (GCS 31; Leipzig: Hinrichs, 1922), and so hereafter.

32. Streeter, *The Four Gospels*, 436 n. 141.

33. Lightfoot, *Biblical Essays*, 119.

34. Joseph B. Lightfoot, *The Apostolic Fathers: Clement, Ignatius, and Polycarp*, part 1, vol. 2 (London: Macmillan, 1890), 332.

35. Lightfoot, *Apostolic Fathers*, part 1, vol. 1, 332.

36. Frank Williams, trans., *The Panarion of Epiphanius of Salamis*, vol. 1: *Book I (Sects. 1–46)* (2nd rev. ed.; NHMS 63; Leiden: Brill, 2009), 122.

37. Lightfoot, *Biblical Essays*, 119. Cf. chapter 5 for the likely Hippolytan origin of Epiphanius's account of Cerinthus.

38. J. Rendel Harris, *Hermas in Arcadia and the Rest of the Words of Baruch* (Cambridge: Cambridge University Press, 1896), 52.

39. The sole manuscript of this work, from the twelfth or thirteenth century, attributes it to "Hippolytus, Archbishop of Rome and Martyr." See Caroline P. Hammond Bammel, *Tradition and Exegesis in Early Christian Writers* (Aldershot, Hampshire: Variorum, 1995), 196.

40. Lightfoot, *Biblical Essays*, 119. Cf. Smith, "Gaius," 220. See also the important observations of Harris, *Hermas in Arcadia*, 50–52.

41. Extant manuscripts attribute the *Refutation of all Heresies* to Origen, and there is some doubt as to whether it was written by Hippolytus. See, e.g., Ronald E. Heine, "Hippolytus, Ps.-Hippolytus and the early canons," in *The Cambridge History of Early Christian Literature*, ed. Frances Young, Lewis Ayres and Andrew Louth (Cambridge: Cambridge University Press, 2004), 147–48.

42. Lightfoot, *Biblical Essays*, 119.

43. Smith, "Gaius," 233.

44. . Hill, *Johannine Corpus*, 187.

45. Lightfoot, *Biblical Essays*, 50.

46. Brown, *John (I–XII)*, xcii.

47. Bruce, *Canon of Scripture*, 178.

48. Bruce, *Canon of Scripture*, 169.

49. C. Marvin Pate, *The Writings of John: A Survey of the Gospel, Epistles, and Apocalypse* (Grand Rapids: Zondervan, 2011), 23 n. 16.

50. E.g., Brent, *Hippolytus*, Hill, *Johannine Corpus*, 185; Manor, *Epiphanius'* Alogi. According to Luthardt, this view was first proposed by Volkmar (*St. John the Author*, 9).

51. Brent, *Hippolytus*, 140.

52. Brent, *Hippolytus*, 143.

53. See Watson, *Gospel Writing*, 486.

54. See the discussion in M. David Litwa, *Refutation of All Heresies: Text, Translation, and Notes* (WGRW 40; Atlanta: SBL, 2015), xxxvi–xxxix.

55. Brent, *Hippolytus*, 3.

56. Cerrato, *Hippolytus Between East and West*, 11.

57. Brent, *Hippolytus*, 172.

58. Brent, *Hippolytus*, 172.

59. LSJ 1857; BDAG 1030–31.

60. Cf. Lightfoot, *Apostolic Fathers*, part 1, vol. 2, 394; Streeter, *The Four Gospels*, 437; Heine, "Hippolytus," 144.

61. The Syriac text is given in Lightfoot, *Apostolic Fathers*, part 1, vol. 2, 350; cf. Watson, *Gospel Writing*, 480–81. Since Ebed-Jesu only separates the two titles by the word "and" (*waw*), Smith argues that he was referring to only one work (Smith, "Gaius," 224–27).

62. Francis Watson, *Gospel Writing: A Canonical Perspective* (Grand Rapids: Eerdmans, 2013), 481.

63. CSCO, Scriptores Syri, 2.101.10–11; cf. John Gwynn, "Hippolytus and his 'Heads against Caius,' " *Herm* 6 (1888): 397–418; further fragments were published by Pierre Prigent and Ralph Stehly, "Les fragments du De Apocalypsi d'Hippolyte," *TZ* 29 (1973): 313–33.

64. Brent, *Hippolytus*, 175.

65. See, e.g., Klijn and Reinink, *Patristic Evidence*, 5; Norelli, *Papia di Hierapolis*, 281; Pierre Prigent, *Commentary on the Apocalypse of St. John*, trans. Wendy Pradels (Tübingen: Mohr Siebeck, 2004), 553–54; Weinrich, *Revelation*, xxi; Boxall, *Patmos*, 34; Constantinou, *Blessed End*, 24 n. 38; Watson, *Gospel Writing*, 489.

66. Translated by the author from CSCO, Scriptores Syri, 2.101.1–2.

67. Watson, *Gospel Writing*, 489.

68. CSCO, Scriptores Syri, 2.101.10.

69. Translated by the author from the Greek text in Holl.

70. The English translation of Williams, *Panarion*, vol. 2, 65.

71. E.g., Smith, "Gaius," 238–39.

72. The original Latin text read *quidam*, which had been corrected to *Gaius* based on a marginal note found in the Syriac text from which it was translated. Smith notes that another unpublished Syriac manuscript omits the name of Gaius (Harris, *Hermas in Arcadia*, 48–49; Smith, "Gaius," 36–37; 201 n. 2).

73. Translated by Smith, "Gaius," 591, from the unpublished Syriac manuscript *Cod. Paris. syr.* 67. A Latin translation can be found in Harris *Hermas in Arcadia*, 48.

74. See Smith, "Gaius," 591; cf. Harris, *Hermas in Arcadia*, 48.

75. The Latin text is transcribed by Roger Pearse from an unpublished manuscript prepared by Dudley Loftus (Roger Pearse, "Notes from the Commentary on the four gospels," accessed February 2, 2017, http://www.tertullian.org/fathers/dionysius_syrus_revelation_01.htm).

76. Smith, "Gaius," 59; cf. Harris, *Hermas in Arcadia*, 48.

77. Manor, *Epiphanius'* Alogi, 198.

78. Translated by the author from the Greek text in Erwin Preuschen, ed., *Origenes Werke*, ed. vol. 4 (GCS 10; Leipzig: Hinrichs, 1903), and so hereafter. Chapter references, however, are given according to the English version in *ANF* 8.297–408.

79. Cf. Smith, *The Fourth Gospel*, 166: Origen "goaded the 'conservative' church exegetes who were attempting to assimilate John to the synoptics on the historical level."

80. So, Schwartz, "Über den Tod," 44–45; Smith, "Gaius," 195–96; contra *Epiphanius'* Alogi, 13.

81. Hill frames this suggestion as a rhetorical question: "Either Epiphanius too had Hippolytus' work, and thus the 'Alogi' may in fact be identified with Gaius himself, or, could bar Salibi simply have adapted this from Epiphanius' work?" (*Johannine Corpus*, 179).

82. Hill, *Johannine Corpus*, 185.

83. Hill, *Johannine Corpus*, 191.

# SIX
# Eusebius and the Domitianic Exile Tradition

While Eusebius in his *Ecclesiastical History* (c. 324) identified the Apostle and Evangelist, his reconstruction differed from Hippolytus's in privileging Irenaeus's tradition of John's peaceful death in the reign of Trajan over the martyrdom tradition. Central to his reconstruction was his contextualization of John's exile during a persecution late in Domitian's reign (r. 81–96 CE) which, it will be argued, supplied him with further evidence for John's death in old age (probably against the martyrdom tradition, which Eusebius does not discuss), for which he was otherwise largely dependent upon Irenaeus.

This dating also served to place the Patmos exile, the setting of Revelation, closer to the time of John the Elder, whom Eusebius suggested as Revelation's author; furthermore, his identification of the Apostle with the John who died in Trajan's reign served to place the activities of the Elder, who was active a generation after the Apostle according to Papias, too far into the second century for him to have been a personal disciple of Jesus, thus removing apostolic authority from the book of Revelation.

### EUSEBIUS ON THE AUTHORSHIP OF REVELATION

While Gaius's rejection of the Johannine works failed to persuade his contemporaries, his criticisms of Revelation influenced Dionysius of Alexandria (cf. Eusebius, *Hist. eccl.* 7.25.1–3), who suggested that the work had been written by a secondary John (7.25.12–16). Dionysius's criticisms were in turn rehearsed by Eusebius (7.24–26), who seems to have quietly shared Dionysius's skepticism.[1]

Constantinou sees evidence for Eusebius's bias against Revelation in his repeating of Gaius's disavowal of Revelation while failing to mention that Gaius also rejected John's Gospel (3.28.1–2)[2] and in his exceptional placement of Revelation among both the "acknowledged" (ὁμολογούμενα) books of the canon and the "spurious" books (νόθα), rather than among the "disputed" books (ἀντιλεγόμονα) (3.25.1–4); she argues that if opinion were truly divided, Eusebius would have included it among the disputed books, and that his dual placement likely implies that Revelation was not generally questioned at the time.[3] The placement of Revelation in the "spurious" category probably represents Gaius's attribution of the work to the heretical Cerinthus.

Elsewhere, Eusebius indicates that Revelation was received by Justin Martyr (4.18.8; cf. Justin, *Dial.* 81), Melito of Sardis (4.26.1–2), Theophilus of Antioch (4.24.1), Irenaeus (3.18.2–3 = Irenaeus, *Haer.* 5.30.3), and Origen (6.25.9–10; cf. Origen, *Comm. John* 14); he does not mention Papias (Fragment 10), Tertullian (*Marc.* 4.2), Hippolytus of Rome (according to the bar Salibi fragments discussed in chapter 5), the eastern Hippolytus (*Antichr.* 36), and Methodius of Olympus (d. 311) (*Symposium* 8.5).

Although Dionysius rejected the apostolic authorship of Revelation, he was unable to suggest another John as the author, possibly because he placed the exile in Claudius's reign, limiting potential candidates (see chapter 4). Eusebius, however, who favored Irenaeus's placement of John's death in Trajan's reign (*Hist. eccl.* 3.23.3), was free to posit a later date for Revelation and consequently to find a potential author in the person of Papias's John the Elder, whose activities Eusebius likely placed in the early second century (concerning which, see below). This paved the way for Eusebius's innovative correlation of Papias's two Johns with the two tombs of John in Ephesus mentioned by Dionysius (3.39.6; cf. chapter 5).

## THE MARGINALIZATION OF PAPIAS AND THE ELDER

Eusebius had, no doubt correctly, understood Papias as disclaiming any personal knowledge of his first enumerated disciples of the Lord, including the Apostle John, who appear to have been active a generation before him (*Hist. eccl.* 3.39.4; cf. chapter 1). Consequently, Eusebius's identification of John the Apostle as the John who died in Trajan's reign necessitated that the activities of Papias, who was active after the Apostle's death, took place later in the second century. This in turn moved the activities of John the Elder, Papias's contemporary, into the second century also, diminishing any likelihood that he could have been an eyewitness disciple of Jesus.

Eusebius does not explicitly deny the eyewitness status of the Elder, though he likely implies his non-apostolic role when he claims that Papias placed him and Aristion outside of the circle of the apostles (*Hist. eccl.* 3.39.5). The Syriac version and Rufinus's Latin translation of Eusebius seem to have understood him this way, for they omit reference to Aristion and the Elder as "disciples of the Lord." The *Roman Martyrology*, on the other hand, specifically attributes to Papias the claim that Aristion was one of the seventy-two disciples of Jesus.[4]

The historian further diminishes the Elder's status by omitting the definite article before his title, claiming that Papias not only "clearly" (σαφῶς) places this John outside the number of the apostles, but that he also "clearly calls him an elder" (σαφῶς τε αὐτὸν πρεσβύτερον ὀνομάζει) (3.39.5). Possibly Eusebius identified him as one of the Asian elders, that second generation of revered figures who had known apostles; possibly he was only identifying him as a congregational elder. Having stripped the second John of his eyewitness status and having relegated him to the status of an elder, Eusebius concludes: "it is likely" (εἰκός) that the second John saw the apocalyptic vision, if not the Apostle (3.39.6). Thus, it is not that Eusebius undermined the credibility of Revelation by creating a second John out of a misreading Papias's words (cf. chapter 1); it is that he diminished the status of the secondary John of whom Papias did write.

Eusebius lastly proceeds to denigrate Papias's intelligence on the basis of his millennialism. After relating some of Papias's anecdotes concerning Justus and the daughters of Philip (3.39.9–10), he goes on to claim that Papias also related "some more fanciful things," namely the millennium after the resurrection (3.39.12). On this basis he adds: "for let me tell you, he was of very little intelligence" (σφόδρα γάρ τοι σμικρὸς ὢν τὸν νοῦν) (3.39.13). Chapman argues that Eusebius "seizes upon an expression used by Papias of himself in quite commonplace humility," which, he suggests, is preserved in Victorinus's *On the Creation of the World* 9: "Nevertheless, as my small mind will be able, I will try to show it" (*tamen ut mens parva poterit, conabor ostendere*), where *mens parva* corresponds to σμικρὸς νοῦς.[5] In any case, while Eusebius disapproved of Papias's chiliasm, his disparaging of Papias's intelligence and his suggestion that Papias lacked credulity may have also been intended to undermine Papias's affirmation of the tradition of the Apostle John's martyrdom.

## Difficulties with Eusebius's Reconstruction

While Eusebius denies that Papias had known John the Evangelist, Irenaeus, whose evidence he follows for his dating of John's death in Trajan's reign, had made Papias a hearer of the Evangelist (*apud* Eusebius, *Hist. eccl.* 3.39.1 = Irenaeus, *Haer.* 5.33.4; cf. discussion in Chapter 3). To meet this difficulty, Eusebius portrayed Irenaeus's claim as contradicting the words of Papias himself, who denied having known the Apostle (3.39.2–4). This argument, which presupposes the identification of the

Evangelist with the Apostle, was very effective, and it continues to convince many within scholarship.[6] Barrett thus argues that Irenaeus's claim, "as Eusebius himself shows, is contradicted by the content of Papias's own work,"[7] while Watson states that it "is incompatible with Papias' own statements."[8] The possibility that the solution lies instead in the distinction of the Apostle and Evangelist has seldom been noted.[9]

It is unlikely that Irenaeus would have made a mistake of this nature, for he had lived in Asia Minor and would have been familiar with its oral history. Possibly he learned this tradition from reading Papias, since other readers of Papias likewise claimed that he had been a hearer or disciple of the Evangelist. Jerome makes Papias a hearer of John, despite his awareness of Eusebius's work (Fragment 9 = Jerome, Letter 75.3) and Apollinarius of Laodicea (fourth century) speaks of Papias as "John's disciple" (Fragment 18) while relating traditions concerning Judas's death, taken from Papias's fourth book. Philip of Sidé in his *History* (439 or earlier) refers to Papias as "the disciple of John the Theologian" when quoting Papias's second book for the tradition of John's martyrdom (Fragment 5), and the Anti-Marcionite prologue to John (written between the fourth and sixth century[10]), again citing Papias, refers to him as "the dear disciple of John" (Fragment 19).[11] Another writer, possibly to be identified as Anastasius of Sinai (d. c. 700), refers to Papias as "a disciple of the Bosom-Friend" while alluding to his exposition of the six days of Genesis (Fragment 12, [Holmes]).

There is also a scholium, attributed by Norelli to John, bishop of Scythopolis (c. 536–550), found in the late fifth-century work of Ps.-Dionysius the Areopagite entitled *On the Heavenly Hierarchy* (chap. 7), which speaks of Papias as a bishop in Hierapolis who "flourished at the same time as the divine Evangelist John" (Fragment 14 in Norelli's edition).[12] Norelli notes that the scholiast's knowledge of Papias is demonstrably independent of Irenaeus and Eusebius elsewhere (though he adds that he probably did not have direct access to Papias's work).[13]

The chronology of Eusebius's earlier *Chronicle* had approvingly cited Irenaeus to the effect that Papias was John's hearer, while placing the activities of Papias around the turn of the second century and the death of John the Evangelist in the third year of Trajan (c. 100).[14] While Eusebius is chronologically vague with respect to Papias in his *Ecclesiastical History*, his framework still presupposes this chronology, as discussed in chapter 1.

## EUSEBIUS'S CONSTRUCTION OF JOHN'S DOMITIANIC EXILE

While Eusebius's authority for the tradition of John's death in old age seems to have been limited to Irenaeus's statement to that effect (*Hist. eccl.* 3.23.3), the tradition of the Apostle's early martyrdom was quite widespread (cf. chapters 2 and 5). Eusebius seems to have solved this problem already when he wrote his earlier *Chronicle* by placing John's exile to Patmos late in Domitian's reign, at the end of the first century, which necessitated John's long life.[15] Although by the time Eusebius wrote his *Ecclesiastical History* he no longer seems to have believed that John the Evangelist wrote Revelation, he nevertheless still maintains John's Domitianic exile to Patmos, presumably because it still provided a useful argument for John's longevity. Indeed, as if to emphasize this point, he twice in his *Ecclesiastical History* unnecessarily reminds his readers that John was still alive at or shortly after the time of Domitian's persecution (*Hist. eccl.* 3.18.1; 3.23.1–2). It is unclear, however, how Eusebius related this exile to the book of Revelation, and he does not address whether his John the Elder, whom he suggests as the author, was also sent to Patmos.

Eusebius chose as the historical context of John's exile the Domitian's persecution of the Roman aristocracy in the 90s, spoken of by Roman historians. Possibly he was influenced in this by the tradition, first extant in Tertullian, that John was sent into exile from Rome, where this persecution took place (*Praescr.* 36; cf. chapter 3).[16] Nevertheless, the Roman historians do not mention John and no ecclesiastical source unambiguously placed John's exile during this persecution. Victorinus's placement of John's exile in Domitian's reign would not have offered support for Eusebius, had he known of it, for Victorinus seems to have made John to have grown old on Patmos, which would have required that he was sent into exile early in Domitian's reign, not late, as in Eusebius.[17]

Eusebius commences his argument for John's Domitianic exile by observing that Domitian had put a great number of distinguished citizens to death in Rome and had exiled and confiscated the property of multitudes of others; he then claims that Domitian became the second after Nero to institute persecution against the Christians (3.17.1). He adds that secular historians referred to this persecution, noting that they indicated the time it happened by relating how Flavia Domitilla, the niece of the consul Flavius Clemens, was banished with many others to the island of Pontia, on account of her testimony to Christ, in the fifteenth year of Domitian (c. 96) (3.18.4). He concludes by observing that according to the Roman historians, the Roman Senate restored the exiles following Domitian's death, and he claims that it was at this time that John returned from banishment (3.20.8–9). This claim was no doubt related to the statement of the historian Dio Cassius (c. 155–235) that Nerva, Domitian's successor, reversed Domitian's acts and restored his exiles (*Roman History*, 68.1–2).

However, while Roman historians did claim that Domitian persecuted the Roman nobility, they do not speak of a persecution of Christians as such, as Eusebius seems to imply.[18] According to Suetonius, who lived through Domitian's reign, Domitian began confiscating the estates of rich

Romans upon various pretexts in order to maintain his armies, after bringing the imperial finances to ruin by his elaborate building projects and public entertainments (*Domit.* 12.1–2).

Dio also discussed Domitian's erratic behavior towards the end of his reign, noting how he became increasingly suspicious and paranoid, accusing nobles of all manner of crimes (*Hist. Rom.* 67.13–14). One such charge was atheism; Dio says of these that many "were making shipwreck on the customs of the Jews" (ἐς τὰ τῶν Ἰουδαίων ἔθη ἐξοκέλλοντες)[19] and were either executed or had their possessions confiscated (*Hist. Rom.* 67.14.2). This accusation may have been directed only against Jews,[20] though others think that Christians might also have been included.[21] Sordi holds that all those so accused from among the Roman nobility were likely Christians.[22] In any case, the persecution only affected the upper classes in the city, and the charge of atheism was just one convenient pretext among many.[23] There is no evidence that Domitian was ever associated with any systematic or empire-wide persecution of Christians,[24] though sporadic persecution of Christians did take place during his reign, even if not to any unusual extent.[25]

The Flavia Domitilla spoken of by Eusebius as the niece of the consul Flavius Clemens was understood to have been a Christian by Brutius (possibly to be identified as Gaius Bruttius Praesens, who served as consul in 150 and 180[26]), whom Eusebius quotes (possibly from a garbled Christian source[27]) in his *Chronicle*.[28] Suetonius refers to the execution in 95 CE of Domitian's cousin and consul Titus Flavius Clemens, though he only states that it was carried out on the basis of a "very weak suspicion" (*Domit.* 15.1). According to Dio Cassius, the consul Flavius Clemens was executed on the charge of "atheism" (ἀθεότητος) and Flavia Domitilla, his wife (not niece, as in Eusebius) and a relative of the emperor (*Hist. Rom.* 67.14.1–2), was charged with the same offense, though she was only exiled to Pandateria (not to Pontia, as in Eusebius, which was also off the western coast of Italy) (*Hist. Rom.* 67.14.3). Due to these variances, some maintain that Eusebius's account is corrupt[29] while others posit that Eusebius's Domitilla was a different one from Dio's.[30]

Domitian's persecution of the Roman nobility seems like an unlikely setting for John's exile, for even if Domitian did specifically target Christians from among the nobility, John did not belong to Rome's aristocracy; Eusebius's use of the Roman historians as evidence for John's exile at this time is thus tenuous at best.

*Hegesippus, Tertullian, and the Unnamed Source*

Eusebius goes on to claim that "an account holds it" (κατέχει λόγος) that John "was still continuing in life" (ἔτι τῷ βίῳ ἐνδιατρίβοντα) at the time of Domitian's persecution (suggesting that Eusebius intended for this narrative to provide evidence for John's longevity), and that he was banished at that time (*Hist. eccl.* 3.18.1). The source of this statement is not specified, though Lawlor noted that when Eusebius employs λόγος κατέχει, the source is usually referred to in the immediate context or in writers mentioned in the preceding accounts.

One possibility is Irenaeus, whom Eusebius cites immediately afterwards to the effect that Revelation was seen at the end of Domitian's reign (3.18.2–3),[31] which will be discussed below. Lawlor suggests Hegesippus, who is cited elsewhere in this section of the work,[32] noting in support that a fragment of Philip of Sidé speaks both of John's exile in the time of Domitian and of other facts garnered directly from Hegesippus.[33] However, he later admits that Philip summarized this account from Eusebius while adding additional details from Hegesippus (i.e., the names of Jude's descendants),[34] throwing doubt on his claim.

Indeed, although Eusebius goes on to quote from Hegesippus in support of his narrative, no such claim there is made. Citing Hegesippus's *Memoirs*, Eusebius relates the story of how Domitian summoned the grandsons of Jude to appear before him, since they belonged to the lineage of David and were related to Christ. They then explained to Domitian that they lived simple lives as farmers, and Domitian subsequently dismissed them and brought a cessation to the persecution of the church (3.19.1–3.20.6). There is nothing that would suggest an association with the persecution of the Roman aristocracy related by the Roman historians,[35] and where Hegesippus concluded Domitian's persecution with the dismissal of Jude's grandchildren, the Roman historians brought Domitian's persecution of the Roman nobility to an end by his death. Eusebius, however, either does not notice the contradiction[36] or is untroubled by it.[37]

Bauckham further points out that the grandsons of Jude were accused of being descendants of David, not Christians, adding that this fits well with the context supplied by Hegesippus, who related that after the capture of Jerusalem (70 CE), Vespasian sought out the Davidic royal family so that a threat of persecution again hung over the Jews (not the Christians) (3.12.1).[38] Bauckham concludes that any connection of this account with Domitian's persecution of the nobility "seems historically gratuitous."[39]

Hegesippus had probably gone from relating the martyrdom of James, the brother of the Lord (*apud* Eusebius, *Hist. eccl.* 2.23.4–18), to the gathering of the disciples of the Lord following the destruction of the city to elect Simeon, a descendant of David and cousin of Jesus, as James's replacement (3.11.1; 4:22:4).[40] He then likely proceeded to the law of Vespasian against the descendants of David (3.12.1), in which context he recounted the accusation brought against the grandchildren of Jude followed by their subsequent summons to Domitian; it would have concluded with their acquittal and the cessation of the persecution against the relatives of the Lord (3.20.5).

Domitian is not recorded as ever having set foot in Judea[41] and it is improbable that Judean peasants would have been summoned to appear before Domitian in faraway Rome.[42] Sordi suggests that the name of Domitian in Hegesippus was a mistake for his brother Titus, who left Palestine in 71 (or for his father, Vespasian, who left in 69), and she thinks that the relatives of David might have been sought out by Titus, who remained in Jerusalem after the war, because Messianic (Davidic) apocalyptic fervor had fueled the Jewish revolt.[43]

Tertullian, whom Eusebius next quotes, seems to share Hegesippus's conception of Domitian's persecution as one that was short-lived:

> Domitian also once tried to do the same as he, for he was a Nero in cruelty, but, I believe, inasmuch as he had some sense, he stopped at once and recalled those whom he had banished (*apud* Eusebius, *Hist. eccl.* 3.20.7 = Tertullian, *Apol.* 5.4 [Lake, LCL]).

The account is again inconsistent with Domitian's persecution of the Roman nobility, which ceased only with Domitian's assassination. Furthermore, while Tertullian mentions exiles in his account, Domitian himself restores them, unlike those exiles mentioned by the Roman historians who were restored after Domitian's death. Possibly Tertullian was following Hegesippus's account of the persecution of the relatives of Jesus.[44]

### The Case for John's Longevity from Irenaeus and Clement

After relating from the Roman historians that Domitian's exiles were restored by the Roman Senate following Nerva's accession (*Hist. eccl.* 3.20.8, presumably following Dio Cassius, *Hist. Rom.* 68.1), Eusebius goes on to claim that according to "an ancient Christian tradition," it was "then" (τότε) that John took up residence in Ephesus following his banishment (3.20.9), though again he does not specify his source.

After briefly relating some details concerning the accession of Trajan and the then-serving bishops of Alexandria, Rome and Antioch (3.21–22), Eusebius adds, like before, that John was "still alive" (ἔτι τῷ βίῳ περιλειπόμενος) in Asia at this time, at the end of the first century (3.23.1), only this time he appeals to Irenaeus and Clement in support (3.23.2). His apologetic tone is evident, for he points out that his claim is confirmed (πιστώσασθαι) by these two witnesses, who "should be trustworthy (πιστοὶ δ' ἂν εἶεν) since they maintained the orthodoxy of the church" (3.23.2). He thus unintentionally hints that his readers might have had reasons to question his claim concerning John's longevity, probably because, as suggested above, it conflicted with the tradition of the Apostle John's early martyrdom.

Eusebius first provides the two quotations from Irenaeus which claim that John lived in Asia and Ephesus until the reign of Trajan (3.23.3–4 =

Irenaeus, *Haer.* 2.22.5; 3.3.4). He then quotes a lengthier extract from Clement, to the effect that John governed the churches for some time following his return from exile, after the death of "the tyrant" (*apud* Eusebius, *Hist. eccl.* 3.23.6–19 = Clement, *Quis div.* 42). Eusebius assumes that the tyrant was Domitian and is thereby able to allege Clement in support for his statement that John was still alive in the late first century, but Clement himself does not name the tyrant in question. Possibly Eusebius inferred this identification by correlating John's return from Patmos with the restoration of Domitian's exiles during the reign of Nerva.

Eusebius's employment of Clement's ambiguous statement suggests that Irenaeus was the only unambiguous source at his disposal supportive of John's long life in Asia. It would have been problematic to rely solely on this writer, however, not least because Eusebius had already impugned his reliability in order to deny that Papias had known the Evangelist.

In citing Clement, Eusebius passes over any mention of evidence irreconcilable with his own reconstructions, since in Clement's *Stromata*, a work with which Eusebius was familiar (5.11.2), Clement makes the ministry of the twelve apostles (among whom Eusebius included John the Evangelist) to have been completed by the end of Nero's reign (*Strom.* 7.17); Eusebius is either ignorant of this or is untroubled by the inconsistency, just as he is seemingly untroubled by the inconsistencies his reconstruction created between Irenaeus and Papias, and between Hegesippus and the Roman historians.

## The Case for John's Longevity from Irenaeus's Claim Concerning Revelation

Longer discussion is required for Eusebius's earlier quotation of Irenaeus to the effect that the apocalyptic vision was seen at the end of Domitian's reign, which he alleged in support of his contention that John was exiled at that time (*Hist. eccl.* 3.18.3). The quotation itself is introduced with the qualifying particle τοι (3.18.2), which gives emphasis to the reliability of a statement,[45] and thus also hints that Eusebius is consciously arguing against a rival narrative.

In the larger context of the passage, preserved in a Latin translation, Irenaeus was defending the reading of 666 in Rev 13:18 against the variant of 616 found in some copies; he argues that 666 was found in the ancient copies of Revelation, that it was attested by those men who saw John face-to-face, and that it was in accordance with a calculation of the name in Greek letters (*Haer.* 5.30.1).

Irenaeus does not identify those who saw John and attested the number 666, but since he appeals to their authority, he no doubt expected his readers to be familiar with their identity. Later in his work he relates from Papias an eschatological tradition of "the elders who saw John, the disciple of the Lord" (*Haer.* 5.33.3), where he is almost certainly referring to the same group.⁴⁶

Irenaeus then addresses the question of the meaning of 666, the number of the Antichrist, arguing that its meaning would only be known when the time of its fulfilment drew near. It is at this point that Eusebius takes up the quotation:

> For if it were necessary for his [the Antichrist's] name to be openly proclaimed at the present time (τῷ νῦν καιρῷ), by that one it would have been declared, who also saw the apocalyptic vision (δι' ἐκείνου ἂν ἐρρέθη τοῦ καὶ τὴν ἀποκάλυψιν ἑορακότος), for (γὰρ) it [or "he"] was not seen (ἑωράθη) a long time ago, but almost in our generation (σχεδὸν ἐπὶ τῆς ἡμετέρας γενεᾶς), at the end of Domitian's reign (πρὸς τῷ τέλει τῆς Δομετιανοῦ ἀρχῆς) (*apud* Eusebius, *Hist. eccl.* 3.18.3 = Irenaeus, *Haer.* 5.30.3).

As with Clement, there is some ambiguity in this passage, since the subject of the verb ἑωράθη is not expressed. Eusebius identified the apocalyptic vision as that which was seen late in Domitian's reign, and scholars generally concur with this.⁴⁷ Guericke alternatively suggested that Δομετιανός, without the definite article, was adjectival, referring to the Domitianic reign, which he understood as a reference to Nero, whose birth *nomen* was Domitius (his full name at birth was Lucius Domitius Ahenobarbus).⁴⁸ However, this use is unsubstantiated, and Josephus employs similar wording in a statement that clearly refers to Domitian: ἥτις ἐστὶν τρισκαιδεκάτου μὲν ἔτους τῆς Δομετιανοῦ Καίσαρος ἀρχῆς ("which is the thirteenth year of the reign of Caesar Domitian") (*Ant.* 20.267; Greek text from Niese's edition). In any case, Nero's later official name (Claudius Nero Caesar) and imperial name (Nero Cladius Divii Claudi filius Caesar Augustus Germanicus) did not include Domitius, and Guerick's view has failed to find any support in scholarship.

Others have argued that Irenaeus intended John as the subject, so that John, rather than the apocalyptic vision, was seen late in Domitian's reign.⁴⁹ It is noted that Irenaeus does apply the same verb to John at the beginning of the chapter, speaking of those who testified to the reading of 666 as those "who saw (ἑορακότων) John face to face" (*apud* Eusebius, *Hist. eccl.* 5.8.5 = Irenaeus, *Haer.* 5.30.1), and it is consequently suggested that ἑωράθη refers back to this prior reference to John being seen rather than to the immediate reference to John having seen the apocalyptic vision.⁵⁰

Furthermore, it has been pointed out that Irenaeus's argument is that John, who saw the apocalyptic vision, would have declared the meaning to those who saw him face-to-face, had its fulfilment been imminent. Since John, who lived almost in Irenaeus's own day, did not declare the meaning to them, its fulfilment could not have been imminent and consequently the name was not meant to be known at that time.⁵¹ This argument is thus predicated on the lateness of John's non-announcement of the name to those who saw him, rather than on the lateness of his having seen the apocalyptic vision.[52] The force of this argument has been acknowledged by scholars favorable to the standard view.[53]

Chase also notes in support of John as the subject that John is emphatically marked in the sentence, both by the demonstrative ἐκείνου ("of that one") and by its emphatic position in the sentence. The Greek thus reads, δι' ἐκείνου ἂν ἐρρέθη τοῦ καὶ τὴν ἀποκάλυψιν ἑορακότος ("through *that one* it would have been declared, who also saw the apocalyptic vision"), not ἐρρέθη ἂν διὰ τοῦ καὶ τὴν ἀποκάλυψιν ἑορακότος ("it would have been declared through him who also saw the apocalyptic vision").[54] The emphasis is on *that one*, on the seer,[55] and the words τοῦ καὶ[56] τὴν ἀποκάλυψιν ἑορακότος only parenthetically define ἐκείνου.[57]

*Objections*

The interpretation of John as the subject of the verb has been challenged on the basis that if the lateness of John's ability to expound on the name were informing Irenaeus's argument, then he would have brought this ability as close to his own time as possible, that is, down to the time of Trajan, in whose reign John died.[58] Hort and Robinson, though supportive of an earlier dating of Revelation, give weight to this objection.[59]

Chase attempted to mitigate the difficulty by suggesting that John later withdrew from public sight, so that in this way he was no longer seen.[60] Böhme made a similar suggestion, attributing John's withdrawal to the weakness ("Altersschwäche") of his old age.[61] These understand John's being seen in terms of a general visibility in public life, but this sense is unlikely, for the subject is said to have been seen, not habitually over decades, which could have been rendered with, "until (μέχρι) the end of Domitian's reign," but rather "at the end (πρὸς τῷ τέλει) of Domitian's reign," where a specific time seems to be intended. Chase seeks to meet this objection by cautioning that πρός with a dative in a temporal sense "does not seem to express quite so sharply as the English preposition 'at' the notion of a point in time."[62] This may be so, but πρός would still encompass a specific period at the end of Domitian's reign,[63] rather than a continuous period antedating and leading up to the end of his reign, which could have been indicated with μέχρι.

Furthermore, the verb is the aorist ἑωράθη rather than the imperfect ἑωρᾶτο which might have been expected, had Irenaeus intended habitual association over many years or decades. As Aune notes, ἑωράθη "does not appear to be the most appropriate way to describe the length of a person's life."[64] Certainly, as Chase notes, the aorist can comprehend the imperfect aspect,[65] but the aorist does not necessarily comprehend it, as the imperfect does. The employment of both the aorist and πρός together indicates a specific period or occasion at the end of the Domitian's reign;

it would be: "John was seen at the end of Domitian's reign," not: "John used to be seen (ἑωρᾶτο) until (μέχρι) the end of Domitian's reign."

Perhaps a better solution is that Irenaeus was speaking of a specific occasion on which John was seen face-to-face by the elders. Such an occasion may have been conceived of as that on which, according to a widely disseminated tradition, the Asian elders gathered to John in his old age and urged him to write his Gospel, as attested in a number of works, including the Muratorian Canon, Clement of Alexandria, Victorinus, Jerome, and Theodore of Mopsuestia (see chapters 8 and 9).

Irenaeus himself may have referred to this tradition when he spoke of all the elders who conferred or met with John in Asia, to whom John delivered a tradition (*Haer.* 2.22.5). He then adds that John remained (παρέμεινεν) with the elders until (μέχρι) the time of Trajan (*Haer.* 2.22.5= Eusebius, *Hist. eccl.* 3.23.3), suggesting that he was thinking of an occasion late in Domitian's reign. That John's conference with the elders took place late in his life is also suggested by the elders' status as a second generation of Christian leaders, only some of whom had known other apostles besides John (*Haer.* 2.22.5).

Support for this proposal is provided by the Latin translation of the text,[66] which may have been produced in Africa or Gaul, probably between the late second century and the fourth century.[67] Two features of the Latin text are important to note. First, where the Greek speaks of the elders who conferred with John (συμβεβληκότες, from συμβάλλω[68]), the Latin speaks of the elders who "having convened" or "having assembled" to him, using *convenerunt*, which suggests that the translator had in mind a particular occasion on which the elders came to John. The same form of the verb, *convenerunt*, is used by Victorinus in his version of the narrative of the Asian bishops assembling to John and imploring him to write his Gospel (*Comm. Apoc.* 11.1; chapter 8).

Secondly, ἑωράθη is rendered with *visum est*, which excludes the apocalyptic vision as the subject, since *apocalypsis* is feminine (as is the Greek ἀποκάλυψις), which would have been rendered with *visa est*.[69] It is usually taken for granted that *visum* is a neuter participle and therefore could not have been referring to John as the subject of ἑωράθη either, since this would have been rendered with *visus est*.[70] The neuter noun *nomen* ("name") has consequently sometimes been suggested as the Latin translator's intended subject,[71] but this would require that the translator passed over two close antecedents. It would also, like the apocalyptic vision, not be consistent with Irenaeus's argument, which is predicated on the lateness of John's ability to reveal the name rather than on his seeing of the apocalyptic vision or the name (and it would, in any case, be rather odd to speak of the name being seen).

Another possibility is that *visum* represents a copyist error for *visus*, which would then refer to John. This has been characterized as a weak argument,[72] but as the Romance linguist Adam Ledgeway notes: "the addition and omission of final –M is notoriously unsystematic and cannot be consistently interpreted as reliable evidence for the accusative status of the subject."[73] He mentions in support an example from the work of Gregory of Tours (c. 538–594), a learned writer, in which the accusative *causam* is in apposition with the nominative *haec*: *eice, eice haec a te, o sacerdos, ne faciat scandalum haec causam* ("Get those things away from you, get them away, priest, lest this thing creates a scandal").[74]

Some linguists posit an extended use of the accusative in later Latin, whereby "the accusative may occur in subject function," and this is said to be attested "roughly by the 4th–5th century A.D, with earlier attestations by the 2nd–3rd century A.D. from African Latin."[75] The extended accusative is attested in Italy, Spain, and Gaul "in texts from various periods, spanning from the 4th to the 8th–11th century."[76] It was particularly found "in clauses involving passive or intransitive verbs,"[77] as in Irenaeus's passage. Thus, the *Mulomedicana Chironis*, in the second half of the fourth century reads: *catulum lactentem vivum in aqua fervente coctum . . . conditur eodem modo* ("The live suckling kitten, cooked in boiling water . . . is flavoured in the same way"),[78] with the subject "kitten" in the accusative; Anthimus, an early sixth-century Byzantine physician, writes *qualis omnes cibos comedantur* ("that all the food be eaten"), with "food" in the accusative.[79] There is therefore the possibility that Irenaeus's *visum est* represents the masculine accusative acting as the subject of a passive verb. It could not, however, have referred to the apocalyptic vision.

*Irenaeus and his Readers*

Without knowing the assumptions Irenaeus would have made concerning his readers' familiarity with the Johannine narrative, his meaning cannot be determined with certainty. Had his readers been aware of a specific gathering of the elders to John late in John's life, in Domitian's reign, then Irenaeus's prior notice of those who saw John, together with the emphatic placement of John in the sentence and the development of the argument itself, might have reasonably signaled to his readers that John was the intended subject of ἑωράθη. A few extant sources may in fact indicate that this convocation was held to have taken place at that time (see chapter 9).

There would have been little room for misconstruing his meaning had John's exile been generally understood as having occurred at an earlier time. Indeed, there is no independent attestation of a late Domitianic exile from this period, and this view seems to have been the construct of Eusebius, who was unable to offer any unambiguous evidence for it from earlier ecclesiastical writers. On the other hand, there is evidence suggesting that writers of this period, including Tertullian, Clement, and possibly Irenaeus himself, placed John's Revelation within a Neronian context (see chapter 7).

For Irenaeus's readers, therefore, the passage might have been read as follows: "John himself expounded concerning the beast to the elders, when, as you know, they gathered to him and saw him face to face in his old age. Nevertheless, he did not provide the meaning of the name to them at that time. This being the case, we should also be cautious in trying to deduce the meaning. In fact, the meaning will only be important when the fulfilment is imminent, and it cannot be imminent now, for if it were, then it would have been explained by that one who himself also saw the apocalyptic vision, for, as you know, he was seen face to face by the elders nearly in our generation, at the end of Domitian's reign, but they received no such information."

## CONCLUSION

Eusebius, assuming the identification of the Apostle and Evangelist, consciously set about constructing a revised Johannine narrative which maintained the Asian template of John's long life at the expense of the martyrdom tradition. This narrative worked in turn to marginalize John the Elder, Eusebius's suggested author of Revelation, since he had been active after the Apostle's death according to Papias, and in Eusebius's reconstruction this placed his activities too far into the second century for him to have personally known Jesus.

As a further argument for John's longevity, besides the sole evidence of Irenaeus, Eusebius constructed a historical setting for John's exile in the implausible context of the persecution of the Roman nobility towards the end of Domitian's reign, which he buttressed with a statement from Clement which he interpreted as placing John's return from exile after Domitian's death and with a statement from Irenaeus which he interpreted as dating John's apocalyptic vision in Domitian's reign. Finally, he conflated this persecution with an earlier and probably historically mistaken reference to Domitian's attempt at apprehending potential Messianic agitators in Judea, ignoring the obvious inconsistencies of the two narratives in the process.

Eusebius thus created a *pastiche* of ill-fitting secular and ecclesiastical sources, held together by the thread of misinterpreted statements from Clement and Irenaeus, to construct the fiction of the Domitianic banishment of John. Nevertheless, despite the glaring discrepancies in his construction, he was remarkably successful in persuading his readers, ancient and modern, that the old authorities were to be discounted and that his own retelling of the Johannine narrative reflected a critical use of historical sources. In the process, Papias's Elder was transformed into an obscure, non-apostolic figure and Papias was largely dismissed as a credulous hoarder of legends who was lacking in intelligence; even Irenaeus's testimony concerning Papias's knowledge of John was successfully nullified.

While the traditional retelling of the Johannine narrative would generally go on to reject Eusebius's theory of the separate authorship of John's Gospel and Revelation, the innovations Eusebius introduced to accommodate his theory of a non-apostolic John were to form the substance of the "traditional" narrative that would dominate until the advent of critical study.

## NOTES

1. Bruce, *Canon of Scripture*, 199; Hengel, *Johannine Question*, 21; Carson and Moo, *Introduction*, 717; ODCC 1402; Constantinou, *Blessed End*, 30–31.
2. Hengel, *Johannine Question*, 21; Constantinou, *Blessed End*, 30.
3. Constantinou, *Blessed End*, 31–32.
4. *The Roman Martyrology*, ed. Benedict XIV (Baltimore: Murphy, 1916), 55.
5. John Chapman, "Papias on the Age of Our Lord," *JTS* 9 (1908): 53; cf. 48–63; Schoedel, *Polycarp*, 104.
6. Bacon, "The Elder John," 2; Barclay, *Introduction to John*, 45–48; Körtner, *Papias von Hierapolis*, 128; Culpepper, *John*, 109; Beasley-Murray, *John*, lxvii–lxviii; Lincoln, *Saint John*, 19; Hill, *Lost Teaching*, 11 n. 24.
7. Barrett, *St. John*, 105.
8. Watson, *Gospel Writing*, 465 n. 50.
9. E.g., Burney, *Aramaic Origin*, 141–42; Annand, "Four Gospels," 47; Perumalil, "Papias," 362, 366.
10. Culpepper, *John*, 130.
11. Translated by the author from the Latin text in Kurt Aland, ed., *Synopsis Quattuor Evangeliorum: Locis parallelis evangeliorum apocryphorum et patrum adhibitis edidit* (15th ed.; Stuttgart: Deutsche Bibelgesellschaft, 2001), 549.
12. Author's translation.
13. Norelli, *Papia di Hierapolis*, 420.
14. Helm, *Die Chronik*, 193.
15. For the *Chronicle*'s placement of the exile in Domitian's reign, see Robinson, *Redating*, 222.
16. Cf. Eusebius, *Demonstr. evang.* 3.5, which does not mention the immersion in oil but otherwise follows Tertullian, *Praescr.* 36.
17. Cf. Ellis, *New Testament Documents*, 211.
18. Thompson, "Ordinary Lives," 31.
19. Translated by the author from the Greek text in Earnest Cary, trans., *Dio Cassius, Roman History*, vol. 8, books 61–70 (LCL 176; Cambridge, Mass.: Harvard University Press, 1925).
20. Paul Keresztes, "The Jews, the Christians, and Emperor Domitian," *VC* 27 (1973): 7–15; E. Mary Smallwood, *The Jews under Roman Rule from Pompey to Diocletian. A Study in Political Relations* (Leiden: Brill, 2001), 376–84; Stephen Spence, *The Parting of the Ways: The Roman Church as a Case Study* (Leuven: Peeters, 2004), 165; Cook, *Roman Attitudes*, 130–31; Koester, *Revelation*, 77.
21. See, e.g., Leslie William Barnard, "Clement of Rome and the Persecution of Domitian," *NTS* 10 (1963): 259; Marta Sordi, *The Christians and the Roman Empire*, trans. Annabel Bedini (London: Routledge, 1994), 44; G. K. Beale, *The Book of Revelation: A Commentary on the Greek Text* (NIGTC; Grand Rapids: Eerdmans, 1999), 7–9; Marius Heemstra, *The Fiscus Judaicus and the Parting of the Ways* (WUNT 277; Tübingen: Mohr Siebeck, 2010), 117–18; Stephen P. Kershaw, *A Brief History of the Roman Empire* (London: Robinson, 2013), 169.

22. Sordi, *The Christians*, 38–53.
23. Cf. Spence, *The Parting of the Ways*, 165.
24. Barnard, "Clement of Rome," 254; Prigent, *Apocalypse*, 71; Spence, *Parting of the Ways*, 138–56; Cook, *Roman Attitudes*, 248; Koester, *Revelation*, 77; Kershaw, *A Brief History*, 169. An exception is Sordi, who claims that Domitian's persecution of Christians among the Roman nobility "affected not only Rome but the whole Roman empire" (*The Christians*, 53).
25. On the potential evidence for this persecution in 1 Clement, Suetonius, and Melito of Sardis, see J. Christian Wilson, "The Problem of the Domitianic Date of Revelation," *NTS* 39 (1993): 587–606. On the evidence of Pliny the Younger, see William L. Schutter, *Hermeneutic and Composition in I Peter* (WUNT 2.30; Tübingen: Mohr Siebeck, 1989), 13; Cook, *Roman Attitudes*, 135–36.
26. So, e.g., Lightfoot, *Apostolic Fathers*, part 1, vol. 1, 46–49; George Edmundson, *The Church in Rome in the First Century* (London: Longmans, 1913), 230 n. 1; cf. Andrew Cain, ed. and trans., *Jerome's Epitaph on Paula: A Commentary on the Epitaphium Sanctae Paulae* (OECT; Oxford: Oxford University Press, 2013), 196.
27. Cook, *Roman Attitudes*, 118. Possibly it was found in Africanus' *Chronology*: see Lightfoot, *Apostolic Fathers*, part 1, vol. 1, 48.
28. The Latin text is given by Lightfoot, *Apostolic Fathers*, part 1, vol. 1, 108; and Cook, *Roman Attitudes*, 117.
29. Lightfoot, *Apostolic Fathers*, part 1, vol. 1, 42–50; Spence, *Parting of the Ways*, 167–68.
30. Keresztes, "Emperor Domitian," 15–20; Sordi, *The Christians*, 49.
31. Philip Sellew, "Eusebius and the Gospels," in *Eusebius, Christianity, and Judaism*, ed. Harold Attridge and Gohei Hata (Detroit: Wayne State University Press, 1992), 119; Thompson, "Ordinary Lives," 32.
32. Hugh Jackson Lawlor, *Eusebiana: Essays on the Ecclesiastical History of Eusebius Pamphili, c. 264–349* (Oxford: Clarendon Press, 1912), 22–23.
33. Lawlor, *Eusebiana*, 41–42; cf. Hill, *Johannine Corpus*, 88–89; Tobias Nicklas, "Probleme der Apokalypserezeption im 2. Jahrhundert Eine Diskussion mit Charles E. Hill," in *Ancient Christian Interpretations of "Violent Texts" in the Apocalypse*, ed. Joseph Verheyden, Andreas Merkt, Tobias Nicklas (NTOA 92; Göttingen: Vandenhoeck & Ruprecht, 2011), 42–44).
34. Lawlor, *Eusebiana*, 48; cf. 43.
35. Cf. Richard Bauckham, *Jude and the Relatives of Jesus in the Early Church* (London: T. & T. Clark, 2004), 100.
36. Robert M. Grant, *Eusebius as Church Historian* (Oxford: Clarendon Press, 1980), 65–66.
37. Thompson, "Ordinary Lives," 32.
38. Bauckham, *Jude*, 100.
39. Bauckham, *Jude*, 100.
40. . Cf. Bauckham, *Jude*, 84.
41. Cook, *Roman Attitudes*, 118 n. 40.
42. Bauckham, *Jude*, 104; Cook, *Roman Attitudes*, 118 n. 40.
43. Sordi, *The Christians*, 39–42.
44. Sordi, *The Christians*, 40; cf. Ekkehard W. Stegemann and Wolfgang Stegemann, *The Jesus Movement: A Social History of its First Century*, trans. O. C. Dean (Edinburgh: T. & T. Clark, 1999), 453–54; Ramelli, "John the Evangelist's Work," 43.
45. BDAG 1009.
46. So, e.g., Charles E. Hill, "The Fragments of Papias," in Paul Foster, ed., *The Writings of the Apostolic Fathers* (London: T. & T. Clark, 2007), 44–45; Oskar Skarsaune, "Fragments of Jewish Christian Literature Quoted in Some Greek and Latin Fathers," in *Jewish Believers in the Jesus: The Early Centuries*, ed. Oskar Skarsaune and Reidar Hvalvik (Peabody, Mass.: Hendrickson, 2007), 334; W. C. van Unnik, "The Authority of the Presbyters in Irenaeus' Works," in *Sparsa Collecta. Part 4: Neotestamentica—Fla-*

*vius Josephus—Patristica*, ed. Cilliers Breytenbach and Pieter W. van der Horst (Leiden: Brill, 2014), 342.

47. See, e.g., Guthrie, *Introduction*, 956; Mounce, *Revelation*, 16; Aune, *Revelation 1–5*, lix; Beale, *The Book of Revelation*, 19; Carson and Moo, *Introduction*, 717; Trebilco, *Early Christians*, 294; ODCC 1239; Harrington, *Revelation*, 9; Koester, *Revelation*, 74.

48. Heinrich Ernst Ferdinand Guericke, *Historisch-kritische Einleitung in das Neue Testament* (Leipzig, 1843), 285 n. 4.

49. Johannes J. Wetstein, *Nouum Testamentum Graecum*, vol. 2 (1751), 746; anon., "The Date of the Apocalypse," BRCM (1846): 175; Eduard Böhme, *Über Verfasser und Abfassungszeit der Johanneischen Apokalypse und zur biblischen Typik* (Halle: 1855), 30–32; James Madison MacDonald, *The Life and Writings of St. John* (2nd ed.; London: Hodder & Stoughton, 1880), 168–71; F. H. Chase, "The Date of the Apocalypse: The Evidence of Irenaeus," *JTS* 8 (1907): 431–435; Edmundson, *The Church in Rome*, 164–65; Ellis, *New Testament Documents*, 210; Stolt, "Om dateringen," 204–5; Martin Karrer, *Die Johannesoffenbarung als Brief: Brief: Studien zu ihrem literarischen, historischen und theologischen Ort* (Göttingen: Vandenhoeck & Ruprecht, 1986), 18 n. 6; Gentry, *Before Jerusalem Fell*, 48–57. Boxall acknowledges the ambiguity in his translation of the passage (*Patmos*, 39).

50. Anon., "The Date of the Apocalypse," 176; MacDonald, *The Life and Writings of St. John*, 169; Chase, "The Date of the Apocalypse," 432; Edmundson, *The Church in Rome*, 165 n. 1.

51. J. Bovon, "L'Hypothèse de M. Vischer Sur l'Origine de l'Apocalypse," *RTP* (1887), from an extract in Hort, *The Apocalypse*, 41.

52. Anon., "The Date of the Apocalypse," 175–76; Böhme, *Über Verfasser*, 30–31; Bovon, "L'Hypothèse," in Hort, *The Apocalypse*, 41; Chase, "The Date of the Apocalypse," 431; Edmundson, *The Church in Rome*, 165; Stolt, "Om dateringen," 204.

53. Hort, *The Apocalypse*, 42; Robinson, *Redating*, 221 n. 5.

54. See Chase, "The Date of the Apocalypse," 432; cf. Böhme, *Über Verfasser*, 30–31.

55. Chase, "The Date of the Apocalypse," 432.

56. The καί is often untranslated. See, e.g., ANF 1.569. Contrast this with the Latin, which reads *qui et apocalypsim viderat* ("who also had seen the apocalyptic vision").

57. Chase, "The Date of the Apocalypse," 434.

58. Hitchcock, "A Defense," 27; cf. Bovon, "L'Hypothèse," in Hort, *The Apocalypse*, 41.

59. . Hort, *The Apocalypse*, 42; Robinson, *Redating*, 221–22 n. 5.

60. . Chase, "The Date of the Apocalypse," 435.

61. Böhme, *Über Verfasser*, 31.

62. Chase, "The Date of the Apocalypse," 434.

63. The words πρὸς τῷ τέλει are used of being near death (Lucian, *Vit. Phil.* 4.42), of the final phase of an illness (Hippocrates, *Aph.* 2.32), of the things that will be repeated at the end of a speech (Plato, *Leges* 957b) and of being in the final stages of victory (Josephus, *Bell.* 6.28).

64. Aune, *Revelation 1–5*, lix.

65. Chase, "The Date of the Apocalypse," 434.

66. The Latin text reads, *per ipsum utique dictum fuisset qui et apocalypsim viderat: neque enim ante multum temporis visum est sed pene sub nostro saeculo ad finem Domitiani Imperii*. The Latin text is from *S. Irenaei Libros quinque Adversus Haereses*, ed. W. Wigan Harvey, 2 vols. (Cambridge: Typis Academicis, 1857), and so hereafter

67. Dominic J. Unger, trans., *St. Irenaeus of Lyons Against the Heresies, Book 1* (ACW 55; New York: Newman Press, 1992), 14–15.

68. BDAG 956.

69. Robinson, *Redating*, 222 n. 5; Beale is mistaken when he asserts that the Latin translation supports the apocalyptic vision as the subject (*The Book of Revelation*, 20). Gentry (*Before Jerusalem Fell*, 54) and Hitchcock ("A Defense," 26) mistakenly understand physical objects in Latin to be neuter in gender and suggest that the subject is "book" (*liber*), which is masculine in Latin.

70. Thomas Witulski, *Die Johannesoffenbarung und Kaiser Hadrian: Studien zur Datierung der Neutestementlichen Apokalypse* (Göttingen: Vandenhoeck & Ruprecht, 2007), 31.
71. Robinson, *Redating*, 222 n. 5; cf. Aune, *Revelation 1–5*, lix; Boxall, *Patmos*, 32 n. 14.
72. Robinson, *Redating*, 222 n. 5; Beale, *The Book of Revelation*, 20.
73. Adam Ledgeway, *From Latin to Romance: Morphosyntactic Typology and Change* (OSDHL; Oxford: Oxford University Press, 2012), 329.
74. Ledgeway, *From Latin to Romance*, 329–30.
75. . Michela Cennamo, "Argument structure and alignment variations and changes in late Latin," in *The Role of Semantic, Pragmatic, and Discourse Factors in the Development of Case*, ed. Jóhanna Barðdal and Shobhana Lakshmi Chelliah (Amsterdam: John Benjamins, 2009), 315.
76. Cennamo, "Argument Structure," 317.
77. Alison Goddard Elliott, *Medieval Latin*, ed. K. P. Harrington and Joseph Pucci (Chicago: University of Chicago Press, 1997), 19.
78. Latin and English translation from Chiron, 199, cited by Cennamo, "Argument Structure," 318.
79. Anthimus 1, cited by Cennamo, "Argument Structure," 318.

# Section 3

## *Toward a Reconstruction of the Earliest Tradition*

In the final section of this work, an attempt will be made at reconstructing the Johannine narrative as it likely existed before the identification of the Apostle and Evangelist. In particular, evidence will be presented for the following three propositions: (1) that John's exile was contextualized in the reign of Nero; (2) that Papias identified the Evangelist with his second John, the Elder; and (3) that the publication of the Gospel of John was placed within the context of the Asian elders imploring John to write at the end of Domitian's reign.

# SEVEN
## The Tradition of John's Neronian Exile

It is commonly held that early ecclesiastical writers contextualized John's Patmos exile in the reign of Domitian,[1] but the evidence to be discussed in this chapter will suggest instead an early association of John's exile with Nero's reign. The study will commence by examining some of the most important pre-Eusebian writers on the question, including Irenaeus, Tertullian, Clement, and the *Acts of John*; it will then consider how the Neronian narrative continued to influence and shape Johannine narratives even after the publication of Eusebius's influential *Ecclesiastical History* popularized the Domitianic banishment narrative.

### IRENAEUS ON THE NICOLAITANS

The key text of Irenaeus, which has done so much to persuade scholars that Irenaeus placed John's apocalyptic vision, and hence his banishment, late in Domitian's reign (*apud* Eusebius, *Hist. eccl.* 3.18.3 = Irenaeus, *Haer.* 5.30.3) was discussed at length in the previous chapter. Another passage in Irenaeus's *Against Heresies* is suggestive of an earlier context for John's exile. There, Irenaeus relates that John wrote his Gospel "to carry away that error which had been sown among men by Cerinthus, and a long time previously by those called Nicolaitans," whom he then describes as a Gnostic sect (*Haer.* 3.11.1). He adds that John in his Gospel refuted their error by asserting that there was one God who made all things through his Word (3.11.1).

Irenaeus thus distinguishes Cerinthus and the Nicolaitans chronologically; while Cerinthus was disseminating his doctrines at the time John wrote his Gospel, the Nicolaitans had been active "a long time previously," where the words *multo prius* (the ablative of degree of difference) likely indicate a period of decades.[2] Elsewhere, Irenaeus relates the story of how John, walking with Polycarp, refused to enter the baths at Ephesus as Cerinthus was inside (*Haer.* 3.3.4). The inclusion of Polycarp in this anecdote suggests that Irenaeus envisioned Cerinthus as being active at the end of the first century; presumably he placed the activities of the Nicolaitans closer to the middle of the century, which would agree with Hippolytus, who placed the activities of the Nicolaitans in Asia Minor towards the end of Paul's life, during Nero's reign, writing that the Hymenaeus and Philetus mentioned in 2 Tim 2:17–18, who taught that the resurrection had already passed, were following the teaching of Nicolas, the founder of the sect (*De resurr.* fr. 1).[3] Irenaeus seems to envision the Nicolaitans as no longer active at the time that Cerinthus was spreading his teaching, which agrees with the notice of Eusebius that the Nicolaitans "subsisted for a very short time" (ἐπὶ σμικρότατον συνέστη χρόνον) (*Hist. eccl.* 3.29.1).[4]

While Irenaeus places a considerable interval between the activities of the Nicolaitans and the writing of John's Gospel, he elsewhere notes that the Nicolaitans were active at the time of the writing of Revelation, in which their practices (adultery and eating foods sacrificed to idols) were condemned (Rev. 2:6) (*Haer.* 1.26.3). Irenaeus therefore presumably considered Revelation, written at a time when the Nicolaitans were active, to have also been written "a long time before" the writing of John's Gospel.

## THE ANTI-MARCIONITE PROLOGUE TO LUKE

While the probably late second-century[5] Anti-Marcionite prologue to Luke does not provide any specific information concerning when Revelation was written, it is consistent with (though it does not require) an earlier dating of Revelation, for it records that "John first wrote Revelation in the island of Patmos, and afterward the Gospel (the Latin text adds: "in Asia").[6]

## TERTULLIAN AND THE LEGEND OF THE BOILING OIL

Tertullian (c. 200) is the first extant writer to relate the tradition that John was plunged into boiling oil and emerged unscathed, which he associates with John's banishment. He thus speaks in his *Prescription Against Heretics* of Rome as the place "where Peter attains to the suffering of the Lord, where Paul is crowned with the departure of John, where the apostle John, after he was plunged into boiling oil, having suffered nothing, is exiled to an island" (*Praescr.* 36).

Jerome, who accepted Eusebius's narrative of John's Domitianic banishment (*Vir.* 9.6–7), attributed to Tertullian a Neronian setting for the boiling oil legend: "moreover, Tertullian relates that, having been thrown into a terracotta jar of burning oil by Nero (*a Nerone missus in ferventis olei dolium*), he came out cleaner and more vigorous than when he entered" (*Jov.* 1.26).[7] Since Tertullian speaks as though John's exile followed upon his immersion in oil, this would suggest that he placed the exile during Nero's reign also.

There is no extant text of Tertullian that relates this, however, and Robinson thinks that Jerome inferred the Neronian dating from the text in Tertullian's *Prescription Against Heretics* because he there speaks of John's oil immersion in the same context as the martyrdoms of Peter and Paul, which took place in Nero's reign.[8] Certainly, Tertullian's mention of the fates of the three apostles together is suggestive that he considered them to have suffered at the same time. However, Tertullian's passage does not mention the terracotta jar (*dolium*)[9] or record anything about John emerging from the oil cleaner and more vigorous, suggesting that Jerome may have known another version of the story from one of Tertullian's lost works, with which he is known to have been familiar.[10]

Interestingly, while all the codices containing Jerome's *Against Jovinianus*, in which this claim is found, state that John was thrown into the burning oil *a Nerone* ("by Nero"), Vittori corrected Jerome's text in his 1564 printed edition to read *Romae* ("at Rome"), on the basis that Tertullian himself associated the oil immersion with John's exile, and "this happened in the time of Domitian, not Nero."[11] This reading was subsequently adopted for Migne's edition,[12] and from thence found its way in the standard English edition of the fathers,[13] obscuring Tertullian's placement of the episode in Nero's reign.

Jerome refers to the same tradition of the boiling oil in another work, citing "ecclesiastical histories" as relating that John was sent "immediately" (*statim*) to Patmos following the oil immersion (*Comm. Matt.* 20.23).[14] While this could have been inferred from Tertullian's statement that John was sent to Patmos after being plunged in oil, Ramelli points out that Tertullian was likely not Jerome's source as his *Prescription Against Heretics* was not an ecclesiastical history.[15]

Thus, the plunging in oil seems to have been associated both with Nero's reign and with John's banishment to Patmos by sources which are no longer extant, but which were known to Jerome. Possibly both Tertullian and Jerome were dependent upon Hegesippus for this tradition, as Ramelli suggests,[16] noting that Hegesippus seems to have been the source for Tertullian's claim that Domitian initiated and brought an end to a persecution of the Christians (*Apol.* 5.4; cf. chapter 6).[17] As a resident of Rome, Hegesippus would have been familiar with such local legends, and his *Memoirs* could have been considered an ecclesiastical history. Another possibility is that the tradition was found in the lost beginning of the *Acts of John*.

## JOHN'S EXILE AND CLEMENT'S TYRANT

In the late second century, Clement related the story of a young man who fell away from the faith and was restored to repentance by John (*Quis div.* 42). This is said to have occurred during John's travels to various neighboring regions following his return to Ephesus from exile, during which time he ordained bishops and ordered the churches. While Clement places John's return "after the death of the tyrant," he does not name the tyrant in question, perhaps because he expected his readers to be aware of his identity.[18] Many scholars, influenced by Eusebius's identification of this tyrant (see chapter 6), have assumed that Clement intended Domitian,[19] though this assumption has not gone unchallenged.[20] The identity of the particular tyrant intended by Clement has important implications for understanding his Johannine chronology, since Nero and Domitian died nearly thirty years apart: Nero took his own life in June 68, while Domitian was assassinated in September 96.

Clement's characterization of the emperor as a "tyrant" could potentially have described Nero or Domitian. Thus, Apollonius of Tyana (c. 15–c. 100), after likening tyrants to beasts with many heads, adds that even beasts do not devour their mothers as Nero had done (Philostratus, *Vit. Apoll.* 4.38).[21] A later writer, Lactantius (c. 260–330), speaks of Nero as a tyrant and a wild beast (*Mort. pers.* 2). On the other hand, Domitian's tyrannical actions were described by Dio, who relates among other things that he executed a sophist for, ironically, speaking against tyrants in a speech (Dio, *Hist. Rom.* 67.12.5). His tyranny is likewise spoken of by Suetonius (*Dom.* 1.3). Nero, however, was considered "the quintessential vicious tyrant,"[22] whose wicked and despotic reign continued to inspire fear and apprehension long after his death.

Clement does provide potential clues as to the intended identity of the tyrant. In his account of John's travels, he tells of an occasion when John came to a city not far from Ephesus (the name of which was said to have been related by some but is not given) and committed a young man to the pastoral care of the bishop of the church there. This bishop, it is said, "reared him" (ἔτρεφεν) in the faith, "kept him and at last (τὸ τελευταῖον) enlightened [i.e., baptized] him." At this point, the bishop relaxed his care, and the young man began at first (πρῶτον) attending extravagant feasts with youths his own age; next (εἶτά) they took him on night-time robberies and then (εἶτά) they urged him on to greater crimes. Gradually (κατ' ὀλίγον) he became accustomed to this way of life until he finally (τελέως) renounced salvation; casting aside all restraint, Clement continues, he went on to form his own band of robbers and excelled in violence and murder.

After an interval of some time (χρόνος ἐν μέσῳ), John returned to the city on account of some business and made inquiries after the young man. When he was informed of what had transpired, he called for a horse and set out for the robbers' outpost, intending to be taken into custody so that he might be brought before the young man, their leader. When the young man recognized John, he is said to have turned and fled rather than face him. John, however, "forgetful of his age (ἡλικία), rigorously (ἀνὰ κράτος) pursued him, shouting out, 'why do you flee from me, child, from your own father, from this unarmed old man (γέρων)?'" John is said to have successfully entreated him to return to the faith and to have subsequently brought him back to the church, joining with him in continual fasting. Clement concludes by relating that John did not leave him until he had restored him to the church (*Quis div.* 42).

The temporal markers used by Clement in the account do not give an impression that these events were conceived of as having unfolded rapidly. Indeed, Chrysostom—whether as an inference from Clement or from independent knowledge of the tradition—states that the young man "first became a disciple of John, but later was a chief of robbers for a long time (ἐπὶ πολὺν χρόνον)" (*ad Theod.* 1. 17),[23] where the reference is only to the period in which he presided as a robber chief. Clement probably envisioned the narrative of the young man's instruction, baptism, gradual falling away, time as a robber bandit and eventual restoration to the faith as taking place over the course of a number of years. This would leave insufficient time for Clement to have placed the events in the period following Domitian's assassination in 96 and John's death, probably at the end of the first century.[24]

It is sometimes objected that the expression "forgetful of his age" and the reference to John as an old man (γέρων) would lose their force if they had described John following a return from exile under Nero, when he would have probably been no older than sixty.[25] But this objection mistakenly assumes that these events had to have unfolded immediately upon John's return to Ephesus,[26] whereas it is only the Domitianic view that must require their immediate commencement, in order to condense the account into the brief space of time between John's return from exile and his death. If Nero was the intended tyrant, the story could have been understood as having occurred in the 70s or 80s, at a time when John might still have been able to run after the young man "strenuously" (ἀνὰ κράτος) but before the onset of his extreme old age.[27] Indeed, a tradition attributed to Pythagoras claims that a γέρων was someone aged between sixty and eighty (*Diog. Laer.* 8. 10),[28] which would correspond to this period. This would be consistent with the tradition known to Jerome, according to which John was unable even to walk in his extreme old age and had to be carried into the meetings (Jerome, *Comm. Gal.* 6.10).

## JOHN'S ASIAN MINISTRY IN THE *ACTS OF JOHN* AND RELATED TEXTS

The *Acts of John* is variously dated from as early as the second quarter of the second century to the first half of the third.[29] Although its provenance is unknown, many favor Egypt, Syria, or Asia Minor as the place of composition.[30] It relates various events purported to have taken place during John's long residence in Asia Minor, one of which is the story of how John raised a dead man to life in Ephesus (§§ 45–47), which may be related to the similar tradition mentioned by Apollonius (*apud* Eusebius, *Hist. eccl.* 5.18.14).

The beginning of the work is lost and the extant account commences with John sailing from Miletus to Ephesus (18), where he remains a "long time" (πολὺν χρόνον) (37.3).[31] John is then called upon to journey to Smyrna, which he promises to do after he has confirmed those at Ephesus in the faith (45.5–7). The excerpts from this work contained in the eleventh-century manuscript classified as Q relate that John left Ephesus and resided in the region of Smyrna for four years, during which time he ordained Polycarp.[32]

The record of John's journeys following his departure from Smyrna and his later return to Ephesus is no longer extant, but the account does record that John returned to Ephesus from Laodicea (58). John had thus travelled from Ephesus to Smyrna and had ended his travels at Laodicea before returning to Ephesus. It may not be coincidental that Ephesus, Smyrna and Laodicea are the first, second, and last churches addressed in Revelation, and some have suggested that the lost sections of the work depicted John visiting all the seven churches of Revelation in order.[33] That he did visit the other cities is suggested by the message of those from Smyrna who came to Ephesus and urged him to come "to Smyrna and to the other cities" (εἰς τὴν Σμύρναν καὶ εἰς τὰς λοιπὰς πόλεις) (55.5), where the definite article perhaps denotes the cities spoken of in connection with the seven churches of Revelation. Moreover, the *Suffering of John* (usually referred to by its Latin title, *Passio Iohannis*) of Ps.-Melito (thought to have originally been written in Greek in the second half of the fifth century[34]) and the *Virtues of John* (usually referred to as the *Virtutes Iohannis*) of Ps.-Abdias (possibly written in Gaul in the late sixth century[35]), both of which seem to depend on a Greek text related to the *Acts of John*,[36] speak of John's journey to Pergamum.[37] Tertullian seems to have been aware of a tradition of John having established the bishops in the seven churches, for he states: "although Marcion rejects his Revelation, the order of the bishops [i.e., of the seven churches of Revelation] when reckoned to its origin will nevertheless stand on John as the founder" (Tertullian, *Marc.* 4.5).[38]

While the *Acts of John* concludes with John's death in Ephesus, there is no mention in the extant text of John's banishment to Patmos, leading

Lalleman to propose that it had been narrated at the lost beginning of the work; in support, he notes that the extant text begins in Miletus, which would have been a natural stopping point between Patmos and Ephesus.[39] This would be in agreement with Clement, who also places John's Asian ministry after the return from exile. Indeed, since the travels and events related in the *Acts of John* were likely conceived of as having transpired over the course of a decade or more (as noted above, according to one manuscript of the *Acts of John*, John stayed four years just in Smyrna), this reconstruction would also agree with the proposal above that Clement placed John's travels in Asia Minor in the last decades of the first century, after Nero's death, rather than in the short space of time after the death of Domitian and the end of the first century.[40]

*Modifications of the* Acts of John *Narrative*

A number of events recorded in the *Acts of John* are also found in the two Latin texts mentioned above, the *Suffering of John* of Ps.-Melito and the *Virtues of John* of Ps.-Abdias, including the raising of Drusiana, the destruction of the temple of Artemis and John's laying himself in his own grave (*metastasis*).[41] The *Virtues of John* also relates the story of the young man restored to repentance by John, given by Clement of Alexandria (*Quis div.* 42). But in both works, these events take place after John's exile to Patmos, as it is suggested here that they did in the *Acts of John* also.

Both works, however, follow Eusebius in placing the exile in Domitian's reign. Thus, according to the *Suffering of John*, quoting Eusebius's *History* (*Hist. eccl.* 3.17.1), Domitian "administered a second persecution of the Christians after Nero," at which time John was brought from Ephesus and exiled on Patmos.[42] The *Virtues of John* also seems to follow Eusebius when it claims that the exiles were restored by the Senate following Domitian's death (*Virt. Ioh.* 2; Eusebius, *Hist. eccl.* 3.20.8–9). It also relates the tradition that John was plunged into burning oil and then exiled, though in this work these things takes place in Ephesus at the proconsul's order, not in Rome at Nero's order, as in Tertullian (*Virt. Ioh.* 1–2).[43] Probably the Domitianic placement of John's exile, during a time otherwise associated with John's later Asian ministry, has led to the reshaping of the original Roman context into an Ephesian one.

## THE NERONIAN EXILE IN THE SYRIAC TRADITION

A number of Syriac works reflect awareness of a Neronian tradition. Two Syriac versions of Revelation, dating from perhaps as early as the fourth century, state that John was banished during Nero's reign,[44] and a Neronian banishment is also attested in the Syriac apocryphal work entitled the *History of John*, preserved in two manuscripts from the sixth and ninth century respectively, the text of which may have been written as early as the end of the fourth century.[45] According to this work, John's preaching in Ephesus came to the notice of Nero, "the unclean and impure and wicked king," who ordered him to be exiled.[46] A Domitianic dating of John's exile, however, is found in the work of the Eastern Syrian bishop Isho'dad (c. 850), who was likely influenced by Eusebius (*Comm. John.* prolog.).[47]

## TYCONIUS ON THE SEVEN KINGS OF REVELATION

Tyconius of Carthage, who wrote his *Exposition of the Apocalypse* in the late fourth century, seems to have presupposed John's Neronian exile in his comments on Rev 17:10 ("there are seven kings; five have fallen, one is, one has not yet come"), which he interprets in terms of the seven emperors of Rome, beginning with Julius Caesar (who was never officially an emperor but who established the Julio-Claudian dynasty and was often counted as the first) and concluding with Otho (69 CE), whom he identified as the king who is said to have "not yet come" at the time of John's writing.[48] Nero is thus identified as the sixth king, of whom Revelation states "one is," using the present tense, making John to have seen the vision in Nero's reign.[49]

## THE *ACTS OF JOHN OF PROCHORUS*

The probably fifth-century[50] *Acts of John by Prochorus* (46[51]) places John's exile in Trajan's reign (or Hadrian's in one reading), but it makes John to have arrived in Ephesus from Jerusalem at the age of fifty; he remains in the city for nine years and is exiled to Patmos for fifteen years; he then resides in Ephesus until his death at the age of one hundred, twenty-six years later (162). This work thus places John's exile forty or so years before his death, likely corresponding with the late 50s or early 60s, during Nero's reign. It probably represents a confused recollection of various traditions, one of which may have been that of a Neronian exile.

## THE *ACTS OF JOHN IN ROME*

Gentry sees evidence of a tradition of the Neronian banishment of John in the sixth-century[52] *Acts of John in Rome*,[53] a work which originated independently of the *Acts of John*.[54] In this account, news reaches Domitian in Rome that a certain Hebrew in Ephesus named John "is making it known" (διαφημίζει)[55] that the seat of the Roman Empire would be removed and given to another (§ 5.1–5). He summons John to Rome, from whence he banishes him to Patmos. Noting the reference to the apocalyptic preaching of John in Ephesus, Gentry points out that "the rationale for the exile is suggestive of a prior publication of Revelation" indicating that the work may betray knowledge of a Neronian exile, and he suggests that John could have been banished both under Nero and under Domitian.[56]

However, the reference to the prior publication of John's Revelation, if it be such, is probably only due to the work's conflation of different sources and is not necessarily reflective of any conscious placement of John's exile in Nero's reign. The text seems to recycle the story, found in the *Suffering of John* of Ps.-Melito[57] and the *Virtues of John* of Ps.-Abdias (*Virt. Ioh.* 20), of John convincing the priest of Artemis of his message by drinking a cup of poison. In the account found in the *Acts of John in Rome*, however, John offers to drink the poison for Domitian's sake, not the priest's, and it occurs before John's exile, rather than following it as in those works.

The template for the narrative seems to have been provided by Hegesippus's account of Domitian's persecution of the relatives of Jesus.[58] In Hegesippus, the descendants of the royal Davidic line are brought before the emperor as a potential threat to the throne (*Hist. eccl.* 3.19.1); here, it is John's apocalyptic preaching that is employed as a narrative device to bring John's loyalty to the empire into question and so cause him to be summoned before Domitian.

The story depicts Domitian as intending to expel (ἐκβάλλειν[59]) the Jews from "the city of the Romans" (§ 2.6–7). The Jews, however, inform the emperor of those called Christians who proclaim Jesus as the Son of God, whose family is said to have been connected with the Hebrews (§ 3). These accusers probably correspond to those of the Jewish-Christian sects (cf. *apud* Eusebius, *Hist. eccl.* 4.22.4–5) who were said by Hegesippus to have brought accusations against the grandsons of Jude (3.19.1)[60] and against Simeon (3.32.3),[61] who were referred to as the relatives of the Lord by Hegesippus (3.11.1; 3.19.1).

The summoning of John before Domitian to account for his proclamation of the coming removal of the seat of the Roman Empire, along with the resulting dialogue, similarly seems to be modelled after Hegesippus's account of the summoning of the grandsons of Jude. Whereas it is the grandsons' Davidic lineage that challenges the empire in Hegesippus, it is John's subversive preaching in this work. In Hegesippus, the grandsons assure Domitian that the kingdom they believe in is a spiritual one that will appear at the end of the world (*apud* Eusebius, *Hist. eccl.* 3.20.4). Here, John tells Domitian that the coming king he proclaims is eternal and will come from heaven as a judge, putting down all earthly rule (§ 8.5–12). John also assures the king that his rule would continue for many years and that many others would rule after him (§ 8.4–5), pointing to a setting early in Domitian's reign.

Lastly, in Hegesippus, Domitian brings an end of the persecution with the summoning of Jude's grandsons, while in this account, a similar effect is produced by having Domitian reluctantly banish John to Patmos that he might be seen to uphold the decrees of the Senate (§ 12) (cf. the story of Daniel in the lions' den).

The document may provide further evidence for Sordi's theory that Hegesippus confused Domitian (r. 81-96) with Titus (r. 79-81), for it opens with a reference to the destruction of Jerusalem under Vespasian (70 CE) and then shifts its focus to Domitian, who was reigning "after Vespasian was dead" (Οὐεσπεσιανοῦ δὲ ἀποθανόντος[62]) (§ 2.1). Historically, Titus took control of the operation in Judea following Vespasian's departure and began reigning after his death in 79.

## NON-DOMITIANIC EXILE TRADITIONS IN LATER WRITERS

Andrew (or Andreas), bishop of Caesarea in Cappadocia, noted in his commentary on Revelation, possibly written during the late sixth or early seventh century,[63] that there were those before him who had interpreted some of the apocalyptic visions as references to the fall of Jerusalem in 70 CE (*Comm. Apoc.* 6:12–13; 7:1). He evidently refers to Oecumenius, who suggested that the sealing of the 144,000 referred to those sealed and protected during the Jewish War.[64] Oecumenius himself held to the Domitianic dating (Oecumenius, *Comm. Apoc.* 1),[65] but he may have been repeating older exegetical material that assigned an earlier historical setting to John's apocalyptic vision.

Arethas of Caesarea in Cappadocia (c.850–944), who closely followed Andrew's exegesis,[66] likewise interprets the 144,000 of the believing Jews who did not perish in the destruction of Jerusalem in 70 CE and he specifically places John's apocalyptic visions before the destruction of the city, stating that "the destruction by the Romans had not yet overtaken the Jews, when the Evangelist prophesied these things."[67] However, his chronology probably represents a confused conflation of earlier Johannine traditions.[68]

Lastly, the possibly late tenth-century writer Hippolytus of Thebes in his *Chronicle* (*Chron.* 9a; 9b; 9c)[69] and the Byzantine exegete Theophylact of Ochrid (d. c. 1107) in his *Commentary on John* claimed that John the Seer was in Patmos thirty-two years after the ascension (pref.),[70] which would place his time there in Nero's reign.

## CONCLUSION

The principal writers of the pre-Eusebian period seem to presuppose an early or Neronian dating. According to Irenaeus, the Nicolaitans were active both at the time Revelation was written and "much earlier" than the writing of John's Gospel. Tertullian and other "ecclesiastical histories" (possibly Hegesippus and/or the *Acts of John*) are said by Jerome to have associated John's exile to Patmos with the legend of the plunging of John into boiling oil by Nero. Clement of Alexandria relates that John travelled to the churches in Asia Minor "after the death of the tyrant," which is best explained on the supposition that he placed John's return from exile and his Asian ministry in the last decades of the first century, following the death of Nero. The same chronology seems to have been known to the second- or third-century *Acts of John*, which likely placed John's exile in the lost beginning of its narrative.

With the exception of Victorinus, discussed in chapter 4, no pre-Eusebian writers indicate a dating of John's exile in Domitian's reign, and none place it in the context of Domitian's persecution of the Roman nobility at the end of his reign. While Irenaeus's statement is understandably often interpreted as placing the apocalyptic vision in Domitian's reign, it is nevertheless remarkable in light of the evidence that the pre-Eusebian writers are so often thought to have overwhelmingly attested the Domitianic dating of John's exile.

## NOTES

1. See, e.g., Charles, *Revelation*, vol. 1, xcii; Mounce, *Revelation*, 16; Carson and Moo, *Introduction*, 707–8.
2. Cf. Irenaeus, *Haer.* 3.16.2, where the Latin text states that God promised David the same thing he had "much earlier" (*multo prius*) promised Abraham, where it signifies centuries.
3. An English translation of the passage can be found in Lightfoot, *Apostolic Fathers*, part 1, vol. 2, 397.
4. Cf. Heikki Räisänen, *Challenges to Biblical Interpretation: Collected Essays, 1991–2000* (Leiden: Brill, 2001), 164–65.
5. See, F. F. Bruce, *The Book of the Acts* (NICNT; Grand Rapids: Eerdmans, 1988), 5; Culpepper, *John*, 130.
6. Text given in Aland, *Synopsis*, 549.
7. Latin text given by Ramelli, "John the Evangelist's Work," 43. See also, Gumerlock, *Revelation in the First Century*, 42 n. 17.
8. Robinson, *Redating*, 223–24.
9. Cf. Ramelli, "John the Evangelist's Work," 42–43.
10. Simcox, *Revelation*, xliv.
11. Translated by the author from the Latin notes of Vittori, cited by Henry Dominique Saffrey, "Le témoignage de pères sur le martyre de S. Jean l'Evangéliste," *RSPT* 69 (1985): 268; see also Gumerlock, *Revelation in the First Century*, 42.
12. Gumerlock, *Revelation in the First Century*, 42, citing Saffrey, "Le témoignage," 267–68; cf. Hort, *The Apocalypse*, xvii; Ramelli, "John the Evangelist's Work," 43. Migne's text can be found in *PL* 23:259.
13. However, *NPNF* 2.6.366 states that John was sent "to Rome," as though the Latin read *Romam*.
14. CCSL 77: 178.
15. Ramelli, "John the Evangelist's Work," 43.
16. Ramelli, "John the Evangelist's Work," 43.
17. Ramelli, "John the Evangelist's Work," 43; cf. Stegemann and Stegemann, *The Jesus Movement*, 653–54; Sordi, *The Christians*, 40.
18. . Boxall, *Patmos*, 32.

19. See, e.g., Charles, *Revelation*, vol. 1, xciii; Mounce, *Revelation*, 16; Carson and Moo, *Introduction*, 707–8; Hitchcock, "A Defense," 53; Watson, *Gospel Writing*, 468.
20. E.g., Hort, *The Apocalypse*, xv; Edmundson, *The Church in Rome*, 166; Robinson, *Redating*, 222–23; Gentry, *Before Jerusalem Fell*, 69.
21. Cf. Robinson, *Redating*, 235–36.
22. Anthony A. Barrett, Elaine Fantham and John C. Yardley, *The Emperor Nero: A Guide to Ancient Sources* (Princeton: Princeton University Press, 2016), xi.
23. Translated by the author from *PG* 47:305.
24. Cf. Hort, *The Apocalypse*, xv; Robinson, *Redating*, 223.
25. . Milligan, *The Revelation of St. John*, 305; Hitchcock, "A Defense," 44–45.
26. Cf. Hort, *The Apocalypse*, xv.
27. Simcox, *Revelation*, xliv; Robinson, *Redating*, 223.
28. Cf. BDAG 195. For (Ps.-)Hippocrates, as cited by Philo, it referred to anyone fifty-seven or older (*Opif.* 105).
29. See Bauckham, *Eyewitnesses*, 463.
30. See Trebilco, *Early Christians*, 259; Bauckham, *Eyewitnesses*, 363.
31. From the Greek text in Richard. A. Lipsius and Max Bonnet, eds., *Acta Apostolorum Apocrypha*, vol. 2/1 (Leipzig: 1898).
32. Montague Rhodes James, *The Apocryphal New Testament: Being the Apocryphal Gospels, Acts, Epistles, and Apocalypses* (Oxford: Clarendon Press, 1924), 239.
33. See, e.g., Hengel, *Die johanneische Frage*, 53. This is doubted by Pieter J. Lalleman, *The Acts of John: A Two-stage Initiation into Johannine Gnosticism* (Leuven: Peeters, 1998), 18–19, who thinks that it could have been modelled on an Assize proconsular tour.
34. Annette Volfing, *John the Evangelist and Medieval German Writing: Imitating the Inimitable* (New York: Oxford University Press, 2001), 17. Junod and Kaestli, *Acta Iohannis*, vol. 2, 769, date it to the fifth or sixth century.
35. Volfing, *John the Evangelist*, 17.
36. Junod and Kaestli, *Acta Iohannis*, vol. 2, 790.
37. The Latin text of the *Passio Iohannis* is found in *PG* 5:1239–50; that of the *Virtutes Iohannis* in Johann Albert Fabricius, ed., *Codex Apocryphus Novi Testamenti*, vol. 2 (Hamburg: 1703), 531–90, and in Junod and Kaestli, *Acta Iohannis*, vol. 2, 798–834.
38. Translated from the Latin text in Aemilianus Kroymann, ed., *Tertullianus: Opera I* (CCSL 1; Turnhout: Brepols, 1954).
39. Lalleman, *The Acts of John*, 16.
40. Cf. the suggestion of Theodor Zahn (*Forschungen zur Geschichte des neutestamentlichen Kanons und der altkirchlichen Literatur*, vol. 6: *Apostel und Apostelschuler in der Provinz Asien* [Leipzig: Deichert, 1900], 16–17), that the *Acts of John* were Clement's source for the story of the robber captain who repents, hence his reference to "the μῦθος which is not a μῦθος but an actual account" (*apud* Eusebius, *Eccl. Hist.* 3.23.6).
41. Summarized from the Latin texts of the *Passio Iohannis* in *PG* 5:1239–50 and the *Virtutes Iohannis* in Johann Albert Fabricius, ed., *Codex Apocryphus Novi Testamenti*, vol. 2 (Hamburg: 1703), 531–90.
42. Translated by the author from the Latin text in *PG* 5:1241.
43. Following the chapter divisions of Fabricius' edition, and so hereafter.
44. Koester, *Revelation*, 72.
45. Junod and Kaestli, *Acta Iohannis*, vol. 2, 705. However, it is dated to the fifth or sixth century in Keith Elliott, *The Apocryphal New Testament: A Collection of Apocryphal Christian Literature in an English Translation* (Oxford: Clarendon Press, 1993), 347.
46. William Wright, *Apocryphal Acts of the Apostles: Edited from Syriac Manuscripts in the British Museum and Other Libraries*, vol. 2 (London: Williams and Norgate, 1871), 55. Another version is found in the *Story of John, Son of Zebedee* preserved in a sixteenth-century Arabic manuscript (Agnes Smith Lewis, *The Mythological Acts of the Apostles* [HSem 4; London: Clay, 1904], x), in which the "unclean Philip," apparently the governor of the city, sends John to a desert (166–67).

47. For an English translation, see Margaret Dunlop Gibson, ed. and trans., *The Commentaries of Isho'dad of Merv: Bishop of Ḥadatha (c. 850 A.D.)* (HSem 5, vol. 1; Cambridge: Cambridge University Press, 1911), 212.
48. See Francis X. Gumerlock, review of *Tyconii Afri Expositio Apocalypseos*, ed. Roger Gryson, CCSL 107A (Turnhout: Brepols, 2011) *WTJ* 74 (2012): 470.
49. . See Gumerlock, review of *Tyconii*, 470.
50. Junod and Kaestli, *Acta Iohannis*, vol. 2, 748–49.
51. The page numbers are given according to the Greek text in Theodor Zahn, ed., *Acta Joannis unter Benutzung von C. v. Tischendorf's Nachlass* (Erlangen: Verlag von Andreas Deichert, 1880), 3–165, and so hereafter.
52. Elliott, *Apocryphal New Testament*, 347. Junod and Kaestli think 545 a likely *terminus ad quem* (*Acta Iohannis*, vol. 2, 857).
53. It is titled "The Acts of the Holy Apostle and Evangelist John the Theologian" in ANF 8.560–64. Elliott's title (*Apocryphal New Testament*, 347) is followed here. Gentry confuses it with the *Acts of John* (*Before Jerusalem Fell*, 100–1; cf. ANF 8.357; Lalleman, *The Acts of John*, 26). Hitchcock confuses this work with the *Acts of John* and the *Acts of John by Prochorus* ("A Defense," 67–68).
54. Junod and Kaestli, *Acta Iohannis*, vol. 2, 841–42; Lalleman, *The Acts of John*, 9–10.
55. CCSA 2.865.
56. Gentry, *Before Jerusalem Fell*, 100.
57. PG 5:1247.
58. Cf. Junod and Kaestli, *Acta Iohannis*, vol. 2, 853–54.
59. CCSA 2.865.
60. Cf. Bauckham, *Jude*, 96–97.
61. Cf. Bauckham, *Jude*, 82.
62. CCSA 2.865.
63. Weinrich, *Greek Commentaries on Revelation* (ACT; Downers Grove, Ill.: IVP, 2011), xxxiii–xxxiv. Constantinou argues for 611 as the date of composition (Andrew of Caesarea, *Commentary on the Apocalypse* [FC 123; Washington DC: Catholic University of America Press, 2011], 68–71).
64. Constantinou, *Commentary on the Apocalypse*, 102.
65. Weinrich, *Greek Commentaries*, 17.
66. Constantinou, *Blessed End*, 298.
67. Translated from the Greek text in *PG* 106:605.
68. He seems in the context to have placed John's exile and Ephesian residence in the 40s, for reasons that are explained in Furlong, *John also Called Mark*.
69. Greek text and translations are taken from Franz Diekamp, ed., *Hippolytos von Theben: Texte und Untersuchungen* (Münster, 1898), and so hereafter.
70. PG 123:1133.

# EIGHT
## Papian Traditions on the Gospel of John

Although Eusebius quoted the words of "the Elder" (as related by Papias) concerning the Gospels of Matthew and Mark (*apud* Eusebius, *Hist. eccl.* 3.39.15–16), he does not relate anything from Papias concerning the Gospels of Luke and John. Some have understood this silence to indicate that Papias did not say anything concerning these Gospels,[1] while others explain Eusebius's silence on other grounds. Lightfoot thus suggests that Eusebius only intended to relate some "curious facts" concerning the Gospels and that he did not discuss John as the circumstances of its publication were already well known.[2] Bauckham on the other hand thinks that Eusebius might have disagreed with what Papias said about those Gospels: possibly Papias "distanced Luke further from eyewitness testimony than Eusebius would have liked";[3] possibly he identified John the Evangelist with the Elder, which Eusebius found objectionable.[4]

Some have further argued that fragments from Papias's discussion of John (and Luke) are partially preserved in other texts, including the Muratorian Canon,[5] Irenaeus,[6] Clement of Alexandria,[7] and Victorinus.[8] And Bartlet and Hill have argued that Eusebius paraphrases Papias's account of John's Gospel elsewhere in his work, though without attribution.[9]

In this chapter, these proposed sources will be examined, and the question of whether these sources were dependent on Papias will be evaluated. Chapter 9 will examine Bartlet and Hill's proposed Papian fragment in Eusebius along with its potential implications for the question of whether Papias identified his John with the Elder.

## IRENAEUS

There are three main passages in which Irenaeus speaks about John's Gospel. One occurs within the context of a tradition concerning how the four Gospels came to be published:

> Indeed, Matthew published a writing of the gospel also among the Hebrews, in their own dialect, while Peter and Paul were preaching in Rome and establishing the church. After their departure (ἔξοδος), Mark, the disciple and interpreter of Peter, also himself has handed down (παραδέδωκεν) in writing the things preached by Peter. Luke also, the follower of Paul, put the gospel being preached by him into a book. Then John, the disciple of the Lord, who leaned on the Lord's breast, himself published the Gospel, when residing in Ephesus of Asia. (*apud* Eusebius, *Hist. eccl.* 5.8.2 = Irenaeus, *Haer.* 3.1.1)

Irenaeus echoes Papias's statements on Matthew and Mark, alleging like him that Matthew wrote for Hebrews, and in their dialect, and that Mark was Peter's interpreter (*Haer.* 3.1.1; cf. the words of Papias, *apud* Eusebius, *Hist. eccl.* 3.39.15–16). This strengthens the probability that his statements concerning Luke and John were also derived from Papias. Indeed, the claims that John wrote his Gospel last and that he composed it in Ephesus are found in other proposed Papian fragments (see below).

In another place, Irenaeus places John's residence in Ephesus at the end of the first century, and he also mentions the elders in connection with the Fourth Gospel:

> However, from the fortieth and fiftieth year [a man] declines to old age, at which age our Lord was teaching (*quam habens dominus noster docebat*), just as the Gospel and all the elders, who have conferred (συμβεβληκότες/*convenerunt*) with John the disciple of the Lord in Asia, are testifying (μαρτυροῦσιν/*testantur*), [saying] that John delivered (παραδεδωκέναι/*tradidisse*) it to them. For he also remained with them until the times of Trajan. (*Haer.* 2.22.5, partially quoted in Eusebius, *Hist. eccl.* 3.23.3).

The reference to the elders raises the possibility that Irenaeus was drawing from Papias, since Papias had claimed to have collected the traditions of the elders (Eusebius, *Hist. eccl.* 3.39.4).[10] Indeed, the specific reference to "all the elders" (πάντες οἱ πρεσβύτεροι) may point to a written collection of their testimonies,[11] which Papias is known to have written. A written source is further suggested by the repetition of the phrase, "for he remained with them until the times of Trajan" (παρέμεινεν γὰρ αὐτοῖς μέχρι τῶν Τραϊανοῦ χρόνων) later in his work (Ἰωάννου δὲ παραμείναντος αὐτοῖς μέχρι τῶν Τραϊανοῦ χρόνων, in *Haer.* 3.3.4, *apud* Eusebius, *Hist. eccl.* 3.23.4).[12] Lastly, the use of the present tense μαρτυροῦσιν may also suggest written testimony.[13] Indeed, Irenaeus elsewhere uses this word in the present tense when speaking of Papias's writings: "Papias, an ancient man, the hearer of John and companion of Polycarp, also witnesses (ἐπιμαρτυρεῖ) to these things in writing" (cf. *Haer.* 5.33.4).

Within this context, Irenaeus makes the problematic claim that Jesus lived to be about fifty. Possibly it was the Gospel itself which the elders testified had been delivered by John, which Irenaeus held to have contained this teaching (cf. John 8:57).[14] In that case, Irenaeus would be alluding to the testimony of those identifying themselves by the pronoun "we," found in the epilogue (John 21:24), who bear witness to the truth of the eyewitness's testimony written in the Gospel, and this would indicate that Irenaeus identified the "we" with the elders.[15] An alternative possibility is suggested by Chapman, who provides evidence that Irenaeus drew his arguments about the ages of Jesus's life from a misinterpreted statement of Papias which, he argues, is preserved by Victorinus.[16]

Lastly, Irenaeus elsewhere relates that John wrote in response to the growth of heresies. John, he says, was wanting "by the proclamation of the Gospel to carry away that error which had been sown among men by Cerinthus, and a long time before by those called Nicolaitans" (*Haer.* 3.11.1). He adds that it was in order to circumscribe these teachings that John commenced his account with the words of the prologue, "In the beginning was the Word, and the Word was with God, and the Word was God" (*Haer.* 3.11.1). It has been suggested that Irenaeus may have been reliant for his information here upon Polycarp's lectures,[17] though the theme of John writing to refute heresies will reappear in other proposed Papian fragments discussed below, suggesting the possibility that this may have been derived from Papias.

## CLEMENT AND THE TRADITION OF THE ELDERS ON THE GOSPELS

According to Eusebius, Clement of Alexandria related in his lost work entitled the *Hypotyposes* "a tradition of those who were elders from the first concerning the arrangement of the Gospels" (*apud* Eusebius, *Hist. eccl.* 6.14.5), which claimed that the Gospels containing the genealogies were "written first," and which described how the Gospel of Mark came to be written. The whole account reads as follows:

> Again, Clement in his books has provided a tradition from those who were elders from the beginning concerning the arrangement (τάξις) of the Gospels, in this way: he was saying that those Gospels which had the genealogies were written first, but that the one according to Mark was administered in this manner (ἐσχηκέναι τὴν οἰκονομίαν): That when Peter preached publicly (δημοσίᾳ) in Rome and proclaimed the gospel by the Spirit, those present, being many, called upon Mark (παρακαλέσαι τὸν Μᾶρκον) to write up the things said, as one who

had followed him for a long time (ὡς ἂν ἀκολουθήσαντα αὐτῷ πόρρωθεν) and had remembered those things that were told. And that having done this, he shared this Gospel with those asking him. That, when Peter learned of it, he neither hindered it nor urged it forward. (*apud* Eusebius, *Hist. eccl.* 6.14.5–7)

The derivation of this tradition from those who "were elders from the beginning" may point to Papias as the source, since he recorded the traditions of the elders (*apud* Eusebius, *Hist. eccl.* 3.39.4). Both the theme of "arrangement" or τάξις and the reference to Mark as the follower of Peter do evoke Papias's description of Mark's Gospel, given elsewhere by Eusebius (3.39.15). Furthermore, Papias quotes the Elder as speaking of Mark as the "follower of Peter, as I said before," which presupposes a previous reference to Mark as one who followed Peter, which may refer to this account.

Eusebius then records a brief notice concerning John's Gospel which maintains, as with the description of Mark's Gospel, indirect discourse (i.e., it employs an infinitive and subject accusative), showing that this had also been related by these elders:

That John, the last (τὸν μέντοι Ἰωάννην ἔσχατον), comprehending that the corporeal (σωματικά) things were shown in the Gospels, and urged by his acquaintances (προτραπέντα ὑπο τῶν γνωρίμων), and borne along by the Spirit, composed a spiritual Gospel (πνεύματι θεοφορηθέντα πνευματικὸν ποιῆσαι εὐαγγέλιον) (*apud* Eusebius, *Hist. eccl.* 6.14.7).

## The Gospels with the Genealogies

Clement's account seems to disagree with that of Irenaeus, another proposed Papian source. While Clement states that the Gospels with the genealogies (i.e., Matthew and Luke) were "published first," Irenaeus rehearses the writing of the Gospels in the order of Matthew, Mark, Luke, and John (*apud* Eusebius, *Hist. eccl.* 5.8.2–4 = Irenaeus, *Haer.* 3.1.1). Thus, Norelli, who treats Irenaeus as a Papian source, consequently denies that Clement's passage was derived from Papias.[18]

However, while the verb προγεγράφθαι, translated as "written first" in the translation above, can mean "to write beforehand" (e.g., Eph 3:3), it can also carry the idea of "to set forth publicly" (e.g., Gal 3:1) or "publish openly" (e.g., Plutarch, *Cam.* 39.3; Appian, *Bell. Civ.* 5.113; Aeschines, *Fals. Leg.* 60) and Clement may have meant that the Gospels with the genealogies were officially sanctioned for use in the churches when they were written, not that they were written first.[19]

This definition would explain the contrast in Clement's account between the publishing of those Gospels with the initially private circulation of Mark's Gospel. Thus, Clement states that the Gospels with the genealogies were "set forth publicly," "but Mark's Gospel was administered in this manner" (literally, "had this dispensation or administration"; τὸ δὲ κατὰ Μάρκον ταύτην ἐσχηκέναι τὴν οἰκονομίαν), with the δὲ ("but") indicating a contrast.[20] He then describes how Mark came to write an account of the things that Peter had preached "publicly" and how this account, written without Peter's knowledge, initially had only a private circulation among those who requested it.[21] If προγεγράφθαι is rightly understood as referring to a public publishing of a work, then the account would have contrasted Mark's private and unofficial publication of the Gospel with the apostolically sanctioned ones of Matthew and Luke, though it provided an apology for Mark's Gospel by pointing out that even the privately circulated Gospel recorded Peter's "public" (δημοσίᾳ) preaching.[22]

The same theme is touched on earlier in Eusebius's work, where he relates, again from Clement's *Hypotyposes* (though this time Eusebius notes that the same account was found in Papias), that Peter later confirmed Mark's writing for public use in the churches. Thus, Clement relates that Peter's hearers "entreated Mark, whose Gospel is extant (οὗ τὸ εὐαγγέλιον φέρεται), since he was a follower of Peter, with all kinds of exhortations (παρακλήσεσιν δὲ παντοίαις)," to leave for them in writing a "record" (ὑπόμνημα) of Peter's teaching; he continues: "They say that the apostle, when the deed had been revealed to him by the Spirit, was pleased with the zeal of the men and confirmed (or "ratified"; κυρόω) the writing for study in the churches" (*apud* Eusebius, *Hist. eccl.* 2.15.1–2).

Both of Clement's accounts seem to tell the same story of Mark being a follower of Peter who was exhorted to write by Peter's hearers, and both likely represent the same "tradition of the elders" used by Clement. Both accounts also complement each other.[23] In one, the Gospel is circulated privately to those requesting it from Mark, in contrast to those Gospels that were set forth publicly; in the other, Peter, upon learning of it, approves it for public use. Furthermore, in the former passage (6.14.5–7), Peter is somewhat ambivalent toward the Gospel; in the latter (2.15.1–2), Peter is said to have been pleased with the zeal of those responsible, rather than with the writing itself, suggesting that he was pleased more with their good intentions than with the finished product. Both also offer a defense of Mark's Gospel; while it was not set forth publicly when it was written, one account relates that it did record the public preaching of Peter and the other that Peter himself, when he later learned of it, did ratify it for public use.

But why are only the Gospels with the genealogies mentioned as being set forth publicly, and not John's? The passage fits very well with the narrative found in other proposed Papian sources on the writing of John's Gospel discussed in this final section of the study, according to which John discussed the relative strengths and weaknesses of the τάξις (literary arrangement) of the Gospels prior to writing his own. The two accounts of how Mark came to write, taken in one case from the "tradition of the elders concerning the τάξις of the Gospels" and in the other from Papias, may have been recorded as part of John's discussion of the Synoptic Gospels, which would have contrasted Mark's Gospel with the other two Synoptics.

*Papias and the Gospel of Mark*

In Eusebius's earlier version of the account, he specifically notes that the same tradition was found in Papias: "Clement provides this story (ἱστορία) in the sixth book of his *Hypotyposes*. The bishop of Hierapolis, Papias by name, also testifies (συνεπιμαρτυρεῖ) with him" (2.15.2).[24] Indeed, Clement is said to have added that Peter mentioned Mark in his first letter, written at Rome, and to have cited 1 Pet 5:13 (2.15.2), which is also cited in other proposed Papian sources (see below). Probably both accounts of the writing of Mark's Gospel were derived from the tradition of the elders on the τάξις of the Gospels as recorded by Papias, which would mean that the tradition of the elders concerning John's Gospel was also discussed in Papias.

Eusebius cites the second passage only from Clement's work, even though he acknowledges that it was also found in Papias, and this may indicate that he only knew Papias's work through Clement, as Gustafsson has suggested,[25] noting in support that Eusebius does not specifically cite the volume of Papias's work from which the information was drawn, contrary to his usual practice.[26] He also observes that when Eusebius provides quotations from authors found in secondary sources, he often does so as though he were citing the primary authors themselves.[27]

While Clement in *Hist. eccl.* 2.15.22.15.1–2 records that Peter approved Mark's Gospel, Irenaeus claims that Mark wrote after the "departure" of Peter and Paul, which is often understood as a reference to their deaths:

> After their departure (ἔξοδος), Mark, the disciple and interpreter of Peter, also himself has handed down (παραδέδωκεν) in writing the things preached by Peter. (*apud* Eusebius, *Hist. eccl.* 5.8.2 = Irenaeus, *Haer.* 3.1.1)

Norelli, who holds that Irenaeus is (partially) dependent on Papias here, takes the discrepancy as evidence that Clement's account (apud *Hist. eccl.* 2.15.1–2) was not dependent on Papias,[28] while Winn denies that Irenaeus was dependent on Papias on the basis of the same discrepancy.[29] Others, however, argue that both may have been dependent on Papias, and that Irenaeus was using the word ἔξοδος of physical departure rather than death.[30] This would explain Irenaeus's use of the present participle κηρυσσόμενος, which implies that Peter was still alive at the time in which "the things being preached by Peter" were written down by Mark.[31]

Another version of this story found in the fourth-century commentary on the *Diatessaron* by the Syriac deacon Ephrem does speak of geographical departure:[32]

> Matthew wrote it [i.e., his Gospel] in Hebrew, and it was then translated into Greek. Mark, however, was following Simon Peter. When he had departed to Rome (*cum abiisset Romam*), they [the faithful] persuaded him [i.e., Mark], that they might recall the tradition, and lest it might fall into oblivion after a long duration of time, and he wrote that which he had comprehended.[33]

It is also noteworthy that Ephrem speaks only of Peter, rather than of both Peter and Paul (it is *abiisset* not *abiissent*), and Peter is also spoken of alone in the version of the narrative known to the Anti-Marcionite Prologue (possibly written as early as the second century[34]), which states: "He [Mark] was Peter's interpreter. After the death/departure (*post excessionem*) of Peter he wrote down (*descripsit*) this same Gospel in the regions of Italy."[35] As with ἔξοδος, the Latin *excessio* may refer to either death or physical departure.[36] Possibly this represents an earlier form of the tradition in which only the departure of Peter was mentioned.

Possibly the reading μετὰ δὲ τὴν τούτων ἔξοδον arose by error, since τούτων and τούτου were often confused by copyists.[37] A scribe reading τούτων and taking ἔξοδος as a reference to the death of Peter might have then supplied the name of the other apostle who was known to have been martyred at Rome at around the same time.

## ORIGEN ON THE FOUR GOSPELS

Origen provided an account of the origins of the four Gospels which has been partially preserved by Eusebius, and his comments on the Gospels of Matthew and Mark contain familiar Papian elements: Matthew is said to have written in Hebrew and Mark is said to have written "as Peter led the way for him" (ὡς Πέτρος ὑφηγήσατο αὐτῷ); Origen then refers to 1 Pet 5:13 in connection with Mark's relationship to Peter (*Hist. eccl.* 6.25.4–5), just as Clement does in the passage drawn from Papias (*apud* Eusebius, *Hist. eccl.* 2.15.2). Eusebius elsewhere states that Papias quoted 1 Peter, though he does not specify the passage (3.39.17).

Origen adds that Luke was the follower of Paul (6.25.6), possibly echoing the claim found in the Muratorian Canon (concerning which, see below) that Luke was Paul's travelling companion (ll. 3–5). He adds that Paul commended Luke's Gospel, which is perhaps related to tradition found in Clement concerning (as argued here) how the Gospels came to be publicly set forth. Here, it is the Apostle Paul's authority that sanctions Luke's Gospel.

Eusebius records from Origen only that John's Gospel came "after all the others" (ἐπὶ πᾶσιν) (*Hist. eccl.* 6.25.6), which agrees with Clement's statement, drawn from the tradition of the elders, that John was the last to write.

## THE MURATORIAN CANON

The beginning of the text of the Muratorian Canon is not extant, and the first complete description of a Gospel is concerning Luke's, of whom it states: "However, neither did he see the Lord in the flesh" (*dominum tamen nec ipse vidit in carne*) (l. 7), which presupposes that the previously-discussed Evangelist had also not seen the Lord.[38] This is often considered to be a reference to Mark[39] and may reflect Papias's statement that Mark had neither heard nor followed the Lord (*apud* Eusebius, *Hist. eccl.* 3.39.15).[40]

Only a few words survive concerning the evangelist mentioned before Luke: "nevertheless, he was present at these and thus he set them down [sc. "in writing"]" (*quibus tamen interfuit et ita posuit*) (l. 1). Although the evangelist was not an eyewitness, he was evidently present at something that afforded him the opportunity to write things down, which some have seen as a reference to the Papian tradition of Mark being present at Peter's preaching.[41]

A lengthier account is provided concerning John's Gospel:

> Of the fourth of the Gospels. John, one of the disciples, having been urged by his fellow disciples and bishops (*cohortantibus condiscipulis et episcopis suis*), said: "Fast with me today for three days, and if anything is revealed to anyone, let us reveal it to each other." On the same night, it was revealed to Andrew, one of the apostles, that with everyone reviewing [or, "certifying"] (*recognoscentibus cunctis*), John should write down all things in his own name. (ll. 9–16)

The motif of John being exhorted to write is also found in Clement's passage quoted above (*apud* Eusebius, *Hist. eccl.* 6.14.7).[42] Here, the additional detail is given that he was exhorted to write, "with all of them certifying" (*recognoscentibus cunctis*) (ll. 14–15), in possible allusion to the epilogue of John's Gospel in which a collective "we" testifies to the validity of John's testimony (John 21:24).[43]

The account continues:

> And therefore, although different beginnings (*principia*) may be taught in the individual books of the Gospels, nevertheless nothing differs with respect to the faith of those believing, since all things have been declared in them all, by the one principal Spirit, concerning his birth, his suffering, his resurrection, his interaction with his disciples, and concerning his double coming, the first when he was despised in humility, which has been, the second in royal power, illustrious, which is to be. What wonder is it therefore, if John so continually brings forward singular points (*singula*) in his letters, saying of himself: "What things

we have seen with our eyes and heard with our ears, and that our hands have touched, these things we have written to you." For thus he professes (*profitetur*) himself to be, not only an eyewitness and hearer, but also a writer of all the wonders of the Lord in an orderly way (ll. 16–34).

There are a number of literary parallels between this passage and Papias (or rather, the "Elder" whom Papias quotes). As Hill observes, whereas Mark is said to have written "some/several things" (ἔνια) by Papias (*apud* Eusebius, *Hist. eccl.* 3.39.15), John is said in his letters to have written "individual/several things" (*singula*) in the Muratorian Canon (1.28).[44] According to Papias, Mark wrote accurately "though not indeed with arrangement" (οὐ μέντοι τάξει) (3.39.15); Papias adds in explanation that Mark had not heard or followed the Lord but had been a follower of Peter. The Muratorian Canon on the other hand emphasizes that John was an eyewitness and hearer of the Lord and adds that he was "also a writer all the wonders of the Lord in an orderly way" (*scriptorem omnium mirabilium Domini per ordinem*) (1.33), where the Latin *per ordinem* may correspond Papias's τάξει, as Hill argues.[45] The citation from 1 John 1:1, 4 in relation to John's Gospel is also consistent with it having a Papian derivation, since Papias is said to have quoted 1 John and 1 Peter (*apud* Eusebius, *Hist. eccl.* 3.39.17).

*The Role of Andrew*

The Muratorian Canon grants an important role to the Apostle Andrew, to whom it is revealed that John should write. But as Ehrhardt notes, the narrative is clearly defective, for although it speaks of a three days' fast, "the decisive vision was seen by St. Andrew already in the first night, i.e. right at the beginning of the fast."[46]

Furthermore, other sources of the narrative do not mention Andrew. Thus, Jerome, citing "church histories" (*ecclesiastica historia*), states that John was "compelled to write by his brothers" (*cum a fratribus cogeretur ut scriberet*), and John answered that he would do it, "if everyone together would implore God in an appointed fast" (*si indicto ieiunio in commune omnes Deum precarentur*) (*Comm. Matt.* pref.).[47] An apparently unconflated version of this tradition is found in the *Golden Legend* of Jacobus de Voragine (c. 1230–1298), Archbishop of Genoa, who stated that it was the bishops of the country of Ephesus who came to John, urging him to write his Gospel, and that he instructed them to pray and fast for three days that he might truly write his account,[48] not to determine who would write, as in the Muratorian Canon; no mention is made of Andrew. The three-day fast thus seems to represent the original tradition, into which the Andrew narrative was inserted.[49]

## CHROMATIUS OF AQUILEIA

Chromatius of Aquileia (d. 406 or 407), Rufinus and Jerome's literary patron, seems to have either used the Muratorian Canon[50] or to have drawn from a common source[51] for his own discussion of the Gospels (*Tract. in Matt.* prolog. 1–3). Thus, as Lemarié points out,[52] while the Muratorian Canon says of Luke: "nevertheless, neither did he see the Lord in the flesh" (*Dominum tamen nec ipse vidit in carne*) (ll. 6–7), Chromatius[53] states: "Luke also did not see the Lord in the flesh" (*Lucas quoque Dominum in carne non vidit*) (ll. 27–28). Both similarly state that Luke was Paul's companion and wrote in his own name;[54] the Muratorian Canon reports that Paul took Luke with him, "as one studied in law" (*quasi ut iuris studiosum*) (l.4) while Chromatius describes Luke as "most learned in the law" (*eruditissimus legis*) (l.28).[55] Whereas the Muratorian Canon speaks of John as recording "all the wonders of the Lord in order (*per ordinem*)" (ll. 33–34), Chromatius depicts Luke as "describing the whole order of things (*omnem ordinem rerum*) from the beginning (*primordio*)" (ll. 31–32).

Like the Muratorian Canon (ll. 29–31), Chromatius quotes 1 John 1:1, 4 in reference to John's Gospel (ll. 23–25). Both texts also speak of the "different beginnings in the various books of the Gospels" (*varia singulis euangeliorum libris principia* in both) (Muratorian Canon, ll. 16–17; Chromatius, l. 37), while maintaining that they agree, in the words of the Muratorian Canon, "concerning the nativity, the passion, the resurrection and also concerning his twin advent" (*de nativitate, de passione, de resurrectione, de conversatione cum discipulis suis ac de gemino eius adventu*) (ll. 20–23); or, in the words of Chromatius, "concerning the nativity, the passion, the resurrection and also concerning his twin advent" (*de navititate, de passione, de resurrectione, de gemino quoque eius adventus*) (ll. 39–40).[56]

Chromatius's comments on Mark's Gospel are preserved, and he states that it was Mark who had "not seen the Lord in the flesh" (*Dominum in carne non vidit*) (ll. 25–26), lending support to the view that the Muratorian Canon had stated similarly. In Chromatius's account, Mark is portrayed as "the disciple and interpreter of Peter" (*discipulus et interpres Petri*) (l.25), strengthening the view that the accounts are dependent on Papias. Finally, echoing the words of Clement's elders, Chromatius states that John wrote "last of all" (*novissime omnium*) (l. 12).

## VICTORINUS'S DEPENDENCE ON PAPIAS

Victorinus (d. 303 or 304) tells of how the Gospel of John came to be published, relating that neighboring bishops gathered to John and compelled him to write his Gospel in response to the growth of heresies:

For when Valentinus, and Cerinthus, and Ebion, and the remaining school [of Satan] were dispersed throughout the world, all the bishops gathered to him from the neighboring cities and compelled him to write his testimony (*convenerunt ad illum de finitimis civitatibus episcopi et compulerunt eum, ut ipse testimonium conscriberet*) (*Comm. Apoc.* 11.1).[57]

Victorinus places this late in John's life, after his return from Patmos following the death of Domitian (*Comm. Apoc.* 10.11; 11.1). While Irenaeus claims that John wrote to refute Cerinthus (*Haer.* 3.11.1), Victorinus adds the names of Valentinus, who was not active until the middle of the second century, and Ebion, which probably represents a literary construction formed from the name of the Ebionites. Epiphanius similarly claims that John opposed the influence of Ebion and Cerinthus in Asia during his old age (*Pan.* 51.2.3–4).

Harnack suggests that Victorinus was dependent upon Papias for the tradition of the bishops gathering to John, noting in support the similarity of Victorinus's *episcopi de finitimis civitatibus* who compel him to write with the *episcopis suis* of the Muratorian Canon who urge him to write.[58] Papias has also been suggested as the source for Victorinus's account of Mark's Gospel,[59] which he states was not written "in order" (*non ordine*)[60] (*Comm. Apoc.* 4.4), corresponding to Papias's claim that Mark did not write "in order" (οὐ μέντοι τάξει) (cf. the Muratorian Canon's reference to John writing all things *per ordinem*).

Another possible indication of Victorinus's dependence on Papias is provided by his explanation of the twenty-four elders of Revelation as representing the twenty-four books of the Old Testament. According to the Cheltenham (or Mommsen) list of canonical works, written in Latin c. 365,[61] this exegesis was attributed by the "predecessors" (*maiores*) to "the elders" (*seniores*),[62] who are possibly to be identified with Papias's elders.[63]

## JEROME ON THE GOSPELS

The preface to Jerome's Commentary on Matthew shares a number of motifs with other proposed Papian sources, though Jerome is not dependent on any in particular. Like Papias, he relates that Matthew handed down his Gospel in the Hebrew language (*Iudaea sermone*) and that Mark was "the interpreter of Peter" who "did not see the Lord, the Savior"; he adds that he related the account "more according to the faithfulness of the events than according to order (*quam ordinem*)."[64]

Furthermore, as in the Muratorian Canon and Chromatius, Jerome relates that Luke was a physician and a follower of Paul. In common with other proposed Papian sources, he records that John was the "last" (*ultimus*) to write, and that he "was compelled (*coactus est*) to write more loftily of the Savior's divinity (*de divinitate Salvatoris*) by almost all the then bishops of Asia and embassies from many churches." In agreement with Irenaeus (*Haer.* 3.11.1) and Victorinus (*Comm. Apoc.* 11.1), Jerome states that John wrote on account of heretics, and like Victorinus he refers to "Cerinthus, Ebion and others who denied that Christ had come in the flesh." Also echoing Irenaeus, Jerome refers to the opening words of John's Gospel, though he associates them with a prophetic experience, writing that that John, "saturated with revelation (*revelatione saturatus*), gushed forth that preface from heaven (*in illud prooemium coelo veniens eructavit*)."

## PAPIAS IN THE ANTI-MARCIONITE PROLOGUE

The final potential Papian source to be discussed in this chapter is the Latin ("Anti-Marcionite") prologue to John, which is found in a number of medieval copies of the Vulgate. It survives in a shorter and longer recension, the latter of which was likely expanded using material from Jerome's *Lives*.[65] It was possibly originally written in Greek,[66] perhaps as early as the second century.[67] Recent studies have tended to date it between the fourth and sixth century,[68] though this would not rule out its use of earlier material.[69]

The prologue cites Papias as its source for its account of John's Gospel:

> The Gospel of John was made known and given to the churches by John, still in a body, as the Hierapolitan named Papias, the dear disciple of John, related in the exoteric (that is, in the last section) in his five books (*in exotericis* [*id est in extremis*] *quinque libris*). He indeed transcribed the Gospel correctly, as John dictated (*descripsit vero evangelium dictante Iohanne recte*). Truly Marcion the heretic, when he had been rejected by him because he was holding contrary opinions, was thrust out by John (*abiectus est a Iohanne*). Certainly, he had carried writings or letters sent to him from the brothers who were in Pontus (Fragment 19).[70]

This account is problematic since it depicts Marcion being thrust out by John, making them contemporaries,[71] and some have dismissed it for this reason.[72] But Orchard and Riley point out that Marcion was a contemporary of Polycarp and could have been born as early as the 70s, which would allow him to have met John in his early 20s.[73] Annand has avoided the difficulty by suggesting a different punctuation, placing the period after *abiectus est*,[74] so that "he had carried writings or letters from John, sent to him from the brothers who were in Pontus," though Schoedel notes that this would be "a rather strange word order."[75] Lastly, Lightfoot has suggested that John's confrontation with Cerinthus has become confused with Polycarp's confrontation with Marcion.[76]

The account is also questioned because it identifies Papias as John's amanuensis.[77] Lightfoot thought that the statement might have arisen based upon a misunderstanding of an original Greek reading of "they were writing down" in the imperfect, which was wrongly understood as "I was writing down" and attributed to the author, Papias.[78] Bruce suggested the verb in the original Greek might have been in the aorist, noting that the final ν of the aorist third person plural in Greek was sometimes dropped, making it indistinguishable from the first person singular.[79] But Bruce cautions that "this is chronologically possible and nothing that we know for certain rules it out of court."[80] While some argue that Eusebius would have recorded any such tradition had it been related by Papias,[81] Orchard and Riley counter that Eusebius might not have recorded it because he denied that Papias knew the Evangelist.[82]

A similar account of John dictating to Papias is found in an anonymous comment of unknown date contained in a Greek catena on the Gospel of John that was extracted from various Greek fathers:

> For the last of these, John, surnamed "the Son of Thunder," when he was a very old man (as Irenaeus and Eusebius and a succession of other trustworthy historians have handed it down to us) and about the time when terrible heresies had cropped up, dictated the Gospel to his own disciple, the virtuous Papias of Hierapolis, to complete the message of those before him who had preached [or possibly "to fill out what was lacking in those before him who had preached the Word"[83]] to the peoples of the whole world (Fragment 20 [Holmes]).[84]

Here, as in the prologue, it is stated that John was very old at the time of writing and that he dictated his Gospel to Papias, who is called his disciple, but it does not include the problematic mention of Marcion. John is also said to have completed or filled out the message of those who preached before him, in possible allusion to the Gospel of John as a work that included details omitted by the other Gospels (see chapters 9 and 10).

## CONCLUSION

The sources examined in this chapter seem to demonstrate some literary relationship through the use of shared motifs and terminology. In many cases (Irenaeus, Clement of Alexandria, the Anti-Marcionite prologue to John) these writings cite either Papias or the elders as the source for their traditions concerning the Fourth Gospel. It is therefore reasonable to conjecture that Papias likely did relate information concerning the origin of John's Gospel, notwithstanding Eusebius's silence on the matter, and that this material came to be disseminated in a number of later writings. The question of why Eusebius might have been silent concerning Papias's account of John's Gospel will be addressed in the following two chapters.

## NOTES

1. Schoedel, *Polycarp*, 106; Bauer, *Orthodoxy*, 185–91; P. Vielhauer, *Geschichte der urchristlichen Literatur* (Berlin: de Gruyter, 1975), 457; Körtner, *Papias von Hierapolis*, 197; Zuntz, "Papiana," 261. Norelli, *Papia di Hierapolis*, 114–23, is undecided on the question.

2. Joseph B. Lightfoot, *The Gospel of John: A Newly Discovered Commentary*, ed. Ben Witherington III, Todd D. Still and Jeanette M. Hagen (Downers Grove, Ill.: IVP Academic, 2015), 222 n. 26; cf. Andrew Gregory, *The Reception of Luke and Acts in the Period Before Irenaeus* (WUNT 2.169; Tübingen: Mohr Siebeck, 2003), 34.

3. Bauckham, *Testimony*, 57.

4. Bauckham, *Testimony*, 57; cf. Hengel, *Die johanneische Frage*, 88; Gregory, *Reception*, 34–35.

5. Lightfoot, *Supernatural Religion*, 205–7; Ehrhardt, *Framework*, 13; Bauckham, *Testimony*, 59–60.

6. Bauckham, *Eyewitnesses*, 430–31; Watson, *Gospel Writing*, 128.

7. Ehrhardt, *Framework*, 20; Charles Hill, "What Papias Said about John (and Luke): A 'New' Papian Fragment," *JTS* 49 (1998); cf. Gregory, *Reception*, 586.

8. Harnack, "Über den Verfasser," 9–10.

9. Bartlet, "Papias's 'Exposition,' " 26; Hill, "What Papias Said"; 34–35; cf. Gregory, *Reception*, 586.

10. Adolf von Harnack, *Die Chronologie der altchristlichen Litteratur bis Eusebius*, vol. 1 (Leipzig: Hinrichs, 1897), 334–35 n. 2; Chapman, "Papias," 57–58; Culpepper, *John*, 124; Hill, *Johannine Corpus*, 406–7; Bauckham, *Eyewitnesses*, 430–31.

11. Harnack, *Die Chronologie*, 334 n. 2.

12. Chapman, "Papias," 57 n. 1.

13. Harnack, *Die Chronologie*, vol. 1, 334 n. 2; Bacon, "The Elder John," 5.

14. Lightfoot, *Biblical Essays*, 58 n. 1; cf. Harnack, *Die Chronologie*, vol. 1, 334 n. 2; Bauckham *Eyewitnesses*, 430–31; idem, *Testimony*, 63.

15. Bauckham *Eyewitnesses*, 430–31; idem, *Testimony*, 63.

16. Chapman, "Papias," 48–63, esp. 53–63.

17. Hill, "What Papias Said," 592 n. 98.

18. Norelli, *Papia di Hierapolis*, 217.

19. See Stephen C. Carlson, "Clement of Alexandria on the 'Order' of the Gospels," *NTS* 47 (2001): 118–25. Francis Watson's response (*Gospel Writing*, 433 n. 86) relies upon a definition of τάξις as chronological order which will be challenged in chapter 9).

20. Cf. Carlson, "Clement," 123.

21. Cf. Carlson, "Clement," 123.

22. Cf. Carlson, "Clement," 123.

23. Contra Norelli who speaks of the "tensione" of the two passages (*Papia di Hierapolis*, 215–16).

24. Contra Norelli (*Papia di Hierapolis*, 213–14), who holds that Eusebius was referring only to Papias's claim, reported elsewhere, that Mark was Peter's follower and wrote down what he heard from him (*Hist. eccl.* 3.39.15).

25. B. Gustafsson, "Eusebius's Principles in Handling His Sources, as Found in His Church History, Books I to VIII," *StP* 4 (1961) 432; cf. Black, *Apostolic Interpreter*, 85.

26. Gustafsson, "Eusebius's Principles," 432; cf. Black, *Apostolic Interpreter*, 85.

27. Gustafsson, "Eusebius's Principles," 429–432; cf. Philip Sellew, "Eusebius and the Gospels," 136 n. 21.

28. Norelli, *Papia di Hierapolis*, 216.

29. Adam Winn, *The Purpose of Mark's Gospel: An Early Christian Response to Roman Imperial Propaganda* (WUNT 2.245; Tübingen: Mohr Siebeck, 2008), 49.

30. Robinson, *Redating*, 111; Ellis, *New Testament Documents*, 362 n. 28; R. T. France, *The Gospel of Mark : A Commentary on the Greek Text* (NIGTC; Grand Rapids: Eerdmans, 2002), 37; Crossley, *Date of Mark's Gospel*, 6–9.

31. See Ramelli, "John the Evangelist's Work," 33.
32. France, *Gospel of Mark*, 37.
33. Translated from the Latin text in Kurt Aland, ed., *Synopsis Quattuor Evangeliorum: Locis parallelis evangeliorum apocryphorum et patrum adhibitis edidit* (15th ed.; Stuttgart: Deutsche Bibelgesellschaft, 2001), 560; cf. Saint Éphrem, *Commentaire de l'Évangile concordant, texte syriaque (Manuscrit Chester Beatty 709)*, ed. Louis Leloir (CBM 8. Dublin: Hodges Figgis, 1963), 251.
34. Ellis, *New Testament Documents*, 359.
35. Translation in Crossley, *Date of Mark's Gospel*, 8.
36. Martin Hengel (*Studies in the Gospel of Mark* [Eugene: Wipf and Stock, 2003], 3) and Winn (*Purpose of Mark's Gospel*, 47) hold the former sense, whereas Robinson (*Redating*, 111) Ellis (*New Testament Documents*, 362); France, *Gospel of Mark*, 37), and Crossley (*Date of Mark's Gospel*, 8–9) argue for the latter.
37. E.g., Acts 25:20 where the Majority Text is divided, or Mark 10:10 where Aleph reads τούτων against the τούτου of Codices Vaticanus, Alexandrinus, and Ephraemi; cf. LXX Exod 30:23; Num 35:5; Deut 21:6; Ezra 5:17; Neh 5:16; Dan 11:4, 12:8; 2 Macc 10:3; 3 Macc 4:19; Tob 8:6; Josephus, *Ant.* 4.206, 229, 293; 5.318; 8.17; 9.266; 10.255; 11.99; 12.388; idem, *Wars* 1.141; *Mart. Pol.* 23:3.
38. Cf. Lightfoot, *Biblical Essays*, 98; Schwartz, "Über den Tod," 81–82; Ehrhardt, *Framework*, 13; Hahneman, *Muratorian Fragment*, 183–84.
39. Lightfoot, *Biblical Essays*, 98; Ehrhardt, *Framework*, 13; Orchard and Riley, *Order of the Synoptics*, 138; Hahneman, *Muratorian Fragment*, 183–84.
40. Cf. Bauckham, *Eyewitnesses*, 427.
41. Lightfoot, *Supernatural Religion*, 205–6; Bauckham, *Eyewitnesses*, 235 n.100.
42. Cf. Ehrhardt, *Framework*, 20.
43. Bauckham, *Eyewitnesses*, 431.
44. Hill, "What Papias Said," 586.
45. Cf. Hill, "What Papias Said," 586–87. Norelli argues that *per ordinem* modifies *profitetur*, so that John declared himself to have been an eyewitness, hearer and writer, in that order (Norelli, *Papia di Hierapolis*, 506–7).
46. Ehrhardt, *Framework*, 19.
47. Latin text from CCSL 77:3.
48. Jacobus de Voragine, *The Golden Legend, or, Lives of the Saints*, trans. William Caxton, ed. F. S. Ellis, vol. 2 (London: Dent, 1900), 173.
49. Cf. Ehrhardt, *Framework*, 24.
50. Joseph Lemarié, "Saint Chromace d'Aquilée témoin du Canon de Muratori," *REAug*, 24 (1978): 101–2; Verheyden, "The Canon Muratori," 552–53.
51. Travis B. Williams, *Persecution in 1 Peter* (Leiden: Brill, 2012), 139 n. 17; cf. Christoph Markschies, *Kaiserzeitliche christliche Theologie und ihre Institutionen* (Tübingen: Mohr Siebeck, 2008), 230. Possibly he derived his material from Victorinus's lost commentaries on the Gospels (cf. Verheyden, "The Muratorian Canon," 552).
52. Lemarié, "Saint Chromace," 101.
53. Translated by the author from the Latin text in Étaix, R., and J. Lemarié, eds., *Chromatii Aquileiensis Opera* (CCSL 9A; Turnhout: Brepols, 1974)185–86.
54. Lemarié, "Saint Chromace," 101.
55. Cf. Lemarié, "Saint Chromace," 102; Williams, *Persecution in 1 Peter*, 139 n. 17.
56. Cf. Lemarié, "Saint Chromace," 101.
57. Translated by the author from the Latin text in Haussleiter.
58. Harnack, "Über den Verfasser," 9–10.
59. Chapman, "Papias," 48–49; Schoedel, *Polycarp*, 92.
60. Chapman, "Papias," 48.
61. Hahneman, *Muratorian Fragment*, 145.
62. From the Latin text as given by Erwin Preuschen, *Analecta: Kürzere texte zur Geschichte der Alten Kirche und des Kanons, zusammengestellt von Erwin Preuschen* (Leipzig: Mohr, 1893), 139.

63. Chapman, "Papias," 48. Other examples of Victorinus's probable Papian dependence are given by Chapman ("Papias," 48–63) and Schoedel (*Polycarp*, 94, 96, 104, 115–16, 125, 126–27).

64. Translated by the author from the Latin text in CCSL 77:2–3.

65. So, e.g., Engelbert Gutwenger, "The Anti-Marcionite Prologues," *TS* 7 (1946): 399.

66. Lightfoot, *Supernatural Religion*, 213; Schoedel, *Polycarp*, 121; F. F. Bruce, *The Gospel of John: Introduction, Exposition, Notes* (Grand Rapids: Eerdmans, 1983), 9. This is disputed by Gutwenger, "The Anti-Marcionite Prologues," 408.

67. Donatien de Bruyne, "Les plus anciens prologues latins des Évangiles," *RevBén* 40 (1928): 193–214; W. F. Howard, "The Anti-marcionite prologues to the Gospels," *ExpT* 47 (1936): 534–38.

68. Cf. Culpepper, *John*, 130. Hahneman thinks the prologue to John was written in the fourth or fifth century (*Muratorian Fragment*, 108).

69. Orchard and Riley, *Order of the Synoptics*, 141.

70. Translated by the author from the Latin text in Aland, *Synopsis*, 549.

71. E.g., de Bruyne, "anciens prologues," 208–9; Braun, *Jean le Théologien*, vol. 1, 349; Jürgen Regul, *Die antimarcionitischen Evangelienprologe* (*VL* 6; Freiburg: Verlag Herder, 1969), 100–101; Norelli, *Papia di Hierapolis*, 462.

72. E.g., Chapman, *John the Presbyter*, 101; Schoedel, *Polycarp*, 121–22; Smalley, *John*, 77.

73. Orchard and Riley, *Order of the Synoptics*, 153–54.

74. Annand, "Four Gospels," 60.

75. Schoedel, *Polycarp*, 122.

76. Lightfoot, *Supernatural Religion*, 212–13.

77. . E.g., Chapman, *John the Presbyter*, 101; Schoedel, *Polycarp*, 122; Bauckham, *Testimony*, 51 n. 68.

78. Lightfoot, *Supernatural Religion*, 214; cf. Schoedel, *Polycarp*, 122.

79. Bruce, "St John at Ephesus," 346 n. 3; *The Gospel of John*, 9–10; cf. Schoedel, *Polycarp*, 122.

80. Bruce, "St John at Ephesus," 346.

81. Schoedel, *Polycarp*, 123; Culpepper, *John*, 130.

82. Orchard and Riley, *Order of the Synoptics*, 154–55.

83. The alternative translation is suggested by Holmes.

84. Holmes follows the Greek edition of B. Corder or Corderius, *Catena patrum Graecorum in sanctum Ioannem* (Antwerp, 1630). Cf. Culpepper, *John*, 112.

# NINE
## John on the Τάξις of the Gospels

In his *Ecclesiastical History*, Eusebius relates an account of how the Synoptic Gospels were brought to John, who noted their omission of the earlier ministry of Christ; John was then urged to write his own Gospel, which narrated the events left out by the others (*Hist. eccl.* 3.24.5–13).[1] Eusebius does not cite his source, but Bartlet has suggested that he "almost certainly" paraphrased Papias,[2] a position which has been defended at length by Hill, who sees the Papian identification of Eusebius's source as providing evidence that Papias distinguished John the Elder from the Evangelist.[3]

This chapter will revisit Hill's arguments, both for the Papian derivation of the fragment and for his claim that Papias identified the Elder and the Evangelist. It will also consider objections raised against the thesis by Bauckham,[4] and in particular Bauckham's claim that the argument of the unattributed fragment differs from that of Papias and therefore could not have been dependent upon him. While this chapter will argue that Bauckham's objections fail to overturn the thesis of the Papian derivation of the fragment, it will also conclude, contrary to Hill, that the fragment's depiction of the Evangelist is similar to Papias's depiction of the Elder, favoring the suggestion that Papias identified the two figures. It will further argue that Eusebius summarized Papias without attribution so as not to draw attention to these similarities, thus obscuring Papias's identification of the two.

### EUSEBIUS'S UNATTRIBUTED PASSAGE

In the unattributed fragment, Eusebius relates that although "the twelve apostles, the seventy disciples, and besides these countless others" were not ignorant of Christ's works, only two, Matthew and John, left written records (ὑπομνήματα), and only, as "an account holds it" (κατέχει λόγος), due to necessity (3.24.5). Matthew, Eusebius continues, put his Gospel into writing to compensate for his departure to preach to others (3.24.6). But John, he continues, came to write as follows:

> (7) When Mark and Luke had already made the publication (τὴν ἔκδοσιν) of their Gospels, they say (φασί) that John preached the whole time without writing but that he finally came to write for the following reason: With the three that were formerly written having been distributed to all, and to him, it is said that he approved them, bearing witness to their truth on the one hand, saying only on the other that the narrative (τὴν διήγησιν) concerning the things done (πεπραγμένων) by Christ at first and at the beginning of his preaching (κατ' ἀρχὴν τοῦ κηρύγματος) was missing to the writing. (8) And this account is true (καὶ ἀληθής γε ὁ λόγος).

Eusebius then inserts some parenthetical comments:

> In fact, it is possible to see that the three Gospels recorded only the things done by the Savior which took place for one year after the confinement of John the Baptist in prison, and that they indicated this at the beginning of their narrative. (9) In fact, Matthew makes clear the period after the forty-day fast and the temptation which followed, saying: "having heard that John had been delivered up, he withdrew from Judea into Galilee" [Matt. 14:12]; (10) and Mark in like manner says: "after the delivering up of John, Jesus came into Galilee" [Mark 1:14]; and Luke observes almost the same thing before he makes a beginning (ἄρξασθαι) of the deeds of Jesus, saying that Herod, adding to the wicked deeds which he had done, "shut up John in prison" [Luke 3:20].

Eusebius resumes the account as follows:

> (11) They say (φασί) therefore that the apostle John, exhorted (παρακληθέντα) on account of these things, delivered in his own Gospel [an account of] the period which was passed over in silence (παρασιωπηθέντα χρόνον) by the former evangelists and [an account of] the things done by the Savior during it (those were the things done before the confinement of John); and that he indicated the same thing, saying thereafter (τότε): "this beginning of marvels did Jesus" (ταύτην ἀρχὴν ἐποίησεν τῶν παραδόξων ὁ Ἰησοῦς) [John 2:11], and then by having made mention of the Baptist within [his account of] the deeds of Jesus as still at that time baptizing in Aenon near Salem [John 3:23], and [they say] that he clearly shows the same thing in saying: "for John was not yet thrown into prison" [John 3:24].

He proceeds to draw some conclusions, providing a few additional details as he does so:

> (12) John then, in the writing which is his Gospel, hands down the things done with reference to Christ when John had not yet been thrown into prison, but the other three make mention of the things

done after the confinement of the Baptist in prison. (13) For the one paying attention to these things (or "to them," i.e., "the Gospels"), it would no longer seem that the Gospels disagree with each other, in that the one according to John encompasses the first of the deeds of Christ, while the others encompass the narrative of what was done by him at the end of the period. With respect to the genealogy of the flesh of our Savior, therefore, John reasonably maintained silence (ἀποσιωπῆσαι), seeing that it was already written out by Matthew and Luke, and he began with the doctrine of the divinity (τῆς δὲ θεολογίας), as though it were reserved for him as their better/superior from the divine Spirit (*Hist. eccl.* 3.24.5–13).

Eusebius introduces the account with the words κατέχει λόγος (3.24.5), and Hill draws attention to the conclusion of Lawlor that in the majority of cases in which Eusebius introduces an account with these words, a written source is being referred to, or is at least not excluded.[5] Lawlor, however, thought that only the account of the writing of Matthew's Gospel was drawn from a written source, noting that the account of John's Gospel is introduced by φασί ("they say") instead.[6] But as Hill observes, Eusebius records that this λόγος related how both Matthew and John came to write out of necessity, and Eusebius goes on to record details concerning both, presumably from the same λόγος.[7] Hill further notes that after relating how both Gospels came to be written, Eusebius affirms in line 8 that "this account (λόγος) is true," with "the λόγος here naturally referring to the preceding one"[8] and concluding the account begun in line 5. Both accounts therefore seem to derive from the same written source.

The use of φασί does not militate against this, for Eusebius also employs this word in his account of the writing of Mark's Gospel, taken from Clement's *Hypotyposes*, a written source. Presumably he employs φασί because the account was reliant upon the oral tradition of the elders (*apud* Eusebius, *Hist. eccl.* 2.15.1–2) which, as argued above, was drawn from Papias. The same may be the case here.

Hill suggests that lines 8 to 10 represent either Eusebius's own conclusions or those of his source,[9] while Bauckham, in his list of qualifications for Hill's identification of the passage as Papian (see below), probably rightly thinks that these lines represent "Eusebius's own explanatory comment."[10] The source is resumed again in line 11, which Eusebius again introduces with φασί, followed by Eusebius's own concluding remarks in lines 12–13, which Bauckham allows "may pick up some of the vocabulary of the source."[11]

## HILL'S ARGUMENTS FOR PAPIAN DEPENDENCY

Only the most significant of Hill's arguments in favor of the unattributed fragment's Papian dependency can be rehearsed here. First, Hill draws attention to motifs shared by proposed Papian sources and Eusebius's unattributed fragment. Thus, John is exhorted to write (παρακληθέντα) in the unattributed fragment just as Peter's hearers beseech Mark with exhortations (παρακλήσεσιν) in Clement's account (*apud* Eusebius, *Hist. eccl.* 2.15.1).[12] John himself is also urged to write in Clement (προτραπέντα) (6.14.7), the Muratorian Canon (*cohortantibus*) (l. 10), and Victorinus (*compulerunt*) (*Comm. Apoc.* 11.1).[13] Furthermore, while Clement refers to Mark's Gospel as a "record" (ὑπόμνημα) of Peter's preaching (*apud* Eusebius, *Hist. eccl.* 2.15.1), the unattributed fragment relates that Matthew and John left written records (ὑπομνήματα).[14]

Hill also draws attention to the "unconventional" citation of John 2:11 in the unattributed fragment, which speaks of the miracle at Cana as the beginning of Jesus's "marvels" (τῶν παραδόξων), rather than of his "signs" (τῶν σημείων) as in John's Gospel, and he posits a connection between this and the Muratorian Canon's description of John as a writer of "all the wonders of the Lord in order" (*omnium mirabilium Domini per ordinem*), noting that Jerome's Vulgate translates παράδοξος (which only occurs once in the New Testament, at Luke 5:26) with *mirabilium*.[15]

Hill also notes verbal forms common to the unattributed fragment and Papias's Elder; thus, the verb ποιεῖν is used three times in the middle voice in Papias's short excerpt (3.39.15) and once in the unattributed fragment (3.24.7); similarly, while Papias's Elder describes Mark as recording "the things said or done by the Lord" (3.39.15) using the passive aorist participle πραχθέντα, the unattributed fragment uses the passive aorist or perfect participle of the same verb four times in similar contexts (3.24.7, 8, 11).[16]

### *John the Evangelist and John the Elder*

On the basis of the similarities between the language of the unattributed fragment and the words attributed to Papias's Elder on Matthew and Mark in *Hist. eccl.* 3.39.15–16, Hill deduces that Eusebius's fragment was likely reporting the direct words of Papias's Elder on the origins of John's Gospel, just as Eusebius elsewhere records his words on the origins of Matthew and Mark. Thus, it would have been the Elder who related that the Synoptics Gospels were brought to John the Evangelist, who approved them. But if, as Hill argues, the Elder was describing John in the third person, then this would represent "the ultimate proof" that Papias did not identify the Elder and the Evangelist, since the Elder "describes John, obviously, as a person distinct from himself."[17] This significant conclusion will be further discussed below.

## BAUCKHAM'S OBJECTIONS

Bauckham raises a number of qualifications of and/or objections to Hill's identification, of varying strength and relevancy.[18] His first qualification is that Hill does not sufficiently delineate Eusebius's own editorial comments (i.e., lines 8–10 and 12–13) from his source.[19] Hill does, however, allow for Bauckham's delineations with respect to lines 8–10,[20] and while he does not clearly address 12–13, he does refer to line 12 as representing "Eusebius' paraphrase and summary of his source"[21] and to line 13 as ending Eusebius's own "reflections" on the source, thus distinguishing Eusebius's comments in lines 12–13 from the source.[22]

Bauckham also observes that Eusebius was paraphrasing his source,[23] though this does not affect Hill's thesis, and Hill in any case had made this point himself.[24] In his third qualification, Bauckham questions whether φασί ("they say") can be used of a written source, though he acknowledges that it is used by Eusebius when he relates from Clement's *Hypotyposes* an account of the writing of Mark's Gospel (*Hist. eccl.* 2.15.1-2), which Bauckham accepts was drawn by Clement from the "tradition of the elders" (*Hist. eccl.* 6.14.5); he concedes that if Eusebius's source "is Papias, then Papias could be citing what he had heard that the elders had said or what he had heard that John the Elder had said,"[25] which, as Hill notes, is supportive of his thesis.[26]

Bauckham next argues that Papias and Eusebius's source could not both have spoken of Matthew's Gospel in the same context. Papias states that Matthew "made an orderly arrangement" (συνετάξατο) of Jesus's *logia* in Hebrew, demonstrating, Bauckham maintains, that "Papias is concerned with the issue of order in the Gospels," whereas the fragment speaks of Matthew writing from compulsion; he concludes: "The two statements cannot be combined into a single account from the same context."[27] But Mark's "order" is spoken of by Papias, (3.39.15) and, according to Clement, in a passage which Bauckham holds was derived from Papias,[28] Mark is spoken of as having been urged to write (6.14.6; cf. 2.15.1).[29] If Papias made both statements about Mark, as Bauckham himself accepts, then there is no reason to assume he could not have made them about Matthew also. In any case the insistence that Papias had to have made both statements in the same immediate context is unnecessary.

Bauckham in his fifth point claims that the argument of Papias and of the unattributed fragment differ, so that the unattributed fragment could not have been derived from Papias. This is the most significant of Bauckham's objections to Hill's thesis, and it will be examined in more detail below.

The last of Bauckham's points does not challenge the thesis itself, but rather the inference which Hill draws from it, namely that Papias must have distinguished the Evangelist from John the Elder. Bauckham objects that Eusebius, who held the Zebedean authorship of the Fourth Gospel, would have adapted his source "to conform to his own view of the Gospel's authorship," and he suggests that this was Eusebius's reason for choosing to paraphrase his source.[30] This study will return to this question later in the chapter, where it will provide additional support for Bauckham's position.

## BAUCKHAM'S ARGUMENT FROM ΤΆΞΙΣ

In his fifth point, Bauckham objects that while both Papias and the unattributed fragment are concerned with the problem of the varying "order" (τάξις) of the Gospels, their proposed solutions differ, ruling out the possibility that Eusebius's account could have been summarized from Papias.[31] Thus, according to Bauckham, Papias "freely admits that Mark's Gospel is not 'in order' and excuses Mark for this"; he further infers from this that Papias's solution to the problem of the variances of the Gospels would have been that John's Gospel, unlike Matthew and Mark's, did "follow a correct chronological order."[32] By contrast, the unattributed fragment, Bauckham claims, denies that there is any chronological variance between the Gospels and solves any potential discrepancy by placing the beginning of John's narrative before the Galilean ministry.[33]

However, it is not at all clear that the source of the unattributed fragment was seeking to resolve the issue of the discrepancies of the Gospels, for the claim that the Gospels are not in disagreement is found in lines 12 and 13, and as Bauckham himself notes in one of his qualifications, these comments belong to Eusebius, not his source.[34] The fragment itself only states that John's Gospel records the deeds done by Christ at the beginning of Jesus's ministry, before the Baptist was thrown in prison, which were omitted by the others; it does not address the issue of the discrepancies of the Gospels, and it does not deny, or even address, the possibility that Mark's Gospel might not have been written in order.

Furthermore, Bauckham assumes that Papias was proposing a solution to the chronological variance of the Gospels, but Papias only states that Mark was not written "in order," and contrary to Bauckham, he does not deny that Matthew's Gospel was written in order, for he states that Matthew "put in order (συνετάξατο) the oracles in the Hebrew dialect" (*Hist. eccl.* 3.39.16).

More importantly, Bauckham's argument is predicated on understanding Papias's reference to τάξις as denoting chronological order, so that he is able to equate the fragment's (or rather Eusebius's) concern over the variances of the Gospels (which it solves by placing some events in John's Gospel before the Synoptic ministry) with Papias's concern for τάξις. But Stewart-Sykes points out that the Greek historians did not use τάξις of the order of events, noting that Thucydides (*Hist.* 1.97) and Philostratus (*Vita Apoll.* 1.2) speak of a writing's chronological accuracy in terms of its accuracy "with respect to times" (τοῖς χρόνοις).[35] Furthermore, a number of scholars have argued that τάξις refers to literary rather than chronological arrangement,[36] and Bauckham himself accepts that τάξις does not refer to "chronological sequence as such but to the orderly arrangement of material in a literary composition,"[37] though he maintains that chronological order is not excluded from the meaning.[38]

Hengel, who like Bauckham also argues that τάξις can denote chronological order, cites in support the first-century Romano-Jewish historian Josephus (*Ant.* 1.17) and the second-century Syrian rhetorician Lucian (*de Cons. Hist.* 6).[39] Josephus states that he would indicate the things in the Scriptures "according to their proper order" (κατὰ τὴν οἰκείαν τάξιν) without either adding or taking away anything (οὐδὲν προσθεὶς οὐδ' αὖ παραλιπών), while Lucian's writes that the historian must consider:

> what kind of beginning (ἀρχή) it is to commence with, what arrangement (τάξις) is suitable for the deeds, the proportion (μέτρον) of each part; which things must be passed over in silence (σιωπητέον) and which things should be dwelt upon; what things it is better to hurry through; and how to explain and combine these things (*de Cons. Hist.* 6).[40]

However, in neither case is it necessary for τάξις to be understood of chronological ordering. As Stewart-Sykes notes: "Since in each instance the reference is to the task of ordering a series of events into a narrative, a reference to chronology has to be inferred."[41] Indeed, Josephus and Lucian's comments are consistent with a rhetorical concern for the appropriate inclusion and omission of material, which is part of what constituted good τάξις according to rhetoricians (see below).

Bauckham seems to understand τάξις as referring either to thematic or chronological arrangement, which he then employs as an argument for understanding Papias as speaking of chronological ordering, claiming that Papias clearly uses τάξις in the chronological rather than topical sense since Mark's absence at the events he narrates would not have prevented him from applying topical arrangement to the narrative, whereas it would have hindered him from placing it in chronological order.[42] However, while Mark's absence would not have prevented him from organizing his work thematically, it would have prevented him from supplying the sort of literary τάξις described by the rhetoricians, which was concerned, not with topical arrangement, but with the appropriate selection and correlation of material, irrespective of whether it was related chronologically or topically.

Thus, the famous Roman rhetorician Quintilian (35 CE–c. 100) discusses "arrangement" (*disposito* = τάξις) in his *Institutes*, in which he defines it as "the distribution of things and parts to the places which it is expedient that they should occupy" (*Inst. Or.* 7.1.1 [Butler, LCL]). He goes on to note that the arrangement would not always look the same, but might differ, depending on whether the work was ordered chronologically or topically (*Inst. Or.* 7.1.2 [Butler, LCL]).

Quintilian also describes those works which lack "arrangement," speaking of them in such a way as to demonstrate that the literary shape of the work was his main concern. He thus writes that these works

> cannot fail to be confused, but will be like a ship drifting without a helmsman, will lack cohesion, will fall into countless repetitions and omissions, and, like a traveller who has lost his way in unfamiliar country, will be guided solely by chance without fixed purpose or the least idea either of starting-point or goal (Quintilian, *Inst. Or.* 7. prolog. 3 [Butler, LCL]).[43]

Therefore, works lacking arrangement are those that lack cohesion, purpose, a clear starting point, and an end goal; they are also said to contain "countless repetitions and omissions." Whether a work is arranged chronologically or topically does not appear to be a concern.

The issues of both the inclusion and omission of material are mentioned by Lucian, in the passage cited by Hengel, who states that the historian must consider "which things must be passed over in silence and which things should be dwelt upon" (*de Cons. Hist.* 6). And while Quintilian speaks of the omission of material, the Greek rhetorician Dionysius of Halicarnassus (fl. c. 20 BCE) notes that the historian was not simply to include any random fact but was to choose the material for inclusion carefully. He thus criticizes Thucydides for including "petty details" in his history, asking,

> What necessity (ἀναγκαῖον) was there of speaking about the luxurious mode of life in which the Athenians of olden time indulged, stating that they plaited their hair into "buns" on the nape of the neck and wore golden cicadas on their heads and that the Lacedaemonians "were the first to strip themselves and openly removing their clothes anointed themselves with oil as they exercised"? What suitable occasion (καιρός) was there for telling in advance of the narrative (διήγησις) about the Corinthian shipbuilder Aminocles, who was the first man to build triremes for the Samians . . . (*Thuc.* 19).[44]

Colson observes that the "realistic touches" in Mark, such as his notice that Jesus was "with the wild beasts" when he was tempted in the desert (Mark 1:13) and that he was sleeping "on a pillow" (Mark 4:38), as well as his reference to the "green grass" (Mark 6:39) and his inclusion of the story of the young man who fled naked and left his linen cloak (Mark 14:51–52), would have seemed like unnecessary trivialities to Dionysius.[45]

Mark's inclusion of these notices, however, could have also been excused on the basis that he was reliant upon Peter's preaching, for Papias states that he was resolved "not to leave out (παραλιπεῖν) anything of what he had heard" (*apud* Eusebius, *Hist. eccl.* 3.39.15).

*The Starting Point and Goal*

Quintilian's concern for a suitable starting point and goal is also echoed by Dionysius of Halicarnassus, who criticizes Thucydides for his lack of order (τάξις) in having an unsuitable beginning and ending for his narrative:

> Some critics also find fault with his order (αἰτιῶνται δὲ καὶ τὴν τάξιν αὐτοῦ τινες), claiming that he has neither made a proper beginning nor brought it to a suitable close. These people say that the most important feature of a good arrangement (οἰκονομία) is to adopt as a starting-point something that is not preceded by anything else (ἀρχήν τε λαβεῖν, ἧς οὐκ ἂν εἴη τι πρότερον), and to bring the treatise to such a close that it will seem to be really complete and lack nothing (καὶ τέλει περιλαβεῖν τὴν πραγματείαν, ᾧ δόξει μηδὲν ἐνδεῖν), but Thucydides has not properly attended to either of these two matters (*Thuc.* 10). [46]

The *Exercises* (*Progymnasmata*), generally attributed to Theon of Alexandria who lived in the first century CE, discusses what constitutes a suitable beginning for a historical writing:

> In historical writing it is perhaps appropriate to spin things out and to begin far back and to explain some of the things that seem incidental. . . . For example, speaking about Cylon, if one is composing a history of him it is appropriate to say from what ancestors he descended and from what father and mother and many other things, the event in which he competed at Olympia and what victories he earned, and to give the dates of his victories. . . (Theon, *Progym* 83–84). [47]

Lucian, in the passage cited by Hengel, also raises the issue of adequate beginnings, noting that the historian must consider "what kind of beginning" the work "is to commence with" (*de Cons. Hist.* 6). Later in his work Lucian discusses the relationship which the beginning is to have to the rest of the work, arguing that the introduction must be in due proportion to other sections of the narrative. Some historians, he complains, write long and elevated introductions while the body of writing is short and base, which he likens to placing a colossal head on the body of a dwarf (*de Cons. Hist.* 23–24).[48] Others, he adds, produce headless bodies by commencing the narrative without first providing an introduction (*de Cons. Hist.* 23).

These criticisms would have been pertinent to Mark's Gospel. Matthew and Luke did begin their narratives "far back" and they explain the circumstances of Jesus's birth, ancestry, and early life, in conformity with Theon's advice. They also commenced their narratives at the very beginning, with Jesus's birth, in accordance with Dionysius's advice that a work begin with "something that is not preceded by anything else." By contrast, Mark's Gospel was, so to speak, a headless body, opening abruptly with the narrative of the baptism of John; furthermore, it contained only vague references to time and place and lacked any explanation as to who John was. Its beginning was thus deficient with respect to τάξις,[49] but this would have been excusable if Mark was not in possession of the kind of background knowledge and facts that would have enabled him to write a suitable introduction, due to his sole reliance for his information on the preaching of Peter, who did not intend to provide a "complete arrangement" (σύνταξις) of events (that is, a rhetorically balanced history).

## RHETORICAL CONCERNS IN THE UNATTRIBUTED FRAGMENT

These rhetorical concerns are also reflected in the unattributed fragment. An interest in the question of the starting point of the narrative is seen is the claim that John wrote about the things preached by Christ "at first and at the beginning of his preaching," which were missing to the other Gospels; in editorial comments that likely reflect the terminology of his source, Eusebius adds that John "began with the doctrine of the divinity," and he alludes to the inclusion of the genealogies in Matthew and Luke's Gospels (*Hist. eccl.* 3.24.5–13).

According to Lucian, the historian must decide on "which things must be passed over in silence (σιωπητέον)." This also seems to be reflected in the fragment, which relates that John provided an account of "the period which was passed over in silence (παρασιωπηθέντα χρόνον) by the former evangelists," and which adds that John "reasonably maintained silence (ἀποσιωπῆσαι)" concerning the genealogy of Jesus, "seeing that it was already written out by Matthew and Luke." The explanation that John did not need to repeat what had already been discussed before perhaps also reflects the concern for not repeating material, seen in Quintilian's note that oratory lacking "arrangement" would not "will fall into countless repetitions and omissions."[50]

Thus, it is not that Papias denied that Mark lacked chronological order while the unattributed fragment affirmed that the Gospels could be resolved chronologically, as Bauckham argues. Rather, Papias's Elder speaks of the τάξις of Mark and Matthew while the unattributed fragment depicts John the Evangelist as discussing the literary features of the Synoptics in ways that are associated with τάξις by the rhetoricians. Far from making divergent points, as Bauckham holds, both Papias and the unattributed fragment can be seen to be discussing the τάξις of the Gospels.

## ΤΆΞΙΣ AND JOHN THE ELDER

While this definition of τάξις challenges Bauckham's chief objection against the thesis of the unattributed fragment's dependency on Papias, it nevertheless furnishes support for his sixth point and undermines Hill's claim that Papias distinguished John the Evangelist from the Elder.

According to Hill, the unattributed fragment records the direct speech of John the Elder concerning the four Gospels, requiring that the Elder spoke of John the Evangelist in the third person.[51] He would therefore reconstruct Papias as having written something along the lines of: "The Elder said that John wrote for the following reason: when the Gospels were brought to him, he approved them, etc." However, the mention of the three Gospels in the unattributed fragment is subordinated to the narrative of how the Gospel of John came to be written. The Synoptics are brought to John the Evangelist, and he evaluates them in terms of their inclusion and omission of events, that is, with respect to their τάξις, before writing his own Gospel, which rectified the deficiencies of τάξις found in the Synoptics. Turning to Papias, it is the Elder who discusses the τάξις of two Synoptics, Matthew and Mark. Thus, in evaluating the τάξις of Synoptic Gospels, Papias's Elder was doing the very thing which the unattributed fragment ascribed to the Evangelist, suggesting that in Papias, John the Evangelist was "the Elder."

## EUSEBIUS AND THE VARIANCE OF THE GOSPELS

Eusebius's own editorial comments in the fragment exhibit interest in the question of the alleged discrepancies of the Gospels, which evokes the debate which engaged the minds of Gaius, Hippolytus, Origen, and Epiphanius, discussed in chapter 5. Indeed, Origen had argued in his *Commentary on John* against the possibility of harmonizing John's Gospel with the Synoptics at a historical level,[52] and he had challenged those disagreeing with him to resolve the discrepancy concerning when Jesus came to Capernaum, which, he asserts, could not be done:

> Let those who accept the four Gospels and who think the apparent discrepancy (τὴν δοκοῦσαν διαφωνίαν) is not to be solved through the anagogical sense tell us when the Lord came to Capharnaum [i.e., Capernaum] in relation to the difficulty we mentioned earlier concerning the forty days of temptation which can have no place at all in John. For if it occurred six days after the time when he was baptized, since his ministry at the marriage in Cana of Galilee took place on the sixth day, it is clear that he has not been tempted, nor was he in Nazareth, nor had John yet been delivered up (*Comm. John* 10.2).[53]

Eusebius was familiar with Origen's *Commentary on John*, for he quotes from its fifth book (*Hist. eccl.* 6.25.7–10), and he may have been answering

Origen directly (though not by name, perhaps on account of his great respect for him). Manor notes that while Origen speaks of "the apparent discrepancy" (τὴν δοκοῦσαν διαφωνίαν) concerning when Jesus came to Capernaum, Eusebius argues that, "For the one paying attention to these things, the Gospels will no longer seem to disagree (οὐκέτ᾽ ἂν δόξει διαφωνεῖν) with each other" (*Hist. eccl.* 3.24.13), using the related verbal forms, as if in direct response to Origen.[54]

As Manor further observes, while Origen states that it would be impossible for anyone taking the Gospels as a historical account (ἱστορία) to think that what they were recording was true (*Comm. John* 10.3), Eusebius in his editorial comments does refer to the Gospels as histories (ἱστορίας, ἱστορίαν) (*Hist. eccl.* 3.24.8, 13), whereas he calls them "recollections" (ὑπομνήματα) when drawing from his source (*Hist. eccl.* 3.24.5; cf. the reference to Mark's Gospel as a ὑπόμνημα in Clement's account in *Hist. eccl.* 2.15.1).[55]

Eusebius also seems to be responding to Origen's particular argument against the historical veracity of John's Gospel. According to Origen's schema, the Johannine account placed the commencement of Jesus's Galilean ministry just days after his baptism, whereas the Synoptics inserted a period of forty days between these events, demonstrating, to Origen's mind, that John's Gospel was not a historical account. This schema, as discussed in chapter 5, was predicated on two mistaken correlations: the first was the correlation of the Johannine account of Jesus's encounter with the Baptist and the Synoptic account of Jesus's baptism by the Baptist, and the second, which naturally resulted from it, was that of Jesus's subsequent journey to Cana, in John's account, and the journey of Jesus to Galilee following his temptation, as related in the Synoptics.

Eusebius addresses only the second correlation. To rebut it, he observes that the Synoptics fix the time of the Galilean ministry as having taken place after John's imprisonment, and he further observes that they note this only after relating the temptation, thus leaving an unaccounted-for period between the temptation and the imprisonment of John, after which time the Galilean ministry began. This unaccounted-for period in the Synoptics removed any necessity for placing the Synoptic journey to Galilee in temporal proximity to Jesus's baptism, as Origen's correlation required. Eusebius was subsequently free to posit that the Johannine account depicted an earlier visit to Cana in Galilee, noting that "the beginning of Jesus's miracles" (i.e., the miracle at Cana) took place before the Baptist's imprisonment. This would have directly answered Origen's claim that John's Gospel was in error since it depicted Jesus commencing his Galilean ministry before the Baptist's imprisonment. Furthermore, Eusebius was able to claim that there was support for his view in an older (though unspecified) Christian tradition, from which he no doubt drew his information.

Eusebius does not address whether Jesus's encounter with the Baptist was the occasion of his baptism. Had he differentiated these occasions, he could have simply placed the narrative of Jesus's encounter with the Baptist and the subsequent journey to Cana sometime between the baptism and temptation of Jesus and John's later imprisonment, which would have rendered the rest of his argument superfluous. Presumably he did not do so because he, like Origen, also correlated the Johannine account of Jesus's encounter with the Baptist with the Synoptic account of Jesus's baptism, and he focused instead on the fact that the Synoptic Galilean ministry occurred at some undefined time after the temptation. Eusebius may have held that Jesus went to Cana and Capernaum within days of his baptism and that he immediately returned to Judea afterward, where he was tempted.

## CONCLUSION

Hill has made the case that Eusebius's unattributed fragment derives from Papias, drawing attention to motifs and literary parallels which the fragment shares with Papias and proposed Papian sources. Bauckham, however, has argued that the passage cannot be dependent upon Papias as it denies that there is any chronological variance between the Gospels whereas Papias acknowledges Mark's lack of chronological ordering. It was pointed out in response that it is Eusebius who denies the chronological variance of the Gospels in an editorial comment, and not his source. Furthermore, Bauckham is reliant for his argument upon a likely mistaken interpretation of Papias's τάξις as denoting chronological ordering rather than literary arrangement.

However, this definition of τάξις in terms of literary arrangement was seen to undermine Hill's claim that John the Elder spoke of the Evangelist in the third person and that he was consequently not identified as the Evangelist by Papias. Rather, the Evangelist's discussion of the inclusion and omission of material in the Gospels correlates with the mention of the τάξις of Matthew and Mark by Papias's Elder, suggesting that the words which Papias attributed to the Elder may have originally been recorded within the context of the Evangelist's evaluation of the Synoptic Gospels, leading to the conclusion that for Papias, the Elder was the Evangelist. Eusebius, who identified the Evangelist with the Apostle, perhaps failed to cite Papias so as not to draw attention to the obvious similarities between Papias's Elder and the Evangelist of his source.

## NOTES

1. A shorter version of chapters 9 and 10 was previously published by the author as, "Theodore of Mopsuestia: New Evidence for the Proposed Papian Fragment in *Hist. eccl.* 3.24.5-13," *JSNT* 39 (2016): 209–29.
2. Bartlet, "Papias's 'Exposition,'" 26.
3. Hill, "What Papias Said."
4. Bauckham, *Eyewitnesses*, 433–37.
5. Hill, "What Papias Said," 589–90; cf. Lawlor, *Eusebiana*, 22; Chapter 6.
6. Lawlor, *Eusebiana*, 22.
7. Hill, "What Papias Said," 591.
8. Hill, "What Papias Said," 592.
9. Hill, "What Papias Said," 593–94.
10. Bauckham, *Eyewitnesses*, 433.
11. Bauckham, *Eyewitnesses*, 433.
12. Hill, "What Papias Said," 592.
13. Hill, "What Papias Said," 596.
14. Hill, "What Papias Said," 593.
15. Hill, "What Papias Said," 597–98.
16. Hill, "What Papias Said," 595.
17. Hill, "What Papias Said," 613.
18. See Charles Hill's response, "The 'Orthodox Gospel': The Reception of John in the Great Church prior to Irenaeus," in Legacy of John: Second-Century Reception of the Fourth Gospel , ed. Tuomas Rasimus (Leiden: Brill (2009), 288–94.
19. Bauckham, *Eyewitnesses*, 433.
20. . Hill, "What Papias Said," 593–94.
21. Hill, "What Papias Said," 595.
22. Hill, "What Papias Said," 595 n. 42.
23. Bauckham, *Eyewitnesses*, 433.
24. Hill, "What Papias Said," 599.
25. Bauckham, *Eyewitnesses*, 435.
26. Hill, "'Orthodox Gospel,'" 289.
27. Bauckham, *Eyewitnesses*, 435; cf. Hill, "'Orthodox Gospel,'" 289–90.
28. See Bauckham, *Testimony*, 65; cf. Bauckham, *Eyewitnesses*, 433–34.
29. See Bauckham, *Testimony*, 65.
30. Bauckham, *Eyewitnesses*, 437.
31. Bauckham, *Eyewitnesses*, 435–36.
32. Bauckham, *Eyewitnesses*, 435–36.
33. Bauckham, *Eyewitnesses*, 435–36.
34. Bauckham, *Eyewitnesses*, 433.
35. Alistair Stewart-Sykes, "ΤΑΞΕΙ in Papias: Again," *JECS* 3 (1995): 489–90.
36. E.g., F. H. Colson, "Τάξει in Papias (The Gospels and the Rhetorical Schools)," *JTS* 14 (1912): 62–69; Schoedel, *Polycarp*, 106; Josef Kürzinger, *Papias von Hierapolis und die Evangelien des Neuen Testaments* (Regensburg: Pustet, 1983), 49–50. A thorough survey of the literature on the question can be found in Norelli, *Papia di Hierapolis*, 301–8.
37. Bauckham, *Eyewitnesses*, 220.
38. Bauckham, *Eyewitnesses*, 220–21.
39. Hengel, *Studies*, 154.
40. Translated by the author from the Greek text of Lucian, LCL, vol. 6, 8.
41. Stewart-Sykes, "ΤΑΞΕΙ in Papias," 490.
42. Bauckham, *Eyewitnesses*, 221.
43. The Latin text and translation is taken from Quintilian, *Institutio Oratoria*, vol. 3, trans. H. E. Butler (Cambridge, Mass.: Harvard University Press, 1921), and so hereafter. Cf. Hill, "'Orthodox Gospel,'" 291; Schoedel, *Polycarp*, 106; Bauckham, *Eyewitnesses*, 219.

44. William K. Pritchett, *Dionysius of Halicarnassus: On Thucydides* (Berkeley: University of California Press, 1975), 13.

45. Colson, "Τάξει," 66.

46. Pritchett, *Dionysius*, 6. Greek text from *Dionysii Halicarnasei Quae Exstant*, ed. Hermann Usener, vol. 5 (Leipzig: Teubner, 1899), 338.

47. George A. Kennedy, trans., *Progymnasmata: Greek Textbooks of Prose Composition and Rhetoric* (Leiden: Brill, 2003) 32–33; cf. Colson, "Τάξει," 65.

48. Translated by the author from the Greek text in K. Kilburn, *Lucian*, vol. 6 (LCL; Cambridge, Mass.: Harvard University Press, 1959), 32, 34.

49. Dionysius's criticism would also be pertinent if the Gospel originally ended at 16:3 with the words, "for they were afraid" (ἐφοβοῦντο γάρ); cf. Abbott, *Fourfold Gospel*, 84–85; Colson, "Τάξει," 65.

50. Cf. Hill, "'Orthodox Gospel,'" 291; Schoedel, *Polycarp*, 106; Bauckham, *Eyewitnesses*, 219.

51. Hill, "What Papias Said," 613.

52. Cf. Manor, *Epiphanius'* Alogi, 212.

53. Ronald E. Heine, trans., *Origen, Commentary on the Gospel of John, Books 1-10* (FC 80; Washington DC: Catholic University of America, 1989), 256.

54. Cf. Manor, *Epiphanius'* Alogi, 212.

55. Cf. Manor, *Epiphanius'* Alogi, 212.

# TEN
# Papias and the Publication of John's Gospel

This chapter will examine a number of other sources that provide evidence for Hill's thesis of the Papian origin of Eusebius's unattributed fragment. In particular, it will discuss a passage from Theodore of Mopsuestia which relates, like the unattributed fragment, the narrative of the Gospels being brought to John and being evaluated by him, but which exhibits its own independent points of contact with Papian sources, suggestive of an independent Papian derivation.

This chapter will also examine Epiphanius's discussion of the Gospels, arguing that he, too, may have been using material derived from Papias's discussion of the τάξις of the Gospels, though evidence will be presented suggesting that he may have drawn his Papian material from Hippolytus's discussion of the Alogoi.

Lastly, a small number of sources will be discussed which seem to reflect knowledge of the same narrative known to the unattributed fragment and Theodore and which provide further evidence of the Papian provenance of the narrative. The last of these sources, an anonymous preface, may also provide evidence that Papias placed the writing of John's Gospel late in Domitian's reign.

It will be concluded that Papias did depict John as writing his Gospel at the end of Domitian's reign, and that Eusebius largely ignored this tradition both because Papias identified the Elder and Evangelist and because it presented a chronological challenge to his reconstruction of the Johannine narrative which placed John's exile at that time.

## Chapter 10

## THEODORE OF MOPSUESTIA

Theodore of Mopsuestia (c. 350–c. 428), who gives an account of the writing of John's Gospel in the preface to his commentary on John, may provide further support both for the unattributed fragment's interest in τάξις and for the thesis of its dependence upon Papias. After first mentioning Peter's journey to Rome, he continues:[1]

> So the blessed John also dwells at Ephesus, visiting all of Asia and supplying much help to those there through his words (or 'through his suitable words': διὰ τῶν οἰκείων λόγων). In these times, therefore, the publication (ἔκδοσις) by the other Evangelists takes place, Matthew's and Mark's, still yet Luke's, these having written their own Gospels; and it was distributed (διεδόθη) in a short time over the whole inhabited world; and it was zealously pursued by all the faithful with, as is reasonable, great disposition of mind.
>
> But judging the blessed John to be more reliable (ἀξιοπιστότερον) than the rest regarding his testimony of the Gospel, as one who associated with the Lord himself from the beginning and that before Matthew, and as one who enjoyed more of his grace on account of his love, the faithful in the region of Asia brought the books to him, wishing to learn from him which was of good reputation concerning these matters (μαθεῖν ἥντινα περὶ αὐτῶν ἔχει τὴν δόξαν παρ' αὐτοῦ βουλόμενοι).
>
> He indeed praised the writers for their truth (ἐπῄνεσε μὲν τῆς ἀληθείας τοὺς γεγραφότας) but said that brief things had been omitted (βραχέα παραλελεῖφθαι) by them, and especially of some miracles needing to be recounted (ἀναγκαίων λεχθῆναι θαυμάτων), and that all the teachings were only of a little extent (τὰ διδασκαλικὰ ἅπαντα μικροῦ).
>
> Next, he said it was needful for those discussing concerning the coming of Christ in the flesh (τοὺς περὶ τῆς ἐν σαρκὶ τοῦ Χριστοῦ παρουσίας διαλεγομένους) not to pass over the accounts concerning his divinity either (μηδὲ τοὺς περὶ θεότητος λόγους παραλιπεῖν), so that, in the passing of time, people would not become accustomed by these words to think of him only in the way in which he appeared (τοῦτο μόνον αὐτὸν νομίζειν ὅπερ ἐφαίνετο).
>
> On account of these things a request (παράκλησις) came from the brothers to write with speed those things which he judged on the one hand as most necessary (ἀναγκαῖα) for the purpose of teaching, and which on the other he perceived to have been left out by the others (ταῦτα ἃ μάλιστα ἀναγκαῖα μὲν κρίνει πρὸς διδασκαλίαν, παραλελειμμένα δὲ ὁρᾷ τοῖς λοιποῖς), which thing he then also did. For which reason, he also made examination right from the beginning (ἐξ ἀρχῆς) concerning the teachings of the divinity (περὶ τῶν τῆς θεότητος ἐφιλοσόφησε δογμάτων), judging this beginning (τὴν ἀρχήν) of the Gospel to be necessary (ἀναγκαίαν).

And thus, passing to the incarnation (ἡ οἰκονομία), it was at that point that he [John] himself also dealt with the baptism of John, knowing that there was not any other truest beginning (ἀληθεστάτην ἀρχήν) of the things said (λεχθέντων) or done (γεγονότων) by the Lord in the flesh than that one. But also, coming to this point, he rather made it a point of honor to speak the things left out by the others.

But he also took thought to add a certain proper arrangement to the narrative (τάξιν τινὰ ἐπιθεῖναι τῇ διηγήσει), and he has spoken of the things as they took place on the first day, as well as the place, just as "in Bethara across the Jordan" [John 1:28]. And he has spoken of the things which took place on the second day, and then of the disciples who followed (ἀκολουθήσαντας) thereafter. In short, anyone investigating it will find him accurately (ἀκριβῶς) calling to mind (μνημονεύοντα) as many things as orderly progression (ἀκολουθία) requires and of which he judged the omission not to be necessary (ἀναγκαίαν).

And he joins together successively (ἐφεξῆς) the things left out by the others; of which he alone makes mention, clearly declaring with respect to the wedding that it was the beginning of signs (ἀρχὴν σημείων) [cf. John 2:11]. He makes mention of all the teachings a little, of which none of the others make mention, and likewise of the wonders (θαυμάτων). And if perhaps he makes mention of a sign recounted by the others, he makes mention of it no doubt on account of some need (χρείαν), as with the account of the loaves, mentioned by the others. He has inserted it on account of the necessity (ἀναγκαίως) of bringing together the teaching, in which he also touched on the words related to the mysteries [i.e. the Eucharist]. For the miracle (θαῦμα) was the occasion of these things, and it is not possible to make mention of the words without touching on the causes of the word.

Theodore's account shares a number of features in common with the unattributed fragment.[2] In Eusebius, John spends his time preaching but does not write; following the "publication" (ἔκδοσις) of the Synoptic Gospels, they are "distributed (διαδεδομένων) to all, and to him." He praises the writers for their truth while pointing out that they passed over the miracles performed at the beginning of Jesus's ministry. John was then exhorted to write his own Gospel, which is said to have reasonably maintained silence concerning the genealogy of Jesus and to have begun with the doctrine of the divinity (τῆς δὲ θεολογίας), as though this were reserved for him by the Spirit. In Theodore, John is providing help to the disciples in Asia through his words. A publication (ἔκδοσις) is made of the Gospels, each of which is said to have been distributed (διεδόθη) over the whole world; finally, the Asian faithful bring these Gospels to John; he praises the writers for their truth but states that they left out certain miracles that needed to be related, and he adds that their teaching was lacking, such as that concerning the divinity (περὶ τῆς θεότητος). Mention is also made of the Fourth Gospel's inclusion of the things left out by the others at the time of the baptism of John, and like Eusebius, Theodore cites John 2:11.

*Theodore's Interest in Τάξις*

The rhetorical concerns in Theodore's account are far more pronounced than they are in Eusebius's, possibly reflecting a closer use of Papian material, with its interest in the τάξις of the Gospels. He thus draws attention to the omissions of "brief things" in the Synoptics, especially of certain miracles that needed to be recounted; he adds that the teaching is said to have been of a little extent, that is, not in due proportion to the place it ought to occupy (cf. μέτρον in Lucian, *de Cons. Hist.* 6). In particular, he relates, it was necessary not "to pass over" (παραλιπεῖν) the doctrine of the divinity (cf. Quintilian's reference to "omissions" in *Inst. Or.* 7.3).

Theodore also addresses the concern for a suitable beginning for the narrative, stating that John "made examination right from the beginning concerning the teachings of the divinity, judging this beginning of the Gospel to be necessary." Thus, in choosing his starting point, John went back as far as he could, agreeing with Dionysius of Halicarnassus's observation that the starting point ought to be "something that is not preceded by anything else" (*Thuc.*10).[3]

John is also said to have gone from relating the incarnation to the baptism of John; that is, his narrative omitted the accounts of Jesus's ancestry and of his birth and early life, presumably because it had already been related by others, which would agree with the statement in the unattributed fragment (in Eusebius's editorial comments, but probably summarized from his source) that John "reasonably" (εἰκότως) maintained silence with respect to Jesus's genealogy, seeing that it was already written out by Matthew and Luke.

John's baptizing activity had also been recorded in the other Gospels, and the repetition of this in the Fourth Gospel seems to have prompted Theodore's explanation that no other truest beginning point of the narrative of Jesus's teaching and ministry was possible. Theodore adds that John nevertheless supplied additional information concerning the beginning of Jesus's ministry not included by the others, which perhaps helped to justify John's repetition of the baptism as a starting point.

John is also said to have taken thought to add "arrangement to the narrative," where his τάξιν τινὰ ἐπιθεῖναι τῇ διηγήσει closely echoes Lucian's statement that after making a note (ὑπόμνημα; cf. Clement's description of Mark's Gospel in *apud* Eusebius, *Hist. eccl.* 2.15.1) of all the facts, a literary body (σῶμα) of material, the historian, "having added arrangement" (ἐπιθεὶς τὴν τάξιν), is to stylistically enhance the work (*de Cons. Hist.* 48).[4] Theodore's John seems to have added τάξις by providing suitable beginnings, references to the time and place of events, and appropriate teaching.

Lastly, a constant refrain in Theodore is the "necessity" for the material that John includes, which seems to reflect the same concerns that informed Dionysius's critique of Thucydides for including "petty details" for which there was no "necessity" (*Thuc*.19). Even John's inclusion of material that is also found in the Synoptics is justified on the basis that John only repeated material if there was a need to supply details left out by the others (cf. the criticism of "countless repetitions" by Quintilian).

*Theodore's Independent Use of Eusebius's Source*

A number of considerations suggest that Theodore had drawn from Papias or a Papian source independently of Eusebius's fragment. First, Papias's interest in τάξις is clearly reflected in Theodore's discussion but not in Eusebius, who does not employ the word τάξις and whose interest is in the variance of the Gospels. It is difficult to account for why Theodore would have woven the theme of τάξις into his version had he been dependent upon Eusebius's summarized account; it is Eusebius who has instead likely separated the account from its original rhetorical context and subordinated it to his interest in the question of the chronological harmonization of the Gospel narratives (in answer to Origen, as argued in the previous chapter).

Secondly, Theodore fails to demonstrate any familiarity with Eusebius's editorial comments in lines 8–10 of the unattributed fragment, or to show any interest in the question of the apparent discrepancies between the Gospels. While there are affinities with Eusebius's claim that John began with the doctrine of the divinity (line 13), this statement was likely drawn from Eusebius's source, since it exhibits literary concerns (inclusion, omission, and repetition) and it does not seem to add anything to Eusebius's argument concerning the variances of the Gospels with respect to Jesus's ministry before the Baptist's imprisonment.

Thirdly, Theodore provides additional details that are not found in Eusebius. Thus, he supplies the identity of those who brought the Gospels to John, saying that "a request (παράκλησις) arose from the brothers" in Asia, whereas the unattributed fragment states only that John was "exhorted (παρακληθέντα) on account of these things." He also states that John "associated with the Lord from the beginning, before Matthew," which is not found in the unattributed fragment and which may have been mentioned by Papias in order to account for Matthew's omission of the beginning of Jesus's ministry. Matthew's beginning was clearly superior to Mark's, but it was inferior to John's, who recorded those miracles done at the time of the baptism of John, before Matthew began following Jesus.

Lastly, Theodore's passage contains additional literary affinities with Papias that are not shared by the unattributed fragment. Thus, despite the brevity of the extant fragment of Papias on Mark's Gospel, the words τάξις, χρεία, διδασκαλία, παραλείπω, the passive aorist of λέγω, a form of the verb ἀκολουθέω and the use of ἀκριβῶς with the verb μνημονεύω are common to Papias (apud Eusebius, Hist. eccl. 3.39.15) and Theodore but are absent from Eusebius's unattributed fragment.[5]

Furthermore, Theodore and Papias both connect χρεία with διδασκαλία: in Theodore, John only refers to the miracle of the loaves on account of some "need" (χρεία) with respect to teaching (τὴν διδασκαλίαν), whereas in Papias, Peter "framed his teachings (τὰς διδασκαλίας) according to the needs (πρὸς τὰς χρείας)."[6]

Both writers also use the adverb ἀκριβῶς with a form of the subordinator ὅσος and the verb μνημονεύω: in Theodore, John is described as "accurately calling to mind as many things as orderly progression requires" (ἀκριβῶς ... μνημονεύοντα ὅσων ἥ τε ἀκολουθία κατεπείγει); according to Papias, Mark "wrote accurately whatever he called to mind" (ὅσα ἐμνημόνευσεν, ἀκριβῶς ἔγραψεν) (apud Eusebius, Hist. eccl. 3.39.15).

In both writers, the verb παραλείπω is employed with respect to material included or omitted from the Gospels. Theodore says that John: "joins together successively the things left out (τὰ παραλελειμμένα) by the others"; Papias states that Mark was careful not to leave out (παραλιπεῖν) anything of the things he had heard.

Theodore also uses the passive aorist of λέγω in relation to the teachings of Jesus, speaking of "the things said or brought about by the Lord in the flesh" (τῶν ἐν σαρκὶ παρὰ τοῦ Κυρίου ἢ λεχθέντων ἢ γεγονότων), whereas Papias speaks of Mark writing "the things said and done by the Lord" (τὰ ὑπὸ τοῦ κυρίου ἢ λεχθέντα ἢ πραχθέντα).

In addition, both writers employ a form of the verb ἀκολουθέω. According to Theodore, John spoke of the disciples who followed (ἀκολουθήσαντας) Jesus after the second day of the narrative; Papias says that Mark "did not hear or follow him" (οὔτε γὰρ ἤκουσεν τοῦ κυρίου οὔτε παρηκολούθησεν αὐτῷ) but wrote as one who had followed (ὡς ἂν ἀκολουθήσαντα) Peter.

One last possible point of contact with Papian material comes at the conclusion of Theodore's commentary, where he relates that the words of John's epilogue were "not the Evangelist's" but were inserted "outside (ἔξωθεν) by some hardworking person (or "scholar"[7]) (ὑπό τινος φιλοπόνου)." This may be related to the statement of the Latin prologue (cf. chapter 8), which claims that John delivered his Gospel to the churches "while still in a body," as Papias "related in his exoteric, that is, in the last section in his five books" (in exotericis suis, id est in extremis, quinque libris retulit)," where the word exotericus comes from the Greek word ἐξωτερικός,[8] meaning "that which is outside."[9]

Orchard and Riley think that the clause beginning with *id est* is a later gloss which mistakenly attempted to explain the meaning of the obscure *exotericis*,[10] and that the original source would only have claimed that Papias recorded these things in his *exotericis*, which they suggest (apparently without any awareness of Theodore's statement) had originally referred to the epilogue to John's Gospel, which was thus attributed to Papias.[11] Theodore's reference to the scholar who wrote the epilogue, which was "on the outside," may represent the same tradition.

## EUSEBIUS'S USE OF PAPIAS

It was suggested in the previous chapter that Eusebius had failed to cite Papias so as not to draw attention to Papias's likely identification of the Evangelist who evaluated the τάξις of the Synoptics and the Elder who spoke of the τάξις of Matthew and Mark. The important role that the discussion of τάξις plays in Theodore's passage suggests that Eusebius may have also removed any reference to τάξις in his version of the account for the same reason. Perhaps it was in order to avoid a clear allusion to the Papian tradition that Eusebius also failed to disclose the identity of those who came to John, casting the narrative in the passive voice instead, whereas Theodore speaks of the Asian brothers bringing the Gospels to John.

## EPIPHANIUS, PAPIAS, AND THE ΤΆΞΙΣ OF THE GOSPELS

Epiphanius seems to have drawn from a source which had discussed the rhetorical arrangement of the Gospels. In response to the Alogoi's assertion that the Gospel of John has Jesus go from his baptism directly to Galilee, omitting the forty days, Epiphanius answers that the Synoptics also had omissions and differing starting points in their narratives (*Pan.* 51.4.5–12), which echoes the discussion in the unattributed fragment and Theodore. Epiphanius thus points out that Matthew "does not start from the beginning (ἀπ' ἀρχῆς)," that is, from doctrine of the divine Logos, but sets out the genealogy from Abraham" (*Pan.* 51.5.3; cf. Theon's observation that a history should provide ancestry) and recounts the circumstances of Christ's birth (*Pan.* 51.5.4–8). None of this is found in Mark's Gospel, however, which begins with the events at the Jordan (*Pan.* 51.6.4).

Epiphanius goes on to point out that Mark began his proclamation at the fifteenth year of Tiberius (*Pan.* 51.6.12), whereas Luke goes back further, to Christ's birth (τὴν γέννησιν) (*Pan.* 51.7.2), "going through the whole matter [of Christ's generation] in minute detail (λεπτομερῶς τὴν πᾶσαν πραγματείαν διέξεισι) for the sake of accuracy" (τὴν ἀκρίβειαν)" (*Pan.* 51.7.2). Epiphanius adds that Luke begins before Matthew (*Pan.* 51.7.7), with the events in the six months leading up to Jesus's conception and birth (*Pan.* 51.7.8; cf. Dionysius's concern that a narrative begin at the earliest starting point).

Furthermore, Epiphanius notes that Luke supplied contextual details not found in the other Gospels: the birth in Bethlehem, the circumcision, the offering according to the law at the end of forty days, the residence at Nazareth and the annual return to Jerusalem, "not one of which things is discussed by Matthew or Mark, nor indeed by John" (ὧν οὐδὲν τῷ Ματθαίῳ ἐπείργασται οὐδὲ τῷ Μάρκῳ ἀλλὰ μὴν οὐδὲ τῷ Ἰωάννῃ) (*Pan.* 51.7.9). A little later Epiphanius remarks that Matthew skipped over (ἀπεπήδησεν) the events from Jesus' birth to those of two years later, with the visit of the Magi (*Pan.* 51.9.3; cf. Matt 2:1–16; also note Lucian's reference to the things which must be passed over in silence).

In discussing how each gospel writer recorded those things omitted by the others, Epiphanius argues that "the orderly progression and the teaching" (ἡ ἀκολουθία καὶ ἡ διδασκαλία) of the Gospels come from the Holy Spirit (*Pan.* 51.4.11), where ἀκολουθία again represents a rhetorical concern (cf. "της τάξεως ἀκολουθία" in the *Ars. Rhetor.* 10.6, mistakenly attributed to Dionysius of Halicarnassus). Epiphanius explains that it was God who allotted (ἐμέρισεν) to the gospel writers so that they "might each find in what they should labor," with the result that they declared "some things in unison (συμφώνως) and alike (ἴσως), that they might show that they have gushed forth from the same fountain, and that another might describe the things left out (παραλειφθέντα) to each of the others, as he received his proportionate share (μέρος τῆς ἀναλογίας) from the Spirit" (*Pan.* 51.6.2). Thus, it is the Holy Spirit that "compels" (ἀναγκάζει) and "goads" (ἐπινύττει) Luke "to contribute in turn the things left out by the others" (τὰ ὑπὸ τῶν ἄλλων καταλειφθέντα αὖθις ἐπιβάλλεσθαι) (*Pan.* 51.7.1). Concerning John's Gospel, he writes: "Likewise, the things treated and safeguarded (ἠσφαλισμένα) in the Holy Spirit by St. John had this concern, not to speak only of those things already often proclaimed, but of those proclamations (κηρυγμάτων) left to him by necessity by the others" (*Pan.* 51.6.5).

The same theme is repeated later, when Epiphanius writes that the Spirit "bestowed (ἐδωρήσατο) on each of the evangelists for them to describe (διηγεῖσθαι) the things fulfilled in truth (τὰ ἐν ἀληθείᾳ πληρωθέντα) of each time and season (ἑκάστου χρόνου καὶ καιροῦ)" (*Pan.* 51.9.1). Thus, the relative inclusions and omissions of the Gospels and the different time periods which they discussed were, according to Epiphanius, divinely ordered. The underlying rhetorical concerns of Epiphanius's argument are evident, even if they are employed for polemical purposes against the Alogoi.

## Epiphanius's Source

Epiphanius's discussion of the differing beginnings and time periods addressed by the Gospels (that is, their τάξις) may have been drawn from the discussion of the τάξις of the Gospels that Clement attributed to those "who were elders from the first" (*apud* Eusebius, *Hist. eccl.* 6.14.5), which this study has argued was found in Papias's work (chapter 8). This would, at any rate, have been a natural place for such material to have been found.

Epiphanius's use of Papian material would account for the parallels in his account with the discussions found in the unattributed fragment and Theodore, which likewise seem to have been drawn from Papias. Thus, while Epiphanius draws attention to the things that Luke included in the beginning of his account and which the others omitted in theirs, and while he speaks of Matthew "skipping over" events, the unattributed fragment notes that the imprisonment of the Baptist was discussed by John but "passed over in silence" (from παρασιωπάω) by the Synoptics (*Hist. eccl.* 3.24.11), and it observes that the Lord's genealogy was passed over in silence by John's Gospel, adding that John instead included the teaching of the divinity (3.24.13). In each case, the interest is in the inclusion or omission of material at the beginning of the narrative.

Moreover, while Epiphanius claims that the "orderly progression and the teaching" (ἡ ἀκολουθία καὶ ἡ διδασκαλία) of the Gospels come from the Holy Spirit (*Pan.* 51.4.11), Theodore describes John as "accurately (ἀκριβῶς) calling to mind as many things as orderly progression (ἀκολουθία) requires and which he judged to be necessary not to be left out."

Furthermore, the statements that the teaching comes from the Holy Spirit and that God allotted (ἐμέρισεν) material to the gospel writers is perhaps related to the unattributed fragment's claim that John's doctrine of the divinity (τῆς δὲ θεολογίας) was something closely guarded (παραπεφυλαγμένης, from παραφυλάσσω) by the divine Spirit for him.

In further support of the Papian derivation of Epiphanius's account, it can be noted that the Muratorian Canon, another proposed Papian source, speaks of the "various beginnings (*principia*) in the separate books of the Gospels" (ll. 16–17) and states that Luke "began" (*incepit*) with the birth of John (l.8), echoing Epiphanius's claim that Luke related the things that took place in the six months prior to Jesus's conception (*Pan.* 51.7.8).

## Hippolytus's Use of Papias

Since Epiphanius was dependent upon Hippolytus for his chapter against the Alogoi, in which this discussion occurs (see chapter 4), it is likely that his discussion of the variances of the Gospels was also drawn from Hippolytus, who had perhaps found Papias's discussion of the τάξις of the Gospels useful for his defense of the variances between the Gospels, just as Eusebius later would.

A subtle indication of Hippolytus's employment of Papian material for his defense of John's Gospel against Gaius is perhaps provided by the bar Salibi fragments, which record Hippolytus as speaking of "the first day" and "the second day" when discussing the Johannine narrative of the Baptist (cf. chapter 5). While John's Gospel speaks of "the next day" (twice) and "the third day," Theodore, like Hippolytus, speaks of "the first day" and "the second day," possibly because both writers were drawing from Papias or a Papian source.

Both Gaius and Hippolytus identified the Johannine narrative of Jesus's encounter with the Baptist as the occasion of his baptism (see chapter 5), and this misinterpretation of the narrative might have originated from a misreading of a statement like the one found in Theodore that John's Gospel goes from describing the incarnation to relating the baptism of John, as this was the "truest beginning of the things said or done by the Lord in the flesh." While the passage seems to be speaking only of the general baptizing activity of John the Baptist, a reader might have inferred from it a specific reference to Jesus's baptism in the Fourth Gospel, leading to the error found in Gaius and Hippolytus that John's Gospel has Jesus go immediately to Cana in Galilee following his baptism, omitting the forty days (see chapter 5).

Moreover, Papias's discussion of the various inclusions and omissions of events in the Gospels and of their "passing over" and "skipping over" material might have suggested to Hippolytus that John had omitted the mention of the forty days from the baptism narrative because it had already been related by the other Gospels, prompting his tenuous attempt at reinserting them within the sequence of days related in the Fourth Gospel (see chapter 5).

While Papias was interested in the τάξις of the Gospels rather than in resolving apparent variances between them, his discussion of the differing inclusions and omissions of events in the Synoptic Gospels would have allowed Hippolytus to show that the Synoptics had similar apparent variances between them to those which Gaius was alleging between John and the Synoptics, explaining Epiphanius's almost exclusive preoccupation with the Synoptic variances. In any case, Papias's discussion of John's beginning and of its inclusion of the events before the imprisonment of John would not have helped Hippolytus to refute the charge that John went from relating the baptism of Jesus to his Galilean ministry, unless he had challenged either the correlation of Jesus's encounter with the Baptist and his baptism, as Epiphanius did (chapter 5), or the correlation of the journey to Cana with the Synoptic Galilean ministry, as Eusebius did (chapter 9).

## THE PAPIAN NARRATIVE IN OTHER SOURCES

A few other sources also seem to know the tradition of John composing his Gospel, as found in the unattributed fragment and Theodore. Two of these relate the narrative of the Synoptics being brought to John, while another seems to allude to the claim of both that John preached orally before he composed his Gospel. Furthermore, these sources provide a number of independent indications that are supportive of the thesis that this narrative was derived from Papias.

### *The* Martyrdom of Timothy

An extant fragment of the *Martyrdom of Timothy*, preserved by Photius (ninth century),[12] preserves a tradition, howbeit in a garbled form, of John addressing the "order" of the Synoptics:

> At that time he received *papyrus rolls* (τοὺς τόμους), from people who kept bringing them to him. These papyri recorded, in *different languages* (διαφόροις γλώσσαις), the salvific Passion of the Lord and his miracles and teachings (καὶ θαυματα καὶ διδάγματα). He *put them in order* (διέταξε), *articulated them into a structure*, and *attributed them the name of one of the three evangelists*.[13]

Ramelli thinks the reference to papyrus scrolls indicates that the account used an ancient source.[14] She no doubt correctly takes the mention of "different languages" as a reference to Greek and Hebrew/Aramaic Gospels (the latter is attested, for Matthew at least, by Papias).[15] Neither of these are mentioned by Theodore, making it unlikely that it was dependent on his account.

The account of the Gospels being brought to John includes the motif of arrangement, as Theodore's (but not Eusebius's) does, though here it seems to have been conflated with John's written activity. It also shares in common with Papias (but not with Theodore) the mention of "miracles," (θαύματα; lit: "wonders"); while this word is not used in John's Gospel, Philip of Sidé reports that Papias related "other wonders" (ἄλλα θαύματα) (Fragment 5).

A parallel passage in the *Acts of Timothy* (probably from the fifth century[16]) relates:

> For indeed, the ones who followed the disciples of our Lord Jesus Christ did not know how to organize (συνθεῖναι) the papyrus rolls (or "papyri sheets"; χάρται) that were with them, which had been put together randomly, in various languages (διαφόροις γλώσσαις), and which had been composed concerning the wonderful works (θαυματουργήματα) of Jesus Christ our Lord which took place in their time. They came to the city of the Ephesians and by common consent brought them to the all-praiseworthy John the Theologian. He considered all things and was stirred up by them. Having put into arrange-

ment (ἐνθεὶς κατὰ τάξιν) the things said by them in the three Gospels, he entitled them,[17] (Gospel) of Matthew, of Mark and of Luke, having placed on the Gospels their descriptive titles. But having found them tracing out the genealogies concerning the economy of the incarnation, he theologizes (θεολογεῖ) concerning the things not spoken by the others, inasmuch as he had been impressed of them from the divine breast, having also filled out the divine wonderful works (θαυματουργήματα) omitted from being spoken by them.[18]

In Theodore, John adds arrangement to his account (τάξιν τινὰ ἐπιθεῖναι τῇ διηγήσει); this passage speaks of John "having put into arrangement" (ἐνθεὶς κατὰ τάξιν) the accounts in the Synoptics. Here it is those who followed the disciples who brought them (cf. Papias's reference to the elders as the followers of the apostles; *apud* Eusebius, *Hist. eccl.* 3.39.7); in Theodore, it is the Asian brothers.

The *Acts of Timothy* relates that John found the other Gospels "tracing out the genealogies," and that he instead "theologizes (θεολογεῖ) concerning the things not spoken by the others," echoing the claim of the unattributed fragment (but not Theodore) that John was silent concerning the genealogy as it had been recorded by Matthew and Luke, so that he began instead with the doctrine of the divinity (τῆς δὲ θεολογίας) (*Hist. eccl.* 3.24.5–13). As with the unattributed passage and Theodore, it also relates that John supplied an account of the miracles left out by the others. Thus, this work separately interacts with both Theodore and the unattributed fragment, suggestive of its use of a source common to both.

## The Anonymous Preface to John

Another account of the writing of John's Gospel is given by an anonymous preface to Augustine's tractates on John. Possibly some of the material comes from Augustine, though in any case, it was used by Bede and thus must antedate that writer.[19]

> Now, among the writers of the Gospels, John stands out for his profundity in regard to the divine mysteries. For sixty-five years, from the time of the Lord's ascension down to the final days of Domitian (*usque ad ultima Domitiani tempora*), he preached the word of the Lord, orally, with no writing to assist him. But after the murder of Domitian, when, with Nerva's permission, he had returned to Ephesus from exile, at the insistent urging of the bishops of Asia, he wrote about the coeternal divinity of Christ with the Father in opposition to the heretics who, in his absence, had invaded his churches and were denying that Christ had existed before Mary.[20]

In this account, John is urged to write by the bishops of Asia in response to the growth of heresies, in common with other proposed Papian sources (chapter 8). As with the unattributed passage (*Hist. eccl.* 3.24.7, 13) and Theodore, John's Gospel is said to contain the doctrine of Christ's divinity. John is also like them said to have preached orally before committing his preaching to writing, though unlike those works, the preface states that this lasted for sixty-five years, to the final days of Domitian (that is, the year 95 or 96), culminating in the publication of John's Gospel.

Jacobus de Voragine (c. 1230–1298)[21] and Nicephorus Callistus (fl. c. 1320) (*Hist. eccl.* 2.45)[22] similarly claimed that John wrote his Gospel after sixty-six years, from either the crucifixion (Jacob) or ascension (Nicephorus). Eusebius may have omitted mention of John writing his Gospel in Ephesus after sixty-five years as it conflicted with his placement of John's exile at this time, a chronology which Theodore probably also followed.

Corroborating evidence for the Papian derivation of the tradition of John writing at the end of the first century is provided by the Latin (Anti-Marcionite) prologue to John (cf. chapter 8), which states, citing Papias, that the Gospel was made manifest and given to the churches while John was "still in a body" (*adhuc in corpore constituto*).[23] Bruns may have captured the sense when he translates it as "still possessed of a functioning body,"[24] which may presuppose that his body ceased functioning normally in his extreme old age and may be related to the anecdote told by Jerome that before his death John had to be carried into the meetings as he was unable to walk (*Comm. Gal.* 6.10). John's Gospel was apparently written, according to the prologue's source, just prior to this time. A similar account found in a Greek catena on the Gospel of John relates that John wrote "when he was a very old man" (πάνυ γηραλέου αὐτοῦ γενομένου) (Fragment 20 [Holmes]).

As discussed in chapter 6, Irenaeus likely held that the Asian elders gathered to John late in the first century, shortly before Trajan's reign. It was also argued that Irenaeus made John (and not the apocalyptic vision) to have been seen by the elders "towards the end of Domitian's reign" (πρὸς τῷ τέλει τῆς Δομετιανοῦ ἀρχῆς), and that he was likely dependent for this tradition upon Papias. It may or may not be coincidental that this corresponds with the anonymous preface's period of the sixty-five years for John's oral preaching, down to "the final times of Domitian" (*ultima Domitiani tempora*), at which time the Asian bishops implore him to write.

The preface itself has attempted to combine this narrative with that of Eusebius's dating of John's exile at this time by placing the writing of John's Gospel after the assassination of Domitian in September 96 and the subsequent accession of Nerva, who reigned until his death in January 98. The immediate writing of the Gospel upon John's return from exile apparently served to place it as close to the end of Domitian's reign as possible while retaining Eusebius's chronology. This has been facilitated by the contrived explanation that the heretics had invaded the churches during John's absence, which represents a reworking of the tradition that John wrote in response to the growth of heresies. While the account retains the tradition that the bishops of Asia urged John to write, the placement of the event immediately upon John's return from exile conflicts with Clement's older tradition that John only began ordaining bishops in the area following his return (*apud* Eusebius, *Hist. eccl.* 3.23.6–19).

The anonymous preface's source may have been Chromatius of Aquileia (d. 406 or 407); he likewise claimed that John wrote upon his return to Ephesus from Patmos after Domitian's death, but he likely retains a semblance of the tradition of John writing at the end of Domitian's reign when he claims that while John was still on Patmos, after he had written Revelation, it was revealed to him that he would compose a Gospel because of the heresies that were then sprouting up (*Tract. in Matt.* prolog. 1).[25] Thus, John's writing at the end of Domitian's reign is substituted with a revelation that he would write, given to him at about the same time, in an apparent attempt at combining the two narratives.

Other writers also exhibit evidence of attempting to combine the narrative of John writing at the end of Domitian's reign with Eusebius's placement of John's exile at that time. Thus, an undated synopsis found among the works of Athanasius relates that John first dictated his Gospel on Patmos and later published it in Ephesus,[26] in an apparent attempt at retaining the Domitianic dating and Ephesian provenance of the writing of John's Gospel within the context of Eusebius's chronology.

Other texts seem to privilege the chronological placement of the tradition at the expense of its original Ephesian context. Thus, the *Menologium of the Greeks* (written in Constantinople c. 980)[27] and the Armenian *History of James and John*[28] depict John writing his Gospel on Patmos during the reign of Domitian. Both Hippolytus of Thebes at the end of the tenth century (*Chron.* 9b; 9c) and Theophylact around the turn of the twelfth century (*Comm. John* pref.) also place the writing of John on Patmos, though they claim that this took place thirty-two years after the ascension, which probably represents a further conflation with the Neronian exile tradition. Ps.-Dorotheus in the sixth century similarly places the writing of the Gospel during John's exile in Patmos but claims that John was sent there by Trajan (*Indices Apost.*),[29] as discussed in chapter 4.

Another source, the *Suffering of John* of Ps.-Melito, discussed in chapter 7, does not mention the publication of John's Gospel but it evinces evidence that it may have been interacting with the tradition. According to this work, John was sent into exile by Domitian from Ephesus and then returned again to Ephesus later in the same year, after the emperor had been killed by the Roman Senate.[30] Thus, it makes John to have been present in Ephesus for all but the very last days of Domitian by compressing John's exile within the period of a year.

While the *Acts of John by Prochorus* follows the tradition of John writing on Patmos, it moves the writing to the time of his departure from the island, after Domitian's death, relating that a new king arose and released John from exile, probably in an attempt to combine it with Eusebius's notice that John was released upon the accession of Nerva. However, this also enabled the account to accommodate the tradition of John being urged to write, though in this permutation he is urged to write by the local inhabitants in view of his departure from the island (cf. the unattributed fragment's claim that Matthew wrote when he was about to depart, in *Hist. eccl.* 3.24.6) rather than by the Asian elders in Ephesus. It adds that after fasting for three days (cf. the mention of fasting in other proposed Papian sources), John composed his Gospel and instructed the inhabitants to transcribe the work and send the original to Ephesus (154–158),[31] in what presumably represents an attempt at combining the narrative with the tradition of the work's Ephesian provenance.

The *Acts of John by Prochorus* depicts John as receiving the Gospel by revelation on a mountain in Patmos, akin to how Moses received the law at Sinai, with thunder and lightning and the shaking of a mountain, in which context John is said to have spoken the opening lines of his Gospel while Prochorus, his assistant, wrote (155–156). Perhaps the revelatory context of Patmos has suggested a reworking of the tradition, found in Jerome, that the opening lines of John's Gospel came to John in a prophetic experience (*Comm. Matt.* prolog.; cf. chapter 8). The allusion to Sinai is more explicit in a later version of the story found in the *Memorial of Saint John*, which was perhaps written in the ninth century or later,[32] which relates: "And at last John goes down from the mountain, having been handed the law, as Moses the God-beholder came down with the tablets."[33] A similar account to this is also given by Simeon Metaphases in the tenth century.[34]

## CONCLUSION

This chapter has examined a number of texts which seem to be related to the unattributed fragment. Particular attention was drawn to a passage of Theodore of Mopsuestia, which discusses τάξις as the omission and inclusion of events in the Gospels and which exhibits literary affinities with both the unattributed passage and with the Papian fragment on Mark. Attention was also drawn to Epiphanius's discussion of the various beginnings of the Gospels, with their inclusion and omission of material, which, it was argued, was also drawn from Papias's discussion of the τάξις of the Gospels. Additional evidence for the Papian provenance of Eusebius's fragment and Theodore was provided from the *Martyrdom of Timothy* and the *Acts of Timothy*, which also seem to know the story, though in garbled form, of the Gospels being brought to John and of his evaluating their τάξις.

Lastly, an anonymous preface was discussed which claims that John preached orally for sixty-five years, to the final days of Domitian, after which time he wrote his Gospel. It was suggested that this is related to

Irenaeus's claim that John (as argued in chapter 6) was seen by the elders late in Domitian's reign. Later traditions which tend to associate the writing of John's Gospel with Patmos were explained as varied attempts at combining the Papian narrative of John writing his Gospel late in Domitian's reign with Eusebius's narrative of John's late Domitianic exile.

Eusebius does not name the source for his material in the unattributed fragment and he elsewhere provides only scattered allusions to the tradition of the Asian elders coming to John and imploring him to write a Gospel. Two factors have been suggested to explain this: first, Papias seems to have identified John the Elder as the author of the Fourth Gospel, whereas Eusebius considered him a non-apostolic figure who was associated with Revelation; secondly, Papias likely placed the publication of John's Gospel late in Domitian's reign, which would have been untenable for Eusebius, whose construction of the Johannine narrative placed the Domitianic exile at its center.

## NOTES

1. Translated by the author from the Greek text of Robert Devreesse, *Essai sur Théodore de Mopsueste* (StT 141; Vatican City: Bibloteca Apostolica Vatican, 1948), 305–7. George Kalantzis, trans., *Theodore of Mopsuestia: Commentary on the Gospel of John* (ECS 7; Strathfield: St Pauls Publications, 2004), also contains a translation of the Greek text. There is a longer, Syriac version extant, of which an English translation is available: Theodore of Mopsuestia, *Commentary on the Gospel of John*, trans. Marco Conti (ACT; Downers Grove, Ill.: IVP, 2010).
2. This was also noted by Kalantzis (*Theodore*, 42 n. 3).
3. Pritchett, *Dionysius*, 6.
4. Translated by the author from the Greek text of Lucian, LCL, vol. 6, 60.
5. Eusebius uses the related λείπεσθαι (*Hist. eccl.* 3.24.7) and παρακληθέντα (3.24.11). He also uses σύνταξις of Luke's Gospel in 3.24.15 but it does not appear in Eusebius's account of John's Gospel.
6. Papias has traditionally been understood as claiming that Peter framed his teachings according to the needs of his hearers (χρεία, ας, ή, in BDAG, 1088). More recently, some have proposed that χρεία was used by Papias in the sense of "anecdotes" (Kürzinger, *Papias*, 50–56; R. O. P. Taylor, *The Groundwork of the Gospels* [Oxford: Blackwell, 1946], 76; Stewart-Sykes, "ΤΑΞΕΙ in Papias," 487–92; Gundry, *The Old is Better*, 63–64; Bauckham, *Eyewitnesses*, 214–17; this sense is rejected by Körtner, *Papias von Hierapolis*, 158). Norelli, in a balanced summary of the discussion, is undecided (*Papia di Hierapolis*, 310–11). If Theodore is drawing from Papias, it would lend support to the traditional reading.
7. So Kalantzis, *Theodore*, 146 n. 180.
8. Cf. OLD 647.
9. . Cf. Orchard and Riley, *Order of the Synoptics*, 153.
10. Orchard and Riley, *Order of the Synoptics*, 153; cf. Annand, "Four Gospels," 58–59.
11. Orchard and Riley, *Order of the Synoptics*, 153.
12. Ramelli, "John the Evangelist's Work," 40.
13. Translation and Greek text in Ramelli, "John the Evangelist's Work," 44 (italics in original). Ramelli provides the Greek text separately.
14. Ramelli, "John the Evangelist's Work," 44.
15. Ramelli, "John the Evangelist's Work," 44.

16. Cavan W. Concannon, "The Acts of Timothy: A New Translation and Introduction," in *New Testament Apocrypha: More Noncanonical Scriptures*, vol. 1, ed. Tony Burke and Brent Landau (Grand Rapids: Eerdmans, 2016), 396–97.
17. Here I am following the translation of ἀπεγράψατο given by J. H. Crehan, "The Fourfold Character of the Gospel," StE 1 (TU 73; Berlin, Akademie-Verlag, 1959), 5.
18. Translated by the author from the Greek text in Hermann Usener, ed., *Acta S. Timothei* (Bonn: Caroli Georgi Universitas, 1877), 9–10.
19. . John W. Rettig, trans., *Augustine, Tractates on the Gospel of John 1–10* (FC 78; Washington DC: Catholic University of America, 1988), 37.
20. Rettig, trans., *Tractates*, 37. Latin text in *PL* 35:1577.
21. Caxton, *Golden Legend*, vol. 2, 173.
22. From the Greek text in *PG* 145:881.
23. Text given in Aland, *Synopsis*, 549.
24. J. Edgar Bruns, *The Art and Thought of John* (New York: Herder & Herder, 1969), 39.
25. CCSL 9A:185.
26. The Greek text is given in Johann Heinrich August Ebrard, *Wissenschaftliche Kritik der evangelischen Geschichte*, vol. 1 (Frankfurt: Zimmer, 1842), 1042–43.
27. Cited by Culpepper, *John*, 235.
28. Boxall, *Patmos*, 124, citing *Histoire de Jacques et Jean* 4, ed. Leloir, 412–13.
29. Schermann, *Vitae Fabulosae*, 154–55.
30. *PG* 5:1241.
31. The page numbers are given according to the Greek text in Zahn, ed., *Acta Joannis*.
32. Derek Krueger, *Writing and Holiness: The Practice of Authorship in the Early Christian East* (Philadelphia: University of Pennsylvania Press, 2004), 217 n. 19.
33. Translated by the author from the Greek text given in Yuko Taniguchi, François Bovon, and Athanasios Antonopoulos. "The Memorial of Saint John the Theologian (BHG 919fb)," in François Bovon, Ann G. Brock, and C. R. Matthews, eds., *The Apocryphal Acts of the Apostles* (Cambridge: Harvard University Press, 1999), 353. An English translation is also provided.
34. Boxall, *Patmos*, 113, citing *PG* 116: 692–93.

# Conclusion

While it has traditionally been held that the earliest writers identified the Apostle and the Evangelist, this study has shown that the traditional reading of the evidence often qualifies or rejects the most important and earliest of sources. It thus sometimes suggests that Papias spoke of one John but carelessly expressed himself and that he had identified his "elders" as "apostles," contrary to how his earliest readers defined them. If it allows that Papias spoke of two Johns, it is then obliged to dismiss instead the testimony of Irenaeus, one of the foremost witnesses of the Asian tradition, since he made Papias a hearer of the Evangelist while Papias himself claimed to have been a contemporary only of the Elder. The tradition of the Apostle John's martyrdom, attested in a wide array of early sources, is often dismissed or explained away simply because it contradicts presuppositions about the identity of the Evangelist. *Ad hoc* explanations are offered for why Polycrates described John as a priest: perhaps Polycrates confused the Evangelist with a priest of the same name; perhaps John really was a priest and the Synoptics simply failed to mention it. Likewise, the traditional view struggles to account for Tertullian's claim that John underwent *relegatio*, reserved for the ruling classes, or for Jerome's assertion that John was born to wealth and aristocratic status, and it must dismiss Clement of Alexandria's assertion that the teaching ministry of the twelve had ended by Nero's death by attributing it either to imprecision or to a momentary slip of the memory.

This study provided instead a number of reasons for thinking that early Christian sources distinguished the Evangelist and Apostle. First, Papias, who wrote in the early second century or earlier, spoke of two important figures named John from among the disciples of Jesus—John the Apostle and John the Elder—allowing the possibility that the "John" known to early sources was the second one. Secondly, there appears to have been separate traditions concerning the deaths of the Apostle and the Evangelist in the early centuries, one of which placed the Apostle John's martyrdom prior to the end of Nero's reign, and one of which placed the Evangelist's natural death in old age at around the turn of the second century, which is consistent with the chronological information Papias provides concerning his Apostle and Elder respectively. Thirdly, the earliest sources (e.g., Justin, Polycarp, Polycrates, Irenaeus, Tertullian, Clement of Alexandria) fail to identify John the Evangelist explicitly with the John of the Synoptic Gospels. Indeed, some of their statements seem incongruent with such an identification and better harmonize with Papias's Elder. Fourthly, much of the development of the Johannine traditions, such as the variations with respect to the timing of his exile and death, can be accounted for on the supposition that two separate Johns were conflated. Lastly, evidence was presented suggesting that Papias's Elder, who had discussed the "arrangement" of the Synoptic Gospels, was for Papias the same John as the one who was credited with authoring the Fourth Gospel.

The greatest challenge to the reconstruction posited here is no doubt in accounting for the use of the title of "apostle" with respect to John. While it may seem too convenient, or even disingenuous, to exploit the fluidity of this title in early sources to remove the Zebedean identity from the Evangelist, it is, rather, the very ambiguity and fluidity of the title that likely gave rise to the confusion between the two Johns known from the third century onward.

The identification of the Apostle and Evangelist may have originated in the *Acts of John*; alternatively, it may have first been made by Hippolytus in his defense of the Johannine works against Gaius and the Alogoi. In any case, Hippolytus seems to have originated a conflated narrative which identified the two while privileging the Apostle's early martyrdom, thus necessitating the early dating of John's exile, which was placed in the reign of Claudius.

A century later, Eusebius, who also identified the two Johns, constructed a narrative which favored the tradition of the Evangelist's natural death in old age at the expense of the martyrdom tradition. This was an important revision, as it allowed Eusebius to reconceive John the Elder as a later, marginal figure, whom he subsequently also suggested as the author of Revelation

To provide further evidence for the Evangelist/Apostle's long life (presumably against the martyrdom tradition), and possibly to bring John's sojourn on Patmos closer to the time of John the Elder, Eusebius placed John's exile in the unlikely context of the persecution of the Roman nobility late in Domitian's reign, displacing in the process both the Neronian exile narrative and the tradition of the late Domitianic publication of John's Gospel. Eusebius's revision proved remarkably successful and came to form the basis of the "traditional" Johannine narrative.

In the final section of the work, three conclusions were reached: first, that the earliest Johannine narrative contextualized John's exile in Nero's reign; second, that Papias likely identified John the Evangelist with John the Elder rather than with John the Apostle; and third, that Papias likely placed the publication of his Gospel late in Domitian's reign, after sixty-five years of oral preaching, shortly before John's death at Ephesus during the reign of Trajan.

# Bibliography

Abbott, Edwin A. *The Fourfold Gospel: Introduction*. Cambridge: University Press, 1913.
Adams, A. W., ed. *Primasius Episcopus Hadrumetinus, Commentarius in Apocalypsin*. Corpus Christianorum, Series Latina 92. Turnhout: Brepols, 1985.
Afinogenov, Dmitry. "The story of the Patriarch Constantine II of Constantinople in Theophanes and George the Monk: transformations of a narrative." Pages 207–14 in *History as Literature in Byzantium: Papers from the Fortieth Spring Symposium of Byzantine Studies, University of Birmingham, April 2007*. Edited by Ruth Macrides. Society for the Promotion of Byzantine Studies 15. Farnham, Surrey: Ashland, 2010.
Aland, Kurt, ed. *Synopsis Quattuor Evangeliorum*. 15th ed. Stuttgart : Deutsche Bibelgesellschaft, 2001.
Annand, Rupert. "Papias and the Four Gospels." *Scottish Journal of Theology* 9 (1956): 46–62.
Anon. "The Date of the Apocalypse." *The Biblical Review and Congregational Magazine* (1846): 169–82.
Armstrong, Jonathan J. "Victorinus of Pettau as the Author of the Canon Muratori." *Vigiliae Christianae* 62 (2008): 1–34.
Arndt, William, Frederick W. Danker, and Walter Bauer, eds. *A Greek-English Lexicon of the New Testament and Other Early Christian Literature*. 3rd ed. Chicago: University of Chicago Press, 2000.
Aune, David E. *Revelation 1–5*. Word Biblical Commentary 52A. Dallas: Word, 1998.
Bacon, Benjamin Wisner. "The Elder John, Papias, Irenaeus, Eusebius and the Syriac Translator," *Journal of Biblical Literature* 27 (1908): 1–23.
———. *The Fourth Gospel in Research and Debate: A Series of Essays on Problems Concerning the Origin and Value of the Anonymous Writings Attributed to the Apostle John*. New York: Moffat, 1910.
Badham, F. P. "The Martyrdom of St. John." *American Journal of Theology* 3 (1899): 729–40.
———. "The Martyrdom of John the Apostle." *American Journal of Theology* 8 (1904): 539–54.
Barclay, William. *Introduction to John and the Acts of the Apostles*. Philadelphia: Westminster, 1976.
Bargès, Jean Joseph Léandre, trans. *Homélie sur St Marc, Apôtre et Évangéliste par Anba Sévère, Évêque de Nestéraweh*. Paris: Leroux, 1877.
Barnard, L. W. "Clement of Rome and the Persecution of Domitian." *New Testament Studies* 10 (1963): 251–60.
Barrent, Anthony A., Elaine Fantham and John C. Yardley. *The Emperor Nero: A Guide to Ancient Sources*. Princeton: Princeton University Press, 2016.
Barrett, C. K. *The Gospel According to St. John*. 2nd ed. Philadelphia: Westminster, 1978.
Bartlet, Vernon. "Papias's 'Exposition': Its Date and Contents." Pages 15–44 in *Amicitiae Corolla*. Edited by H. G. Wood. London: University of London Press, 1933.
Bauckham, Richard. *Jude and the Relatives of Jesus in the Early Church*. London: T. & T. Clark, 2004.
———. *The Testimony of the Beloved Disciple: Narrative, History, and Theology in the Gospel of John*. Grand Rapids: Baker, 2007.
———. "For what Offence was James put to Death?" Pages 199–232 in *James the Just and Christian Origins*. Edited by Bruce D. Chilton and Craig A. Evans. Novum Testamentum Supplements 98. Leiden: Brill, 2014.

———. *Jesus and the Eyewitnesses: The Gospels as Eyewitness Testimony.* 2nd ed. Grand Rapids: Eerdmans, 2017.
Bauer, Walter. *Orthodoxy and Heresy in Earliest Christianity.* Edited by Robert A. Kraft and Gerhard Kroedel. Translated by Paul J. Achtemeier. Philadelphia: Fortress, 1971.
Baum, Armin Daniel. "Papias und der Presbyter Johannes: Martin Hengel und die johanneische Frage." *Jahrbuch für evangelikale Theologie* 9 (1995): 21-42.
———. "Papias als Kommentator evangelischer Aussprüche Jesu: Erwägungen zur Art seines Werkes." *NovT* 38 (1996): 257–76.
Beale, G. K. *The Book of Revelation: A Commentary on the Greek Text.* New International Greek Testament Commentary. Grand Rapids: Eerdmans, 1999.
Beasley-Murray, George R. *John.* Word Biblical Commentary 36. 2nd ed. Dallas: Word, 2002.
Beckwith, Isbon Thaddeus. *The Apocalypse of John.* New York: Macmillan, 1919.
Bernard, J. H. "The Traditions as to the Death of John, the Son of Zebedee." *Irish Church Quarterly* 1 (1908): 51–66.
———. *A Critical and Exegetical Commentary on the Gospel According to St. John.* International Critical Commentary. New York: Scribner, 1929.
Black, C. Clifton. *Mark: Images of an Apostolic Interpreter.* Minneapolis: Fortress, 2001.
Blomberg, Craig L. *The Historical Reliability of John's Gospel: Issues & Commentary.* Downers Grove, Ill.: IVP, 2001.
Böhme, Eduard. *Über Verfasser und Abfassungszeit der Johanneischen Apokalypse und zur biblischen Typik.* Halle: 1855.
Boismard, M.-É. *Le martyre de Jean l'apôtre.* Cahiers de la Revue biblique 35. Paris, Gabalda, 1996.
Boxall, Ian. *Patmos in the Reception History of the Apocalypse.* Oxford: Oxford University Press, 2013.
Braun, François-Marie. *Jean le Théologien et son évangile dans l'Église ancienne.* 3 vols. Études bibliques. Paris: Gabalda, 1959–72.
Brent, Allen. *Hippolytus and the Roman Church in the Third Century: Communities in Tension Before the Emergence of a Monarch-Bishop.* Leiden: Brill, 1995.
Brown, Raymond E. *The Gospel According to John (I–XII): Introduction, Translation, and Notes.* Anchor Bible 29. New Haven, Conn.: Yale University Press, 2008.
———. *The Epistles of John: Translated, with Introduction, Notes, and Commentary.* Anchor Yale Bible 30. New Haven, Conn.: Yale University Press, 2008.
Bruce, F. F. "St John at Ephesus." *Bulletin of the John Rylands University Library* 60 (1978): 339–61.
———. *The Gospel of John: Introduction, Exposition, Notes.* Grand Rapids: Eerdmans, 1983.
———. *The Book of the Acts.* The New International Commentary on the New Testament. Grand Rapids: Eerdmans, 1988.
———. *The Canon of Scripture.* Downers Grove, Ill.: IVP, 1988.
Bruns, J. Edgar. "John Mark: A Riddle within the Johannine Enigma," *Scripture* 15 (1963): 88–92.
———. *The Art and Thought of John.* New York: Herder & Herder, 1969.
Budge, E. A. Wallis, ed. and trans. *The Contendings of the Apostles: Being the Histories and the Lives and Martyrdoms and Deaths of the Twelve Apostles and Evangelists.* Vol. 2: *The English Translation.* Oxford: Oxford University Press, 1901.
———. *The Chronography of Gregory Abû'l Faraj, the Son of Aaron, the Hebrew Physician Commonly Known as Bar Hebraeus.* London: Oxford University Press, 1932.
Burney, Charles Fox. *The Aramaic Origin of the Fourth Gospel.* Oxford: Clarendon, 1922.
Butler, H. E., trans. *Quintilian, Institutio Oratoria.* Vol. 3. Loeb Classical Library. Cambridge, Mass.: Harvard University Press, 1921.
Cain, Andrew, ed. and trans. *Jerome's Epitaph on Paula: A Commentary on the Epitaphium Sanctae Paulae.* Oxford: Oxford University Press, 2013.

Carlson, Stephen C. "Clement of Alexandria on the 'Order' of the Gospels." *New Testament Studies* 47 (2001): 118–25.
Carrier, Richard. "Origen, Eusebius, and the Accidental Interpolation in Josephus, Jewish Antiquities 20.200." *Journal of Early Christian Studies* 20 (Winter 2012): 489–514.
Carson, Donald A. *The Gospel According to John*. Pillar New Testament Commentary. Grand Rapids: Eerdmans, 1991.
Carson, Donald, and Douglas J. Moo, *An Introduction to the New Testament*. 2nd ed. Grand Rapids: Zondervan, 2005.
Cary, Earnest, trans. *Dio Cassius, Roman History*. Vol. 8, books 61–70. Loeb Classical Library 176. Cambridge, Mass.: Harvard University Press, 1925.
Cennamo, Michela. "Argument structure and alignment variations and changes in late Latin." Pages 307–46 in *The Role of Semantic, Pragmatic, and Discourse Factors in the Development of Case*. Edited by Jóhanna Barðdal and Shobhana Lakshmi Chelliah. Amsterdam: John Benjamins, 2009.
Cerrato, J. A. *Hippolytus Between East and West: The Commentaries and the Provenance of the Corpus*. Oxford Theological Monographs. Oxford: University Press, 2002.
Chapman, John. "Papias on the Age of Our Lord." *Journal of Theological Studies* 9 (1908): 48–63.
———. *John the Presbyter and the Fourth Gospel*. Oxford: Clarendon Press, 1911.
Charles, Robert Henry. *A Critical and Exegetical Commentary on the Revelation of St. John*. 2 vols. International Critical Commentary. New York: Scribner, 1920.
Charlesworth, James H., ed. *The Old Testament Pseudepigrapha*. 2 vols. New York: Doubleday, 1983–85.
Charlesworth, James H. *The Beloved Disciple : Whose Witness Validates the Gospel of John?* Valley Forge, Penn.: Trinity Press International, 1995.
Chase, F. H. "The Date of the Apocalypse: The Evidence of Irenaeus." *Journal of Theological Studies* 8 (1907): 431–35.
Colson, F. H. "Τάξει in Papias (The Gospels and the Rhetorical Schools)." *Journal of Theological Studies* 14 (1912): 62–69.
Colson, Jean. *L'énigme du disciple que Jésus aimait*. Théologie Historique 10. Paris: Beauchesne, 1969.
Concannon, Cavan W. "The Acts of Timothy: A New Translation and Introduction." Pages 396–405 in *New Testament Apocrypha: More Noncanonical Scriptures*. Vol. 1. Edited by Tony Burke and Brent Landau. Grand Rapids: Eerdmans, 2016.
Constantinou, Eugenia Scarvelis, trans. *Andrew of Caesarea, Commentary on the Apocalypse*. Washington DC: Catholic University of America Press, 2011.
———. *Guiding to a Blessed End: Andrew of Caesarea and His Apocalypse Commentary in the Ancient Church*. Washington, DC: Catholic University of America Press, 2013.
Conti, Marco, trans. *Theodore of Mopsuestia, Commentary on the Gospel of John*. Downers Grove, Ill.: IVP, 2010.
Cook, John Granger. *Roman Attitudes Toward the Christians: From Claudius to Hadrian*. Wissenschaftliche Untersuchungen zum Neuen Testament 261. Tubingen: Mohr, 2010.
Cox, Homersham. *The First Century of Christianity*. London: Longmans, 1886.
Crehan, J. H. "The Fourfold Character of the Gospel." Pages 3–13 in *Studia Evangelica: Papers presented to the International Congress on "The Four Gospels in 1957" held at Christ Church, Oxford, 1957*. Edited by K. Aland, F. L. Cross, et al. Texte und Untersuchungen zur Geschichte der altchristlichen Literatur 73. Berlin: Akademie-Verlag, 1959.
Crook, John Anthony. *Law and Life of Rome: 90 B.C.-A.D. 212*. London, Thames & Hudson, 1967.
Cross, F. L., and Elizabeth A. Livingstone, eds. *The Oxford Dictionary of the Christian Church*. Oxford: Oxford University Press, 2005.
Crossley, James G. *The Date of Mark's Gospel: Insight from the Law in Earliest Christianity*. London: T. & T. Clark, 2004.

Cullmann, Oscar. *The Johannine Circle*. Translated by John Bowden. London: SCM, 1976.
Culpepper, R. Alan. *John, the Son of Zebedee: The Life of a Legend*. Edinburgh: T. & T. Clark, 2000.
Davies, W. D., and D. C. Allison. *A Critical and Exegetical Commentary on the Gospel according to Saint Matthew*. 3 vols. International Critical Commentary. Edinburgh: T. & T. Clark, 1988–97.
De Bruyne, Donatien. "Les plus anciens prologues latins des Évangiles." *Revue Bénédictine* 40 (1928): 193–214.
Delff, Heinrich Karl Hugo. *Das vierte Evangelium: ein authentischer Bericht über Jesus von Nazret*. Husum: Delff, 1890.
Devreesse, Robert. *Essai sur Théodore de Mopsueste*. Studi e Testi 141. Vatican City: Bibloteca Apostolica Vatican, 1948.
Dewing, Henry B., and Glanville Downey, trans. *Procopius*. Vol. 7. Loeb Classical Library. Cambridge, Mass.: Harvard University Press, 1954.
Diekamp, Franz. *Hippolytos von Theben: Texte und Untersuchungen*. Münster, 1898.
Dulaey, Martine. *Victorin de Poetovio, Premier Exégète Latin*. 2 vols. Collection des Études Augustiniennes. Série Antiquité 139/140. Paris: Institut d'Études Augustiniennes, 1993.
Ebrard, Johann Heinrich August. *Wissenschaftliche Kritik der evangelischen Geschichte*. Vol. 1. Frankfurt: Zimmer, 1842.
Edmundson, George. *The Church in Rome in the First Century*. London: Longmans, 1913.
Ehrhardt, Arnold. *The Framework of the New Testament Stories*. Manchester: Manchester University Press, 1964.
Ehrman, Bart. *The Apostolic Fathers*. 2 vols. Loeb Classical Library. Cambridge, Mass.: Harvard University Press, 2003.
Eisler, Robert. *The Enigma of the Fourth Gospel*. London: Methuen, 1938.
Elliott, Alison Goddard. *Medieval Latin*. Edited by K. P. Harrington and Joseph Pucci. Chicago: University of Chicago Press, 1997.
Elliott, Keith, ed. and trans. *The Apocryphal New Testament: A Collection of Apocryphal Christian Literature in an English Translation Based on M. R. James*. Oxford: Clarendon Press, 1993.
Ellis, F. S., trans., and William Caxton, ed. *Jacobus de Voragine, The Golden Legend, or, Lives of the Saints*. 7 vols. London: Dent, 1900.
Étaix, R., and J. Lemarié, eds., *Chromatii Aquileiensis Opera*. Corpus Christianorum, Series Latina 9A. Turnhout: Brepols, 1974.
Evans, Ernest, ed. and trans. *Tertullian, Adversus Marcionem*. 2 vols. Oxford: The Clarendon Press, 1972.
Fabricius, Johann Albert. *Codex Apocryphus Novi Testamenti*. Vols 1-2. Hamburg: 1703.
Farrar, Frederic W. *The Early Days of Christianity*. London: Cassell, 1885.
Feltoe, C. L. "St John and St James in Western 'Non-Roman' Kalendars." *Journal of Theological Studies* 40 (1909): 589–92.
Fitzgerald, John T. "Theodore of Mopsuestia on Paul's Letter to Philemon." Pages 333–64 in *Philemon in Perspective: Interpreting a Pauline Letter*. Edited by D. Francois Tolmie. Berlin: de Gruyter, 2010.
Fitzmyer, Joseph A. *The Acts of the Apostles: A New Translation with Introduction and Commentary*. AB 31. New Haven, Conn.: Yale University Press, 1998.
Ford, J. Massyngberde. *Revelation: Introduction, Translation, and Commentary*. AB 38. New Haven, Conn.: Yale University Press, 1975.
France, R. T. *The Gospel of Mark: A Commentary on the Greek Text*. New International Greek Testament Commentary. Grand Rapids: Eerdmans, 2002.
Furlong, Dean. "Theodore of Mopsuestia: New Evidence for the Proposed Papian Fragment in *Hist. eccl.* 3.24.5-13." *Journal for the Study of the New Testament* 39.2 (2016) 209-229.
———. "John the Evangelist: Revision and Reinterpretation in Early Christian Sources." Ph.D. dissertation. Vrije Universiteit Amsterdam, 2017.

———. *The John also Called Mark: Reception and Transformation in Christian Tradition*. Wissenschaftliche Untersuchungen zum Neuen Testament II. Tübingen: Mohr Siebeck, forthcoming.

Garitte, Gérard, ed. *Le calendrier palestino-géorgien du Sinaiticus 34 (Xe siècle)*. Subsidia hagiographica 30. Brussels: Société des Bollandistes, 1958.

Gentry, Kenneth L. *Before Jerusalem Fell: Dating the Book of Revelation*. 2nd ed. Atlanta: American, Vision, 1999.

Gibson, Margaret Dunlop, ed. and trans. The Commentaries of Isho'dad of Merv: Bishop of Ḥadatha (c. 850 A.D.). Horae Semiticae 5. Vol. 1. Cambridge: Cambridge University Press, 1911.

Grant, Robert M. *The Earliest Lives of Jesus*. New York: Harper & Row, 1961.

———. "Eusebius and His Church History." Pages 233–47 in *Understanding the Sacred Text: Essays in Honor of Morton S. Enslin on the Hebrew Bible and Christian Beginnings*. Edited by John Henry Paul Reumann. Valley Forge, Pa.: Judson, 1972.

———. *Eusebius as Church Historian*. Oxford: Clarendon Press, 1980.

Gregory, Andrew. *The Reception of Luke and Acts in the Period Before Irenaeus*. Wissenschaftliche Untersuchungen zum Neuen Testament 2.169. Tübingen: Mohr Siebeck, 2003.

Gryson, Roger, ed. *Variorum Auctorum Commentaria Minora in Apocalypsin Johannis*. Corpus Christianorum, Series Latina 107. Turnhout: Brepols, 2003.

Guericke, Heinrich Ernst Ferdinand. *Die Hypothese von dem Presbyter Johannes als Verfasser der Offenbarung*. Halle, 1831.

———. *Historisch-kritische Einleitung in das Neue Testament*. Leipzig, 1843.

Gumerlock, Francis X. *Revelation and the First Century: Preterist Interpretations of the Apocalypse in Early Christianity*. Powder Springs: American Vision, 2012.

———. Review of *Tyconii Afri Expositio Apocalypseos*, ed. Roger Gryson. Corpus Christianorum, Series Latina 107A. Turnhout: Brepols, 2011. *Westminster Theological Journal* 74 (2012): 467–71.

Gundry, Robert H. *The Old is Better: New Testament Essays in Support of Traditional Interpretations*. Tübingen: Mohr Siebeck, 2005.

Gunther, John J. "Early Identifications of the Author of the Johannine Writings." *Journal of Ecclesiastical History* 31 (1980): 407–27.

———. "The Elder John: Author of Revelation." *Journal for the Study of the New Testament* 11 (1981): 3–20.

Gustafsson, B. "Eusebius's Principles in Handling His Sources, as Found in His Church History, Books I to VIII." *Studia Patristica* 4 (1961): 429–41.

Guthrie, Donald. *New Testament Introduction*. 4th rev. ed. Downers Grove, Ill.: IVP, 1996.

Gutwenger, Engelbert. "The Anti-Marcionite Prologues." *Theological Studies* 7 (1946): 393–409.

Gwynn, John. "Hippolytus and his 'Heads against Caius.'" *Hermathena* 6 (1888): 397–418.

Haase, Felix, ed. *Apostel und Evangelisten in den orientalischen Überlieferungen*. Neutestamentliche Abhandlungen 9. Münster: Aschendorff, 1922.

Haenchen, Ernst. *John: A Commentary on the Gospel of John 1, Chapters 1–6*. Translated by Robert W. Funk. Hermeneia; Philadelphia: Fortress Press, 1984.

Hahneman, Geoffrey M. *The Muratorian Fragment and the Development of the Canon*. Oxford Theological Monographs. Oxford: Clarendon, 1992.

Hammond Bammel, Caroline P. *Tradition and Exegesis in Early Christian Writers*. Aldershot, Hampshire: Variorum, 1995.

Hansen, G. C., ed. *Theodoros Anagnostes Kirchengeschichte*. Die Griechischen Christlichen Schriftsteller der ersten drei Jahrhunderte 54. Berlin, 1971.

Harnack, Adolph von. *Die Chronologie der altchristlichen Litteratur bis Eusebius*. Vol. 1. Leipzig: Hinrichs, 1897.

———. "Über den Verfasser und den literarischen Charakter des Muratorischen Fragments." *Zeitschrift für die neutestamentliche Wissenschaft und die Kunde der älteren Kirche* 24 (1925): 1–16.
Harrington, Wilfrid J. *Revelation*. Edited by Daniel J. Harrington. Sacra Pagina 16. Collegeville, Minn.: Liturgical Press, 2008.
Harris, J. Rendel. *Hermas in Arcadia and the Rest of the Words of Baruch*. Cambridge: Cambridge University Press, 1896.
Hartke, Wilhelm. *Vier urchristliche Parteien und ihre Vereinigung zur apostolischen Kirche*. 2 vols. Berlin: Akademie-Verlag, 1961.
Hartog, Paul. *Polycarp's Epistle to the Philippians and the Martyrdom of Polycarp: Introduction, Text, and Commentary*. Oxford Apostolic Fathers. Oxford: Oxford University Press, 2013.
Harvey, W. Wigan, ed. *S. Irenaei Libros quinque Adversus Haereses*, 2 vols. Cambridge: Typis Academicis, 1857.
Haussleiter, Johannes, ed. *Victorini Episcopi Petavionensis Opera*. Corpus Christianorum, Series Latina 49. Vienna: Tempsky, 1916.
Heemstra, Marius. *The Fiscus Judaicus and the Parting of the Ways*. Wissenschaftliche Untersuchungen zum Neuen Testament 277. Tübingen: Mohr Siebeck, 2010.
Heine, Ronald E. "Hippolytus, Ps.-Hippolytus and the early canons." Pages 142–51 in *The Cambridge History of Early Christian Literature*. Edited by Frances Young, Lewis Ayres and Andrew Louth. Cambridge: Cambridge University Press, 2004.
Heine, Ronald E., trans. *Origen, Commentary on the Gospel of John, Books 1-10*. Fathers of the Church 80. Washington DC: Catholic University of America, 1989.
Helm, August. *Die Chronik des Hieronymus*. Berlin: Akademie-Verlag, 1956.
Hengel, Martin. *The Johannine Question*. Translated by John Bowden. London: SCM Press, 1989.
———. *Die johanneische Frage: Ein Lösungsversuch*. Wissenschaftliche Untersuchungen zum Neuen Testament 67. Tübingen: Mohr Siebeck, 1993.
———. *Studies in the Gospel of Mark*. Eugene: Wipf and Stock, 2003.
Hilberg, I., ed. *Sancti Eusebii Hieronymi Epistulae*. Corpus Scriptorum Ecclesiasticorum Latinorum 56. Vienna: 1918.
Hill, Charles E. "What Papias Said about John (and Luke): A 'New' Papian Fragment." *Journal of Theological Studies* 49 (1998): 582–629.
———. *The Johannine Corpus in the Early Church*. New York: Oxford University Press, 2004.
———. *From the Lost Teaching of Polycarp*. Tübingen: Mohr Siebeck, 2006.
———. "The Fragments of Papias." Pages 42–51 in *The Writings of the Apostolic Fathers*. Edited by Paul Foster. London: T. & T. Clark, 2007.
———. "The 'Orthodox Gospel': The Reception of John in the Great Church prior to Irenaeus." Pages 233–300 in  *Legacy of John: Second-Century Reception of the Fourth Gospel*. Edited by Tuomas Rasimus. Leiden: Brill, 2009.
Hitchcock, Mark L. "A Defense of the Domitianic Date of the Book of Revelation." PhD dissertation. Dallas Theological Seminary, 2005.
Holl, Karl, ed. *Epiphanius (Uncoratus und Panarion) II: Panarion haer. 34–64*. Die Griechischen Christlichen Schriftsteller der ersten drei Jahrhunderte 31. Leipzig: Hinrichs, 1922.
———. *Epiphanius (Uncoratus und Panarion) III: Panarion haer. 65–80*. Die Griechischen Christlichen Schriftsteller der ersten drei Jahrhunderte 37. Leipzig: Hinrichs, 1933.
Holmes, Michael William, ed. *The Apostolic Fathers: Greek Texts and English Translations*. 2nd ed. Grand Rapids: Baker, 1999.
Hort, Fenton J. A. *The Apocalypse of St. John 1–3: The Greek Text with Introduction, Commentary, and Additional Notes*. London: Macmillan, 1908.
Hort, Fenton J. A., and Joseph B. Mayor. *Clement of Alexandria, Miscellanies Book VII*. London: MacMillan, 1902.
Houghton, H. A. G. *The Latin New Testament: A Guide to its Early History, Texts, and Manuscripts*. New York: Oxford University Press, 2016.

Howard, W. F. "The Anti-marcionite prologues to the Gospels." *Expository Times* 47 (1936): 534–38.
Huber, Konrad. *Einer gleich einem Menschensohn: die Christusvisionen in Offb 1,9-20 und Offb 14,14-20 und die Christologie der Johannesoffenbarung.* Neutestamentliche Abhandlungen 51. Münster: Aschendorff, 2007.
Hurst, D., and M. Adriaen, eds. *Commentariorum in Matheum libri IV.* Corpus Christianorum, Series Latina 77. Turnhout: Brepols, 1969.
Jackson, H. Latimer. *The Problem of the Fourth Gospel.* Cambridge: University Press, 1918.
James, Montague Rhodes, ed. and trans. *The Apocryphal New Testament: Being the Apocryphal Gospels, Acts, Epistles, and Apocalypses.* Oxford: Clarendon Press, 1924.
Junod, E., and J.-D. Kaestli, eds. *Acta Iohannis.* 2 vols. Corpus Christianorum, Series Apocryphorum. Turnhout: Brepols, 1983.
Kalantzis, George, trans. *Theodore of Mopsuestia, Commentary on the Gospel of John.* Early Christian Studies 7. Strathfield: St Pauls Publications, 2004.
Karrer, Martin. *Die Johannesoffenbarung als Brief: Brief: Studien zu ihrem literarischen, historischen und theologischen Ort.* Göttingen: Vandenhoeck & Ruprecht, 1986.
Keener, Craig S. *The Gospel of John: A Commentary.* 2 vols. Grand Rapids: Baker, 2012.
Keim, Théodor. *Geschichte Jesu von Nazara in ihrer Verkettung mit dem Gesamtleben seines Volkes.* 3 vols. Zurich: Orell, 1867–72.
Kelhoffer, James A. *Miracle and Mission: The Authentication of Missionaries and Their Message in the Longer Ending of Mark.* Tübingen: Mohr Siebeck, 2000.
Kellerman, James, trans., and Thomas C. Oden, ed. *Incomplete Commentary on Matthew (Opus Imperfectum ).* 2 vols. Downers Grove, Ill.: IVP, 2010.
Kennedy, George A., trans. *Progymnasmata: Greek Textbooks of Prose Composition and Rhetoric.* Leiden: Brill, 2003.
Keresztes, Paul. "The Jews, the Christians, and Emperor Domitian." *Vigiliae Christianae* 27 (1973): 1–28.
Kershaw, Stephen P. *A Brief History of the Roman Empire.* London: Robinson, 2013.
Kilburn, K., ed. *Lucian.* Vol. 6. Loeb Classical Library. Cambridge, Mass.: Harvard University Press, 1959.
Klijn, A. F. J., and G. J. Reinink. *Patristic Evidence for Jewish-Christian Sects.* Novum Testamentum Supplements 3. Leiden: Brill, 1973.
Klostermann, Erich, and Ernest Benz, eds. *Origenes Werke.* Vol. 10–11. Die Griechischen Christlichen Schriftsteller der ersten drei Jahrhunderte 38. Leipzig: Hinrichs, 1933–35.
Koester, Craig R. *Revelation: A New Translation with Introduction and Commentary.* Anchor Bible 38A. New Haven, Conn.: Yale University Press, 2014.
Kok, Michael J. *The Beloved Apostle? The Transformation of the Apostle John into the Fourth Evangelist.* Eugene: Cascade, 2017.
Körtner, Ulrich H. J. *Papias von Hierapolis: Ein Beitrag zur Geschichte des frühren Christentums.* Forschungen zur Religion und Literatur des Alten und Neuen Testaments 133. Göttingen, 1983.
Köstenberger, Andreas J. *A Theology of John's Gospel and Letters: The Word, the Christ, the Son of God.* Biblical Theology of the New Testament. Grand Rapids: Zondervan, 2009.
Köstenberger, Andreas J., and Stephen O. Stout. "'The Disciple Jesus Loved': Witness, Author, Apostle—A Response to Richard Bauckham's *Jesus and the Eyewitnesses.*" *Bulletin for Biblical Research* 18 (2008): 209–31.
Köstenberger, Andreas J., L. Scott Kellum and Charles L. Quarles. *The Cradle, the Cross, and the Crown: An Introduction to the New Testament.* Nashville: B&H, 2009.
Kroymann, Aemilianus, ed. *Tertullianus: Opera I.* Corpus Christianorum, Series Latina 1. Turnhout: Brepols, 1954.
Krueger, Derek. *Writing and Holiness: The Practice of Authorship in the Early Christian East.* Philadelphia: University of Pennsylvania Press, 2004.

Kruger. Michael J. "The Reception of the Book of Revelation in the Early Church." Pages 159–74 in *Book of Seven Seals: The Peculiarity of Revelation, its Manuscripts, Attestation and Transmission*. Edited by Thomas J. Kraus and Michael Sommer. Wissenschaftliche Untersuchungen zum Neuen Testament 363. Tübingen: Mohr Siebeck, 2016.

Kürzinger, Josef. *Papias von Hierapolis und die Evangelien des Neuen Testaments*. Regensburg: Pustet, 1983.

Lake, Kirsopp, ed. and trans. *Eusebius: The Ecclesiastical History*, 2 vols. Loeb Classical Library. London: Heinemann; 1926.

Lalleman, Pieter J. *The Acts of John: A Two-stage Initiation into Johannine Gnosticism*. Leuven: Peeters, 1998.

Lanéry, Cécile. *Ambroise de Milan hagiographe*. Institut d'Études Augustiniennes, 2008.

Lardner, Nathaniel. *The Works of Nathaniel Lardner*. Vol. 3. London: Thomas Hamilton, 1815.

Lawlor, Hugh Jackson. *Eusebiana: Essays on the Ecclesiastical History of Eusebius Pamphili, c. 264–349*. Oxford: Clarendon Press, 1912.

Ledgeway, Adam. *From Latin to Romance: Morphosyntactic Typology and Change*. Oxford Studies in Diachronic and Historical Linguistics. Oxford: Oxford University Press, 2012.

Leloir, Louis, ed. *Saint Éphrem: Commentaire de l'Évangile concordant, texte syriaque (Manuscrit Chester Beatty 709)*. Chester Beatty Monographs 8. Dublin: Hodges Figgis, 1963.

Lemarié, Joseph. "Saint Chromace d'Aquilée témoin du Canon de Muratori." *Revue des études augustiniennes* 24 (1978).

Liddell, Henry George, Robert Scott, Henry Stuart Jones and Roderick McKenzie, eds. *A Greek-English Lexicon*. Oxford: Clarendon Press, 1996.

Lightfoot, Joseph B. *The Apostolic Fathers: Clement, Ignatius, and Polycarp*. 5 vols. London: Macmillan, 1889–90.

———. *Biblical Essays*. London: Macmillan, 1893.

———. *Essays on Supernatural Religion*. 2nd ed. London: Macmillan, 1893.

———. *The Gospel of John: A Newly Discovered Commentary*. Edited by Ben Witherington III, Todd D. Still and Jeanette M. Hagen. The Lightfoot Legacy Set vol. 2. Downers Grove, Ill.: IVP, 2015.

Lincoln, Andrew T. *The Gospel According to Saint John*. Black's New Testament Commentary. London: Continuum, 2005.

Lipsius, Richard. A., and Max Bonnet, eds. *Acta Apostolorum Apocrypha*. Vol. 2/1. Leipzig: 1898.

Litwa, David M., ed. and trans. *Refutation of All Heresies: Text, Translation, and Notes*. Writings from the Greco-Roman World 40. Atlanta: SBL, 2015.

Luthardt, Christoph Ernst. *St. John the Author of the Fourth Gospel*. Revised and translated by Caspar Rene Gregory. Edinburgh: T. & T. Clark, 1875.

MacDonald, Dennis R. *Two Shipwrecked Gospels: The Logoi of Jesus and Papias's Exposition of Logia about the Lord*. Atlanta: SBL, 2012.

MacDonald, James Madison. *The Life and Writings of St. John*. 2nd ed. London: Hodder & Stoughton, 1880.

Manor, T. Scott. *Epiphanius' Alogi and the Johannine Controversy: A Reassessment of Early Ecclesial Opposition to the Johannine Corpus*. Supplements to Vigiliae Christianae 135. Leiden: Brill, 2016.

Marcovich, Miroslav. *Iustini martyris Dialogus cum Tryphone*. Patristische Texte und Studien 47. Berlin: de Gruyter, 1997.

Markschies, Christoph. *Kaiserzeitliche christliche Theologie und ihre Institutionen*. Tübingen: Mohr Siebeck, 2008.

Marshall, I. Howard. *The Epistles of John*. The New International Commentary on the New Testament. Grand Rapids: Eerdmans, 1978.

Martin, Ralph P. *James*. Word Biblical Commentary 48. Dallas: Word, 1998.

Mattingly, David J. *Imperialism, Power, and Identity: Experiencing the Roman Empire.* Princeton: Princeton University Press, 2011.
McDowell, Sean. "A Historical Evaluation of the Evidence for the Death of the Apostles as Martyrs for their Faith." PhD dissertation. Southern Baptist Theological Seminary, 2014.
McNamara, Martin. *Targum Neofiti 1: Deuteronomy.* The Aramaic Bible 5. Collegeville, Minn.: The Liturgical Press, 1997.
Michaels, J. Ramsey. *The Gospel of John.* The New International Commentary on the New Testament. Grand Rapids: Eerdmans, 2010.
Milligan, William. *The Revelation of St. John.* London: Macmillan, 1886.
Moloney, Francis J. *The Gospel of John.* Edited by Daniel J. Harrington. Sacra Pagina 4. Collegeville, Minn.: Liturgical Press, 1998.
Mommsen, Theodor, ed. *Chronica Minora.* Vol. 1. *Monumenta Germania Historica.* Berlin, 1892.
Morris, Leon. *Studies in the Fourth Gospel.* Grand Rapids: Eerdmans, 1969.
―――. *The Gospel According to John.* The New International Commentary on the New Testament. Grand Rapids: Eerdmans, 1995.
Mounce, Robert H. *The Book of Revelation.* The New International Commentary on the New Testament. Grand Rapids: Eerdmans, 1997.
Munck, Johannes. "Presbyters and Disciples of the Lord in Papias." *Harvard Theological Review* 52 (1959): 223–43.
Murphy-O'Connor, Jerome. "The Cenacle—Setting for Acts 2:44–45." Pages 303–21 in *The Book of Acts in its Palestinian Setting.* Edited by Richard Bauckham. The Book of Acts in its First Century Setting 4. Grand Rapids: Eerdmans, 1995.
Nicklas, Tobias. "Probleme der Apokalypserezeption im 2. Jahrhundert Eine Diskussion mit Charles E. Hill." Pages 28–45 in Ancient Christian Interpretations of "Violent Texts" in the Apocalypse. Edited by Joseph Verheyden, Andreas Merkt, Tobias Nicklas. Novum Testamentum et Orbis Antiquus 92. Göttingen: Vandenhoeck & Ruprecht, 2011.
Niese, Benedict, ed. *Flavii Iosephi Opera.* 6 vols. Berolini: Weidmannos, 1888–95.
Norelli, Enrico. *Papia di Hierapolis, Esposizione degli Oracoli del Signore: Iframmenti.* Milan: Paoline, 2005.
Oberweis, Michael. "Das Papias-Zeugnis vom Tode des Johannes Zebedäi." *Novum Testamentum* 38 (1996): 277–95.
Orchard, Bernard and Harold Riley. *The Order of the Synoptics: Why Three Synoptic Gospels?* Macon, Ga.: Mercer University Press, 1987.
Orchard, John B. "Some Guidelines for the Interpretation of Eusebius' Hist. Eccl. 3.34–39." Pages 393–403 in *The New Testament Age: Essays in Honor of Bo Reicke.* Edited by William C. Weinrich. 2 vols. Macon, Ga.; Mercer University Press, 1984.
Painter, John. *Just James: The Brother of Jesus in History and Tradition.* Edinburgh: Fortress, 1999.
Pate, C. Marvin. *The Writings of John: A Survey of the Gospel, Epistles, and Apocalypse.* Grand Rapids: Zondervan, 2011.
Pearse, Roger. "Notes from the Commentary on the four gospels." Accessed February 2, 2017. http://www.tertullian.org/fathers/dionysius_syrus_revelation_01.htm.
Perrin, Bernadotte, ed. *Plutarch. Lives.* Vol. 3. Loeb Classical Library. Medford, Mass.: Harvard University Press, 1916.
Perumalil, A. C. "Papias." *Expository Times* 85 (1974): 361–66.
Petrie, C. Stewart. "The Authorship of 'The Gospel According to Matthew': A Reconsideration of the External Evidence." *New Testament Studies* 14 (1967): 15–32.
Preuschen, Erwin, ed. *Analecta: Kürzere texte zur Geschichte der Alten Kirche und des Kanons, zusammengestellt von Erwin Preuschen.* Leipzig: Mohr, 1893.
―――. *Origenes Werke* Vol. 4. Die Griechischen Christlichen Schriftsteller der ersten drei Jahrhunderte 10. Leipzig: Hinrichs, 1903.
Prigent, Pierre. *Commentary on the Apocalypse of St. John.* Translated by Wendy Pradels. Tübingen: Mohr Siebeck, 2004.

Prigent, Pierre, and Ralph Stehl. "Les fragments du De Apocalypsi d'Hippolyte." *Theologische Zeitschrift* 29 (1973): 313–33.
Pritchett, William K., trans. *Dionysius of Halicarnassus: On Thucydides*. Berkeley: University of California Press, 1975.
Räisänen, Heikki. *Challenges to Biblical Interpretation: Collected Essays, 1991–2000*. Leiden: Brill, 2001.
Ramage, Nancy H., and Andrew Ramage. *Ancient Rome*. London: British Museum, 2008.
Ramelli, Ilaria. "John the Evangelist's Work: An Overlooked Redaktionsgeschichtliche Theory from the Patristic Age." Pages 30–52 in *The Origins of John's Gospel*. Edited by Stanley E. Porter and Hughson T. Ong. Leiden: Brill, 2016.
Ramsay, William. *The Letters to the Seven Churches of Asia*. 2nd ed. London: Hodder & Stoughton, 1906.
Ratzinger, Joseph. *Jesus of Nazareth: The Infancy Narratives*. Translated by Philip J. Whitmore. New York: Doubleday, 2007.
Regul, Jürgen. Die antimarcionitischen Evangelienprologe. *Vetus Latina; die Reste der alt-lateinischen Bibel* 6. Freiburg: Verlag Herder, 1969.
Rettig, John W., trans. *Augustine, Tractates on the Gospel of John 1–10*. Fathers of the Church 78. Washington DC: Catholic University of America, 1988.
Riesner, Rainer. *Paul's Early Period: Chronology, Mission Strategy, Theology*. Translated by Doug Stott. Grand Rapids: Eerdmans, 1998.
Robinson, John A. T. *Redating the New Testament*. London: SCM, 1976.
Robinson, Theodore H. "The Authorship of the Muratorian Canon." *Expositor* 7 (1906): 481–95.
Rolfe, J. C., trans. *Suetonius*. 2 vols. Loeb Classical Library. London: William Heinamann, 1914.
Ropes, James H. *A Critical and Exegetical Commentary on the Epistle of St. James*. International Critical Commentary. New York: Scribner, 1916.
Rose, Els. *Ritual Memory: The Apocryphal Acts and Liturgical Commemoration in the Early Medieval West (c. 500-1215)*. Leiden: Brill, 2009.
Saffrey, Henry Dominique. "Le témoignage de pères sur le martyre de S. Jean l'Evangéliste." *Revue des sciences philosophiques et théologiques* 69 (1985): 265–72.
Sanday, William. *The Criticism of the Fourth Gospel*. Oxford: Clarendon Press, 1905.
Sanders, Joseph N. *The Fourth Gospel in the Early Church*. Cambridge: Cambridge University Press, 1943.
———. "St John on Patmos." *New Testament Studies* 9 (1963): 75–85.
Schermann, Theodor, ed. *Prophetarum Vitae Fabulosae Indices Apostolorum Discipulorumque Domini*. Leipzig: Teubner 1907.
Schoedel, William R. *The Apostolic Fathers*. Vol. 5, *Polycarp, Martyrdom of Polycarp, Fragments of Papias*. Camden, N.J.: Nelson, 1967.
Schutter, William L. *Hermeneutic and Composition in I Peter*. Wissenschaftliche Untersuchungen zum Neuen Testament 2.30. Tübingen: Mohr Siebeck, 1989.
Schwartz, Eduard. "Über den Tod der Söhne Zebedäi. Ein Beitrag zur Geschichte des Johannesevangeliums" *Gesammelte Schriften* 5 (1963): 48–123.
Sedlácek, I., ed. *Dionysius bar Salibi. In Apocalypsim, Actus et Epistulas Catholicas*. Corpus Scriptorum Christianorum Orientalium, Scriptores Syri 2/101. Rome: de Luigi, 1910.
Stählin, Otto, ed. *Clemens Alexandrinus*. Vol. 2: *Stromata 1–6*. Die Griechischen Christlichen Schriftsteller der ersten drei Jahrhunderte. Leipzig: Hinrichs, 1906.
Sellew, Philip. "Eusebius and the Gospels." Pages 110–38 in *Eusebius, Christianity, and Judaism*. Edited by Harold Attridge and Gohei Hata. Detroit: Wayne State University Press, 1992.
Shanks, Monte A. *Papias and the New Testament*. Eugene: Wipf and Stock, 2013.
Shelton, Brian W. *Martyrdom from Exegesis in Hippolytus: An Early Church Presbyter's Commentary on Daniel*. Studies in Christian History and Thought. Eugene: Wipf and Stock, 2008.

Simcox, William. H. *The Revelation of S. John the Divine.* Cambridge Greek Testament for Schools and Colleges. Cambridge: Cambridge University Press, 1909.

Skarsaune, Oskar. "Fragments of Jewish Christian Literature Quoted in Some Greek and Latin Fathers." Pages 325–78 in *Jewish Believers in the Jesus: The Early Centuries.* Edited by Oskar Skarsaune and Reidar Hvalvik. Peabody, Mass.: Hendrickson, 2007.

Smalley, Stephen. *John, Evangelist and Interpreter.* 2nd ed. London: Paternoster, 1997.

Smallwood, E. Mary. *The Jews under Roman Rule from Pompey to Diocletian. A Study in Political Relations.* Leiden: Brill, 2001.

Smith, Dwight Moody. *The Fourth Gospel in Four Dimensions: Judaism and Jesus, the Gospels and Scripture.* Columbia, S.C.: University of South Carolina Press, 2008.

Smith, Joseph D. "Gaius and the Controversy over the Johannine Literature." PhD dissertation. Yale University, 1979.

Sordi, Marta. *The Christians and the Roman Empire.* Translated by Annabel Bedini. London: Routledge, 1994.

Souter, Alexander. *The Text and Canon of the New Testament.* New York: Scribner, 1913.

Spence, Stephen. *The Parting of the Ways: The Roman Church as a Case Study.* Leuven: Peeters, 2004.

Stanton, Graham N. "The Fourfold Gospel," *New Testament Studies* 43 (1997): 317–46.

Stegemann, Ekkehard W., and Wolfgang Stegemann. *The Jesus Movement: A Social History of its First Century.* Translated by O. C. Dean. Edinburgh: T. & T. Clark, 1999.

Stewart-Sykes, Alistair. "ΤΑΞΕΙ in Papias: Again." *Journal of Early Christian Studies* 3 (1995): 487–92.

———. *Melito of Sardis: On Pascha.* Crestwood, N.Y.: St Vladimir's Seminary Press, 2001.

Stolt, Jan. "Om dateringen af Apokalypsen." *Dansk Teologisk Tidsskrift* 40 (1977): 202–7.

Stott, John R. W. *The Letters of John: An Introduction and Commentary.* Tyndale New Testament Commentaries. Downers Grove, Ill.: IVP, 1988.

Strecker, Georg. *The Johannine Letters: A Commentary on 1, 2, and 3 John.* Translated by Linda M. Maloney. Hermeneia; Minneapolis: Fortress, 1996.

Streeter, Burnett Hillman. *The Four Gospels: A Study of Origins.* London: Macmillan, 1964.

Swete, Henry Barclay. *The Gospel according to St. Mark. The Greek Text with Introduction, Notes and Indices.* London: Macmillan, 1898.

———. *The Apocalypse of St. John.* 2nd ed. New York: Macmillan, 1907.

Taniguchi, Yuko, François Bovon and Athanasios Antonopoulos. "The Memorial of Saint John the Theologian (BHG 919fb)." Pages 333–52 in *The Apocryphal Acts of the Apostles.* Edited by François Bovon, Ann G. Brock, and C. R. Matthews. Cambridge: Harvard University Press, 1999.

Taylor, R. O. P. *The Groundwork of the Gospels.* Oxford: Blackwell, 1946.

Thompson, Leonard L. "Ordinary Lives: John and his First Readers." Pages 25–47 in *Reading the Book of Revelation: A Resource for Students.* Edited by David L. Barr. Atlanta: SBL, 2003.

Trebilco, Paul. *The Early Christians in Ephesus from Paul to Ignatius.* Grand Rapids: Eerdmans, 2007.

Turcan, Marie, ed. *La toilette des femmes: Introduction, texte critique, traduction, et commentaire.* Sources Chrétiennes 173. Paris: Cerf, 1971.

Unger, Dominic J., trans. *St. Irenaeus of Lyons Against the Heresies, Book 1.* Ancient Christian Writers 55. New York: Newman Press, 1992.

Usener, Hermann, ed. *Acta S. Timothei.* Bonn: Caroli Georgi Universitas, 1877.

———. *Dionysii Halicarnasei Quae Exstant.* Vol. 5. Leipzig: Teubner, 1899.

Van den Broek, Roelof, ed. *Pseudo-Cyril of Jerusalem On the Life and the Passion of Christ: A Coptic Apocryphon.* Supplements to Vigiliae Christianae 118. Leiden, Brill, 2012.

Van Unnik, W. C. "The Authority of the Presbyters in Irenaeus' Works." Pages 336–50 in *Sparsa Collecta . Part 4: Neotestamentica—Flavius Josephus—Patristica.* Edited by Cilliers Breytenbach and Pieter W. van der Horst. Leiden: Brill, 2014.

Verheyden, Joseph. "The Canon Muratori: A Matter of Dispute." Pages 487–556 in *The Biblical Canons*. Edited by J.-M. Auwers and H. J. de Jonge. Bibliotheca Ephemeridum Theologicarum Lovaniensium 163. Leuven: Peeters, 2003.
Vielhauer, P. *Geschichte der urchristlichen Literatur*. Berlin: de Gruyter, 1975.
Volfing, Annette. *John the Evangelist and Medieval German Writing: Imitating the Inimitable*. New York: Oxford University Press, 2001.
Von Wahlde, Urban C. *The Gospel and Letters of John*. Vol. 3. Grand Rapids: Eerdmans, 2010.
Watson, Francis. *Gospel Writing: A Canonical Perspective*. Grand Rapids: Eerdmans, 2013.
Weidmann, Frederick W. *Polycarp and John: The Harris Fragments and Their Challenge to the Literary Traditions*. Notre Dame, Ind.: University of Notre Dame Press, 1999.
Weinrich, William C., ed. *Revelation*. Ancient Christian Commentary on Scripture: New Testament 12. Downers Grove, Ill.: IVP, 2005.
———, trans. *Greek Commentaries on Revelation*. Ancient Christian Texts. Downers Grove, Ill.: IVP, 2011.
Wenham, John. *Easter Enigma: Are the Resurrection Accounts in Conflict?* 2nd ed. Grand Rapids: Baker, 1992.
Westcott, Brooke Foss. *A G eneral S urvey of the H istory of the C anon of the New Testament D uring the First Four Centuries*. Cambridge: Macmillan, 1855.
Wetstein, Johannes. J. 2 vols. Amsterdam: Ex Ocina Dommeriana, 1751–52.
Williams, F., trans. The Panarion of Epiphanius of Salamis. Book I (Sects 1–46) . Nag Hammadi and Manichean Studies 35. Leiden: Brill, 1994.
———, trans. The Panarion of Epiphanius of Salamis. Books II and III (Sects 47–80, De Fide) . Nag Hammadi and Manichean Studies 36. Leiden: Brill, 1994.
Williams, Travis B. *Persecution in 1 Peter*. Leiden: Brill, 2012.
Wilson, J. Christian. "The Problem of the Domitianic Date of Revelation." *New Testament Studies* 39 (1993): 587–606.
Winn, Adam. *The Purpose of Mark's Gospel: An Early Christian Response to Roman Imperial Propaganda*. Wissenschaftliche Untersuchungen zum Neuen Testament 2.245. Tübingen: Mohr Siebeck, 2008.
Witulski, Thomas. *Die Johannesoffenbarung und Kaiser Hadrian: Studien zur Datierung der Neutestementlichen Apokalypse*. Göttingen: Vandenhoeck & Ruprecht, 2007.
Wright, William. "An Ancient Syrian Martyrology." *Journal of Sacred Literature* 8 (1866): 423–32.
———. *Apocryphal Acts of the Apostles: Edited from Syriac Manuscripts in the British Museum and Other Libraries*. 2 vols. London: Williams and Norgate, 1871.
Yarbrough, Robert W. "The Date of Papias : A Reassessment." *Journal of the Evangelical Theological Society* 26 (1983): 181–91.
Zahn, Theodor. *Forschungen zur Geschichte des neutestamentlichen Kanons und der altkirchlichen Literatur*. Vol. 6, *Apostel und Apostelschuler in der Provinz Asien*. Leipzig: Deichert, 1900.
Zahn, Theodor, ed. *Acta Joannis unter Benutzung von C. v. Tischendorf's Nachlass*. Erlangen: Verlag von Andreas Deichert, 1880.
Zelyck, Lorne. "Irenaeus and the Authorship of the Fourth Gospel." Pages 239–58 in *The Origins of John's Gospel*. Edited by Stanley E. Porter and Hughson T. Ong. Leiden: Brill, 2016.
Zuntz, Günther "Papiana." *Zeitschrift für die neutestamentliche Wissenschaft und die Kunde der älteren Kirche* 82 (1991): 242–263.

# Index

*The Acts of Andrew*, 26
The Acts of the Apostles, 7, 11, 28, 39, 61, 65, 69
*The Acts of John*, 19, 50, 76, 111, 114–115, 119, 174
*The Acts of John of Prochorus*, 116, 168, 169
*The Acts of John in Rome*, 116
*The Acts of Timothy*, 165–166
ad metalla, 62, 64, 67, 68
Agapius of Hierapolis, 6
Allison, D. C., 28, 49
Alogoi, 59, 76–79, 80, 81, 83, 84, 155, 161, 162, 163, 174
Anastasius of Sinai, 92
Andrew, the Apostle, 131
Andrew of Caesarea, 6, 118
Annand, Rupert, 134
*The Anonymous Preface to John*, 166, 167
Anti-Marcionite Prologue to John, 92, 134, 160, 167
Anti-Marcionite Prologue to Luke, 110
Anti-Marcionite Prologue to Mark, 129
Aphrahat, 22
Apollinarius of Laodicea, 92
Apollonius of Ephesus, 46, 114
Apollonius of Tyana, 112
apostles, 39–40, 41
*The Apostolic Constitutions*, 38
Apringius, 65
Arethas of Caesarea, 118
Aristion, 11, 13, 38, 42, 91
*Ars Rhetorica*, 162
Athanasius, 168
Augustine, 166
Aune, David E., 99

Bacon, Benjamin, 46
Badham, Francis, 21, 22, 49
Barclay, William, 8, 24, 49, 60

Bar Hebraeus, 68
Barrett, C. K, 28, 92
Bartlet, Vernon, 123, 139
Bauckham, Richard, 45, 123, 139, 141, 143–145, 148, 149, 151
Baum, Armin, 10, 24, 29
Beckwith, Isbon Thaddeus, 9
Bede, 166
Bernard, John Henry, 28
Blomberg, Craig, 45
Böhme, Eduard, 99
Boxall, Ian, 60
Brent, Allen, 73, 78–79, 79, 80, 84
Brown, Raymond, 9
Bruce, F. F., 9, 78, 135
Bruns, J. Edgar, 69, 167
Burney, Charles Fox, 43

Cerinthus, 38, 60, 73, 75, 77, 80, 84, 109–110, 133, 134
Chapman, John, 13, 28, 91, 125
Charles, Robert, 8, 23, 28, 61
Chase, F. H., 99
Cheltenham list, 133
Chromatius of Aquileia, 132, 168
*Chronicon Paschale*, 6
Chrysostom, 21, 50, 51, 113
Claudius, 30; and John's exile, 59–60, 60, 61, 63, 64, 65, 69, 174
Clement of Alexandria, 30, 48–49, 96–97, 112–113, 115, 119, 123, 125–127, 128, 163, 173
Colson, F. H., 146
*The Commentary on the Revelation of the Apostle John*, 64
Constantinou, Eugenia Scarvelis, 90
*The Contendings of the Apostles*, 30
Crossley, James, 28
Cyprian, 21
Cyril of Jerusalem, 21

Cullmann, Oscar, 8

Davies, W. D., 28, 49
*The Didache*, 40
Dio Cassius, 93, 94, 96, 112
Dionysius of Alexandria, 50, 69, 75–76, 80, 89, 90
Dionysius the Areopagite (Pseudo), 92
Dionysius bar Salibi, 60, 61, 80–81, 84
Dionysius of Halicarnassus, 146, 147, 158, 159, 162
Domitian, 93–94, 95–96, 111; and John's exile, 1, 49, 62, 63, 64, 89, 93–94, 95–96, 97, 102, 109, 112, 115, 116–118, 119, 174; and date of John's Gospel, 2, 155, 166–167, 167–168, 169–170, 174
Domitilla, Flavia, 93, 94
Dorotheus (Pseudo), 67, 168

Ebed-Jesu, 79
Ehrhardt, Arnold, 131
the elders (of Asia Minor), 8, 9–10, 10–11, 11–13, 14, 41, 43, 91, 97, 100, 124, 125, 126, 127, 133, 167
Ellis, E. Earle, 62
Ephrem, 129
Epiphanius, 30, 59–60, 61, 62, 76–78, 78–79, 80, 81–82, 82–84, 133, 149, 155, 161–163, 164
Eusebius of Caesarea, 1, 7, 12, 13, 25, 89–90, 90–91, 91–92, 92–93, 94–95, 96–97, 102–103, 112, 115, 123, 135, 139, 141, 143–144, 148, 149–150, 155, 157, 159, 161, 164, 167, 174

Farrar, Frederic, 9, 10

Gaius of Rome, 73, 74, 74–75, 78, 80–81, 89, 90, 149, 164, 174
Gentry, Kenneth, 49, 116
George the Sinner. *See* Hamartolos, Georgios
*The Golden Legend*. *See* Voragine, Jacobus de
Gregory of Nyssa, 22
Guericke, Heinrich, 9
Gustafsson, B., 128
Guthrie, Donald, 23, 28

Hamartolos, Georgios, 6, 23–24, 68
Harnack, Adolph von, 133
Harris fragments, the, 19, 42
Hegesippus, 29, 46, 95, 111, 117
Hengel, Martin, 8, 28, 45, 145, 147
Heracleon, 25
Hilary of Poitiers, 50
Hill, Charles, 45, 49, 73, 78, 84, 123, 131, 139, 141, 142, 143, 149, 151, 155
Hippolytus (Eastern), 50, 90
Hippolytus of Rome, 1, 59, 61, 63, 64, 65, 67, 73, 74, 77–78, 78, 80, 81, 84, 90, 110, 149, 155, 163–164, 174; *On the Twelve Apostles*, 29
Hippolytus of Thebes, 118, 168
*The History of James and John*, 168
*The History of John*, 115
Hitchcock, Mark, 61
Hort, Fenton J. A, 99

Ibn Kabar, 30, 62
Ignatius of Antioch, 37
*The Incomplete Commentary on Matthew*, 21, 29
Irenaeus, 6, 12, 20, 40–43, 74, 90, 91–92, 96–97, 97–102, 109–110, 118, 123, 124–125, 126, 128, 134, 173
Isho'dad, 116

James, son of Alphaeus, 29–31, 65
James the Just, 29–31, 95
James, son of Zebedee, 29
Jerome, 9, 22, 30, 50, 76, 92, 110, 113, 131, 133–134, 167, 169, 173
John, the Apostle. *See* John, son of Zebedee
John the Elder, 8, 13, 37, 43, 43–44, 89, 90, 90–91, 93, 123, 126, 139, 142, 148, 149, 155, 162, 170, 174
John, the Evangelist, 1, 12, 19, 27, 37, 38, 40, 43, 44, 48, 50, 76, 92, 123, 124, 127, 131, 132, 133, 139, 142, 148, 149, 151, 155, 156–157, 163, 165, 166, 167, 168, 169, 170, 173
John, Gospel of, 40, 73, 77, 80, 81, 84, 90, 123, 124, 125, 126, 127, 129, 130, 132–133, 134, 140, 144, 149, 156, 157, 158, 162, 163, 164, 166, 167, 168, 169
John of Scythopolis, 92

# Index

John the Seer (author of Revelation), 12, 37, 39, 40, 48, 50, 60, 63, 97, 98; exile of, 48, 61, 62, 64, 65, 90, 93, 109, 110, 114, 115, 168
John, son of Zebedee, 1, 8, 37, 41, 50, 61, 84, 90; martyrdom of, 19, 20–27, 31, 66, 91, 96
Josephus, 98, 145
Justin Martyr, 39, 74, 90

Keener, Craig, 12, 74
Kruger, Michael, 61

Lalleman, Pieter J., 115
Lawlor, Hugh Jackson, 95, 141
Lemarié, Joseph, 132
Lightfoot, Joseph, 6, 9, 25, 78, 123, 134
Ligorio Statue, 79
Lucian, 145, 146, 147, 148, 158
Luke the Evangelist, 43, 129, 130, 132, 133, 140, 147, 162
Luke, Gospel of, 42, 74, 79, 82, 123, 126, 129, 130, 158, 161, 162, 163
Luthardt, Christoph, 11

Manor, T. Scott, 73, 82, 150
Marcion, 134
Mark the Evangelist, 43, 124, 126, 127, 129, 130, 131, 132, 133, 142, 145, 146, 148, 156
Mark, Gospel of, 20, 123, 124, 125–126, 127, 128, 129, 141, 144, 148, 149, 158, 160, 161
Mark (also called John), 69
*The Martyrdom of Isaiah*, 20
*The Martyrdom of Polycarp*, 21
*The Martyrdom of Timothy*, 165
martyrologies, 26–27
Matthew the Evangelist, 43, 124, 129, 133, 139, 142, 147, 158, 159
Matthew, Gospel of, 20, 79, 123, 124, 126, 127, 141, 143, 144, 149, 161, 163
Melito of Sardis, 46, 90
*The Memorial of Saint John*, 169
*Menologium of the Greeks*, 168
Methodius of Olympus, 90
Monarchian prologue to John, 19
Morris, Leon, 23, 24, 28
Munck, Johannes, 8

The Muratorian Canon, 47, 60–61, 63, 74, 123, 130–131, 132, 142, 163

Nero, 25, 49, 60, 93, 97, 98, 112, 116; and John's exile, 109, 110–111, 112, 115–116
Nicephorus Callistus, 167
Nicolaitans, 109–110, 118, 125
Norelli, Enrico, 6, 92, 126, 128, 136n23, 136n24, 137n45, 170n6

Oberweis, Michael, 25, 61
Oecumenius, 118
Orchard, Bernard, 134, 135, 161
Origen, 21, 50, 65–68, 82–84, 90, 129, 149–150

Papias, 5, 8, 11, 23–25, 29, 43, 44, 90, 91, 92, 123, 124, 125, 126, 128, 131, 133, 134, 135, 139, 143, 144, 148, 149, 151, 155, 156, 161, 163, 164, 165, 170, 173; dating of, 6–7; works of, 5–6
*Passio Iohannis*. See *The Suffering of John*
Paul, the Apostle, 26, 39, 42, 60, 61, 69, 75, 110, 111, 124, 128, 129
Peter, the Apostle, 26, 42, 43, 60, 75, 110, 111, 124, 125–126, 126, 128, 129, 130, 131, 132, 133, 142, 146, 156, 160
Philip of Sidé, 6, 24, 29, 68, 92
Philip Sidetes. See Philip of Sidé
Philostratus, 144
Plutarch, 11
Polycarp, 38, 42, 114, 134
Polycrates, 44–46, 173
Procopius, 76

Quadratus, 7
Quintilian, 145, 146, 147, 148, 158, 159

Ramelli, Ilaria, 111, 165
Ramsay, William, 48
Ratzinger, Joseph, 9
Revelation, book of, 39, 64, 73, 75, 80, 89, 90, 97, 110, 117
Riley, Harold, 134, 135, 161
Robinson, John A. T., 99, 111

Sanders, Joseph, 48, 74
Schoedel, William, 8, 25, 134

Severus of Nastrawa, 61
Shanks, Monte, 10, 25
Simeon Metaphases, 169
Sordi, Marta, 94, 96, 118
Stewart-Sykes, Alistair, 144, 145
Suetonius, 93, 94
*The Suffering of John*, 114, 115, 117, 168

Targum Neofiti, 20
Tertullian, 47, 90, 93, 96, 110–111, 114, 118, 173
Theodore of Mopsuestia, 155, 156–160, 163, 165, 166, 167
Theon of Alexandria, 147, 161
Theophilus of Antioch, 46, 90
Theophylact, 68, 70, 118, 168
Thucydides, 144
Trajan, 7, 96; and John's death, 12, 20, 25, 28, 40, 44, 62, 68, 69, 70, 89, 90, 91, 92, 99, 174; and John's exile, 67, 116, 168

Tyconius of Carthage, 116

unattributed fragment (of Eusebius), 139, 142, 143, 144, 148, 149, 151, 155, 156, 157, 158, 159, 160, 161, 163, 165, 166, 169, 170

Victorinus, 62–64, 66, 91, 93, 123, 125, 132–133, 134
*The Virtues of John*, 114, 115, 117
*Virtutes Iohannis. See The Virtues of John*
Voragine, Jacobus de, 131, 167

Watson, Francis, 41, 80, 92
Wenham, John, 45
Westcott, Brooke Foss, 9
Winn, Adam, 128

Zelyck, Lorne, 41–42, 43
Zuntz, Günther, 28

# About the Author

Dean Furlong was born in London, United Kingdom, and resides near Memphis, Tennessee, where he teaches Latin. He received a BA in Classics (*summa cum laude*) from the University of Colorado at Boulder (2009), an MA in Classical and Near Eastern Studies from the University of Minnesota (2011), an MTS in Biblical Studies from the University of Notre Dame (2013), and a PhD in New Testament Studies from Vrije Universiteit Amsterdam (2017). He is currently a research fellow with the Centre for Contextual Biblical Interpretation (CCBI), based in the Netherlands.

www.ingramcontent.com/pod-product-compliance
Lightning Source LLC
Chambersburg PA
CBHW031551300426
44111CB00006BA/274